Kaplan Publis antly finding new ways to make) your studies and our exciting online resources really do offer something different to students looking for exam success.

This book comes with free MyKaplan online resources so that you can study anytime, anywhere

Having purchased this book, you have access to the following online study materials:

CONTENT			AAT		FIA (excluding FFA,FAB,FMA)	
	Text	Kit	Text	Kit	Text	Kit
iPaper version of the book	✓	✓	✓	✓	✓	✓
Interactive electronic version of the book	✓					
Progress tests with instant answers	✓		✓			
Mock assessments online			✓	✓		
Material updates	✓	✓	✓	✓	✓	✓
Latest official ACCA exam questions		✓				
Extra question assistance using the signpost icon*		✓				
Timed questions with an online tutor debrief using the clock icon*		✓				
Interim assessment including questions and answers	✓				✓	
Technical articles	✓	✓			✓	✓

* Excludes F1, F2, F3, FFA, FAB, FMA

How to access your online resources

Kaplan Financial students will already have a MyKaplan account and these extra resources will be available to you online. You do not need to register again, as this process was completed when you enrolled. If you are having problems accessing online materials, please ask your course administrator.

If you are already a registered MyKaplan user go to www.MyKaplan.co.uk and log in. Select the 'add a book' feature and enter the ISBN number of this book and the unique pass key at the bottom of this card. Then click 'finished' or 'add another book'. You may add as many books as you have purchased from this screen.

If you purchased through Kaplan Flexible Learning or via the Kaplan Publishing website you will automatically receive an e-mail invitation to MyKaplan. Please register your details using this email to gain access to your content. If you do not receive the e-mail or book content, please contact Kaplan Flexible Learning.

If you are a new MyKaplan user register at www.MyKaplan.co.uk and click on the link contained in the email we sent you to activate your account. Then select the 'add a book' feature, enter the ISBN number of this book and the unique pass key at the bottom of this card. Then click 'finished' or 'add another book'.

Your Code and Information

This code can only be used once for the registration of one book online. This registration and your online content will expire when the final sittings for the examinations covered by this book have taken place. Please allow one hour from the time you submit your book details for us to process your request.

D1380100

Please scratch the film to access your MyKaplan code.

Please be aware that this code is case-sensitive and you will need to include the dashes within the passcode, but not when entering the ISBN. For further technical support, please visit www.MyKaplan.co.uk

KAPLAN PUBLISHING

EXTERNAL AUDITING

Qualifications and Credit Framework

AQ 2013 Level 4 Diploma in Accounting

British Library Cataloguing-in-Publication Data

A catalogue record for this book is available from the British Library.

Published by
Kaplan Publishing UK
Unit 2, The Business Centre
Molly Millars Lane
Wokingham
Berkshire
RG41 2QZ

ISBN 978 0 85732 876 2

Printed and bound in Great Britain.

We are grateful to the Association of Accounting Technicians for permission to reproduce past assessment materials and example tasks based on the new syllabus. The solutions to past answers and similar activities in the style of the new syllabus have been prepared by Kaplan Publishing.

We are grateful to HM Revenue and Customs for the provision of tax forms, which are Crown Copyright and are reproduced here with kind permission from the Office of Public Sector Information.

CONTENTS

Introduction	v
Unit guide	vii
The assessment	xi
Study skills	xiii

Chapter		*Study text*	*Workbook Activities Answers*
1	Principles of auditing	1	317
2	Business systems	15	317
3	Planning, controlling and recording	49	318
4	Accounting systems and internal controls	81	319
5	Audit evidence, techniques and procedures	113	319
6	Audit verification work 1 – General principles	141	–
7	Audit verification work 2 – Inventory	151	320
8	Audit verification work 3 – Non-current assets	175	321
9	Audit verification work 4 – Receivables, cash and bank	193	321
10	Audit verification work 5 – Liabilities, shareholders' funds and statutory books	225	322
11	Completion stages of an audit	249	323

Chapter		Study text	Workbook Activities Answers
12	The reporting function	269	323
13	The legal and professional framework	287	326
14	Responsibilities and liabilities of the auditor	303	–
Mock assessment questions		329	
Mock assessment answers		347	
Index		I.1	

INTRODUCTION

HOW TO USE THESE MATERIALS

These Kaplan Publishing learning materials have been carefully designed to make your learning experience as easy as possible and to give you the best chance of success in your AAT assessments.

They contain a number of features to help you in the study process.

The sections on the Unit Guide, the Assessment and Study Skills should be read before you commence your studies.

They are designed to familiarise you with the nature and content of the assessment and to give you tips on how best to approach your studies.

STUDY TEXT

This study text has been specially prepared for the revised AAT qualification introduced in 2013.

It is written in a practical and interactive style:

- key terms and concepts are clearly defined
- all topics are illustrated with practical examples with clearly worked solutions based on sample tasks provided by the AAT in the new examining style
- frequent practice activities at the end of the chapters ensure that what you have learnt is regularly reinforced
- ‘pitfalls’ and ‘examination tips’ help you avoid commonly made mistakes and help you focus on what is required to perform well in your examination.

WORKBOOK

The workbook comprises:

Practice activities at the end of each chapter with solutions at the end of this text, to reinforce the work covered in each chapter.

The questions are divided into their relevant chapters and students may either attempt these questions as they work through the textbook, or leave some or all of these until they have completed the textbook as a final revision of what they have studied.

ICONS

The study chapters include the following icons throughout.

They are designed to assist you in your studies by identifying key definitions and the points at which you can test yourself on the knowledge gained.

Definition

These sections explain important areas of Knowledge which must be understood and reproduced in an assessment.

Example

The illustrative examples can be used to help develop an understanding of topics before attempting the activity exercises.

Activity

These are exercises which give the opportunity to assess your understanding of all the assessment areas.

UNIT GUIDE

The unit is designed to test whether students are equipped with the knowledge and skills required to undertake an external audit under supervision. This is achieved by assessing whether students:

- understand the essence and objectives of the audit process and the implications of the regulatory requirements and pronouncements of the professional bodies
- can contribute to the conduct of all stages of an external audit, including planning, gathering evidence, concluding and reporting findings, in accordance with International Standards on Auditing.

Learning objectives

On completion of these units the learner will be able to:

- Understand the organisation's systems and the external auditing procedures
- Plan an audit, identifying areas to be verified and any associated risks
- Conduct an audit under supervision
- Prepare draft reports under approval
- Understanding auditing principles and legal and professional standards.

Learning outcomes and assessment criteria

To perform this unit effectively you will need to know and understand the following:

		Chapter
1	**Understand the organisation's systems and the external auditing procedures**	
1.1K	Describe the accounting systems relevant to the external audit.	2
1.2K	Describe the features of an accounting system.	2, 7, 8, 9, 10
1.3 K	Identify these principles of control and when they should be used: • separation of functions • authorisation • recording custody • vouching • verification.	2
1.4 S	Explain the concept of assurance and why an organisation needs to be audited.	1, 11, 12
2	**Plan an audit identifying areas to be verified and any associated risks.**	
2.1K	Identify the accounting systems under review and accurately record them on appropriate working papers.	3
2.2K	Identify the control framework.	4
2.3S	Assess risks associated with the accounting system and its controls.	3, 4
2.4S	Record significant weaknesses in control.	12
2.5K	Identify account balances to be verified and the associated risks.	6, 8, 9, 10

		Chapter
2.6K	Explain these different sampling techniques selecting a sample for a specific situation: • confidence levels • random numbers • interval sampling • stratified sampling.	5
2.7K	Explain tests of control and substantive procedures and their links to the audit objective.	6
2.8S	Select or devise tests in accordance with the auditing principles and agree them with the audit supervisor.	6, 8, 9, 10
2.9S	Provide clear information and recommendations for the proposed audit plan for submission to the appropriate person for consideration.	5
2.10K	Describe these verification techniques and their uses: • physical examination • reperformance • third party confirmation • vouching • documentary evidence • identification of unusual items.	4, 6, 7, 8, 9, 10
2.11K	Explain the auditing techniques that could be used in an IT environment.	4
2.12K	Explain how management feedback can be used when planning an audit.	12
3	**Conduct an audit under supervision.**	
3.1K	Explain these features of recording and evaluating systems: • conventional symbols • flowcharts • internal control questionnaires (ICQs) • checklists.	4

		Chapter
3.2K	Recognise the importance of audit files and working papers and their role in the audit process.	3
3.3S	Conduct tests, record test results and draw valid conclusions as specified in the audit plan.	5, 6, 7, 8, 9, 10
3.4S	Establish the existence, completeness, ownership, valuation and description of assets and liabilities and gather appropriate evidence to support these findings.	4, 6, 7, 8, 9, 10
3.5S	Identify all matters of an unusual nature and refer them promptly to the audit supervisor.	7, 8, 9, 10
3.6S	Identify and record material and significant errors, deficiencies or other variations from standard and report them to the audit supervisor.	7, 8, 9, 10
4	**Prepare draft reports for approval.**	
4.1S	Prepare and submit clear and concise draft reports with recommendations.	11, 12
4.2S	Use management feedback when reporting.	11, 12
4.3S	Agree preliminary conclusions and recommendations with the audit supervisor.	11, 12
4.4S	Follow confidentiality and security procedures at all times.	11, 12
5	**Understanding auditing principles and legal and professional standards.**	
5.1K	Explain the legal and ethical duties of auditors, including the content of reports and the definition of proper records.	1, 11, 12
5.2K	Explain the liability of auditors under contract and negligence including liability to third parties.	11, 13, 14
5.3K	Explain the relevant legislation and auditing standards.	1, 11
5.4K	Explain audit risk and how it applies to external auditing.	3
5.5K	Explain materiality and how it applies to external auditing.	3
5.6K	Explain how interview and listening skills can be used by an auditor.	4

THE ASSESSMENT

The format of the assessment

The assessment consists of 32 tasks, with a time allowed of two hours. The assessment contains the following question types:

- drag and drop
- pick list
- MCQs
- text selector
- extended writing.

There are three extended writing tasks covering the following assessment criteria:

- 2.9 S: Provide clear information and recommendations for the proposed audit plan for submission to the appropriate person for consideration.
- 3.4 S: Establish the existence, completeness, ownership, valuation and description of assets and liabilities and gather appropriate evidence to support these findings.
- 4.1 S: Prepare and submit clear and concise draft reports with recommendations.

Each of the other assessment criteria may be assessed by any other question type.

STUDY SKILLS

Preparing to study

Devise a study plan

Determine which times of the week you will study.

Split these times into sessions of at least one hour for study of new material. Any shorter periods could be used for revision or practice.

Put the times you plan to study onto a study plan for the weeks from now until the assessment and set yourself targets for each period of study – in your sessions make sure you cover the whole course, activities and the associated questions in the workbook at the back of the manual.

If you are studying more than one unit at a time, try to vary your subjects as this can help to keep you interested and see subjects as part of wider knowledge.

When working through your course, compare your progress with your plan and, if necessary, re-plan your work (perhaps including extra sessions) or, if you are ahead, do some extra revision/practice questions.

Effective studying

Active reading

You are not expected to learn the text by rote, rather, you must understand what you are reading and be able to use it to pass the assessment and develop good practice.

A good technique is to use SQ3Rs – Survey, Question, Read, Recall, Review:

1 **Survey the chapter**

Look at the headings and read the introduction, knowledge, skills and content, so as to get an overview of what the chapter deals with.

2 **Question**

Whilst undertaking the survey ask yourself the questions you hope the chapter will answer for you.

3 Read

Read through the chapter thoroughly working through the activities and, at the end, making sure that you can meet the learning objectives highlighted on the first page.

4 Recall

At the end of each section and at the end of the chapter, try to recall the main ideas of the section/chapter without referring to the text. This is best done after short break of a couple of minutes after the reading stage.

5 Review

Check that your recall notes are correct.

You may also find it helpful to re-read the chapter to try and see the topic(s) it deals with as a whole.

Note taking

Taking notes is a useful way of learning, but do not simply copy out the text.

The notes must:

- be in your own words
- be concise
- cover the key points
- well organised
- be modified as you study further chapters in this text or in related ones.

Trying to summarise a chapter without referring to the text can be a useful way of determining which areas you know and which you don't.

Three ways of taking notes

1 Summarise the key points of a chapter

2 Make linear notes

A list of headings, subdivided with sub-headings listing the key points.

If you use linear notes, you can use different colours to highlight key points and keep topic areas together.

Use plenty of space to make your notes easy to use.

3 Try a diagrammatic form

The most common of which is a mind map.

To make a mind map, put the main heading in the centre of the paper and put a circle around it.

Draw lines radiating from this to the main sub-headings which again have circles around them.

Continue the process from the sub-headings to sub-sub-headings.

Highlighting and underlining

You may find it useful to underline or highlight key points in your study text – but do be selective.

You may also wish to make notes in the margins.

Revision

Kaplan has produced material specifically designed for your final examination preparation for this unit.

This includes a bank of revision questions specifically in the style of the new syllabus.

Further guidance on how to approach the final stage of your studies is given in these materials.

Further reading

In addition to this text, you should also read the "Student section" of the "Accounting Technician" magazine every month to keep abreast of any guidance from the examiners.

Principles of auditing

1

Introduction

This chapter demonstrates the features of an audit and introduces the fundamental principles within audit work. This is the basis for the whole External Audit assessment and introduces some important concepts for the rest of the syllabus.

SYLLABUS AREA

1.4 Explain the concept of assurance and why an organisation needs to be audited.

5.1 Explain the legal and ethical duties of auditors, including the content of reports and the definition of proper records.

5.3 Explain the relevant legislation and auditing standards.

5.4 Explain audit risk and how it applies to external auditing.

5.5 Explain materiality and how it applies to external auditing.

CONTENTS

1 What is an audit?

2 Important principles in audit work

3 Auditing standards

4 Features of an audit

1 What is an audit?

1.1 The purpose of an external audit

The need for an audit arises from the separation between the management and the ownership of companies – directors are responsible for running the company on behalf of the shareholders. Financial statements are prepared by the directors in order to account for their stewardship to the shareholders, and an examination by an independent person (i.e. the external auditor) gives them credibility.

Once the external auditor has conducted his examination, he expresses his opinion in an auditors' report attached to the financial statements.

1.2 Definition of Assurance and an Audit

Definition

Assurance – an assurance engagement is one in which a practitioner expresses a conclusion designed to enhance the degree of confidence of the intended users, other than the responsible party, about the outcome of the evaluation of measurement of subject matter against criteria.

Definition

Audit of financial statements – an audit is a type of assurance engagement and is a process which results in expression of an opinion as to whether the financial statements give a true and fair view of the entity's affairs at the period end, and as to whether they have been properly prepared in accordance with the applicable accounting standards.

All UK companies with a turnover above £6.5m are required by law to have their annual financial statements audited by external auditors (see Chapter 13).

There are a number of benefits of an audit that might mean a company might choose to be audited:

- Adds credibility.
- It is an independent verification.
- There are a number of by-products, such as the fact that an audit can act as a fraud deterrent.

Let's look at this definition in detail, and clear up some common misconceptions. During this section, and indeed throughout this book, we shall be referring to International Standards on Auditing (ISAs) which are produced by the International Auditing and Assurance Standards Board and which, after approval by the UK Auditing Practices Board, must be followed when carrying out audits in the UK and Ireland.

1.3 Expression of opinion – the auditors' report

'Expression of opinion' refers to the reporting function.

ISA 700 *Forming an opinion and reporting on financial statements* indicates the required content of an auditor's report. This includes the audit opinion, which is usually expressed in 'true and fair' terms.

Note that the term 'true and fair', although used in the Companies Act, is not defined. This idea is developed later in this chapter. The wording of the audit opinion is shown below, being an extract from the wording of the standard audit report.

Example

Company incorporated in Great Britain

AUDITORS' REPORT TO THE SHAREHOLDERS OF XYZ PLC (EXTRACT)

Opinion

In our opinion the financial statements:

- give a true and fair view, in accordance with United Kingdom Generally Accepted Accounting Practice, of the state of the company's affairs as at 31 December 20X1 and of its profit for the year then ended; and
- have been properly prepared in accordance with the Companies Act 2006.

Registered Auditors

Date *Address*

1.4 Financial statements

The 'financial statements' comprise:

- statement of financial position
- statement of profit or loss
- statements of cash flows
- statement of changes in equity
- notes to all of the above, including the accounting policies note.

1.5 Misconceptions about the financial statements

There are a number of common misconceptions about the financial statements. The main ones are as follows.

- The statement of financial position is a statement of the value of the business. Wrong – the amounts at which assets and liabilities are stated do not reflect what the business could be sold for.
- That the auditors are responsible for preparing the financial statements on which they report. Wrong – the directors are responsible for selecting suitable accounting policies and preparing the financial statements.
- The amounts in financial statements are stated precisely. Wrong – the majority of figures involve some degree of estimation.

ISA 700 seeks to address these misconceptions in the following ways.

1.6 Directors' and auditors' responsibilities

The auditors' report contains a clear statement of the respective responsibilities of directors and auditors as follows:

The company's directors are responsible for the preparation of financial statements in accordance with applicable law and United Kingdom Accounting Standards. Note that some UK companies, particularly listed groups now follow International Accounting Standards. Our responsibility is to audit the financial statements in accordance with relevant legal and regulatory requirements and International Standards on Auditing.

Readers are warned that the financial statements have been prepared by the company's management (whose interests may be affected by the resulting figures).The auditor expresses an opinion on those figures. This has a number of implications:

- The published figures might not be the only ones that the auditors would have accepted and might not necessarily be the best reflection of the company's performance or financial position.
- The auditor expresses an opinion, which suggests that there is scope for disagreement with the auditor's findings.

1.7 Basis of opinion

"An audit involves obtaining evidence about the amounts and disclosures in the financial statements sufficient to give reasonable assurance that the financial statements are free from material misstatement, whether caused by fraud or error. This includes an assessment of: whether the accounting policies are appropriate to the [describe nature of entity] circumstances and have been consistently applied and adequately disclosed; the reasonableness of significant accounting estimates made by [describe those charged with governance]; and the overall presentation of the financial statements. In addition, we read all the financial and non-financial information in the [describe the annual report] to identify material inconsistencies with the audited financial statements and to identify any information that is apparently materially incorrect based on, or materially inconsistent with, the knowledge acquired by us in the course of performing the audit. If we become aware of any apparent material misstatements or inconsistencies we consider the implications for our report."

Auditors aim to provide reasonable assurance. It would be impractical and unduly expensive to provide a guarantee that all major errors and irregularities have been uncovered during the audit.

1.8 True and fair

The auditor does not certify that the monetary value of each individual figure disclosed is precise and accurate.

Instead the use of the word 'view' indicates that a professional judgement has been reached.

The meaning of 'true and fair' has been much debated. It is not defined in the Companies Acts or International Standards on Auditing. This is deliberate and any 'definitions' cited in textbooks or elsewhere should be regarded with caution.

A starting point for discussion could be that truth relates to factual accuracy (bearing in mind materiality) and correctness, whilst fairness relates to the presentation of information and the view conveyed to the reader.

The word 'fair' in particular is difficult because it is subjective – one person's idea of what is fair is probably not another's. The auditor must consider the overall impression created by the financial statements as a whole; the fact that every individual figure may be justified does not automatically mean that the total picture is 'fair'.

Experience develops in an auditor an understanding of the meaning of the term 'true and fair'. It can then be applied to the particular facts of a case and an opinion can be reached, even though the term itself defies definition.

1.9 Accounting standards

The courts will treat compliance with accepted accounting principles as evidence that financial statements are true and fair.

The Companies Act 2006 requires the notes to the financial statements to state:

- whether the financial statements are prepared in accordance with applicable accounting standards (see below for further definition)
- particulars of and reasons for material departures from accounting standards.

Activity 1

(a) What are the respective responsibilities of the directors and the external auditors regarding the financial statements of a company?

(b) Explain what is meant by a true and fair view.

2 Important principles in audit work

2.1 Introduction

Audit work is a detailed and meticulous process which we shall examine fully in this text. There are, however, some basic principles which apply to audit work which it is useful to examine first, and which should be borne in mind at all times so that we do not get into the position of 'not being able to see the wood for the trees'!

2.2 Materiality

The auditor does not perform tests aimed at detecting all errors however small or insignificant. As part of the planning process, the auditor will determine the maximum amount of error that he is prepared to accept and still be satisfied that the financial statements show a true and fair view. This maximum error can be referred to as 'materiality'.

A material error may be:

- qualitative (e.g. failure to comply with disclosure requirements or generally accepted accounting practice), or
- quantitative (e.g. the monetary value of the disclosed figures is incorrect).

The concept of materiality is developed in Chapter 3.

2.3 Selective testing and audit sampling

The auditor next needs to carry out tests to ascertain whether actual errors in the financial statements are material. These tests must be sufficient to provide evidence of material errors, if such errors exist.

The auditor does not usually test every transaction or item within an account balance, but will limit tests to a selection of items ('selective testing').

Where the auditor tests a representative sample of items in order to draw conclusions about an entire set of data, the selective testing is termed 'audit sampling'.

Audit sampling is detailed in Chapter 5.

2.4 Risk

To apply selective testing procedures, the auditor will wish to target the areas of the financial statements which are most prone to material error ('risky').

In some companies there may be many risk areas. This may be due, in part, to the type of industry in which the company operates, e.g. there may be more risk of material misstatement occurring in the financial statements of a high technology company than there is in a stable industry.

Also, some areas or account headings may be more prone to material error than others, e.g. inventory is usually subject to more material errors than cash at bank, because its valuation is more subjective.

As part of the planning process, the auditor will analyse risk in order to:

- direct audit tests to those areas most prone to material error
- determine the overall assurance required from a test or combination of tests (and therefore what will constitute 'sufficient' audit evidence).

Audit risk and planning are considered in greater detail in Chapter 3.

2.5 Reasonable assurance

The auditors' opinion on the financial statements is based on the concept of reasonable assurance; his report does not constitute a guarantee that the financial statements are free of misstatement.

Because the auditor does not examine every single piece of available audit information and because professional judgement is required when drawing conclusions from the evidence, there is a risk that he will draw an incorrect conclusion: absolute confidence, certainty or assurance is not possible.

Again, the auditors' report sheds some light on this.

'We conducted our audit in accordance with International Standards on Auditing. Those Standards require that we plan and perform the audit to obtain reasonable assurance about whether the financial statements are free of material misstatement.'

There are two levels of assurance you need to be aware of:

	Limited	**Reasonable**
Level	Moderate – negative opinion given.	High – positive opinion given.
Example of engagement	Report on effectiveness of internal controls. Review of business plan.	Statutory audit.
Example of report wording	"Nothing has come to our attention that indicates the internal control systems are not operating effectively."	"Financial Statements show a true and fair view."

Note: Auditors will never give absolute assurance for a number of reasons:

- Audit evidence is persuasive, not conclusive.
- Auditors do not test everything.
- There are areas of judgement in the financial statements.
- There are inherent limitations of internal controls and accounting systems (see session 3).
- Auditors test according to materiality (see later in this session).

2.6 The expectation gap

There is a common misconception that an unmodified audit report provides assurance that no frauds or other irregularities have occurred in the period covered by it. Wrong – the auditor is concerned with material misstatements in the financial statements; fraud is one possible cause of such a misstatement, but it is the misstatement which concerns the auditor, rather than the fraud itself. This is considered in more detail in Chapter 14.

This misconception, together with a lack of comprehension of the auditing principles discussed earlier (selective testing, materiality, etc), have been referred to as part of the 'expectation gap'.

The 'expectation gap' has become a jargon phrase used to describe the difference between:

- public perceptions of the responsibilities of auditors
- the legal and professional reality.

3 Auditing standards

3.1 Introduction

The International Auditing and Assurance Standards Board (IAASB) works to improve the uniformity of auditing practices worldwide by issuing pronouncements (particularly International Standards on Auditing (ISAs) and promoting their acceptance. Their aim is to set standards which facilitate the convergence of national and international auditing standards.

International Standards on Auditing (ISAs) are to be applied in every audit of historical financial information. Failure to apply ISAs could leave the auditor open to accusations of negligence, which could lead to claims for compensation as well as disciplinary action.

The IAASB's Standards contain basic principles and essential procedures (identified in bold type lettering) together with related guidance in the form of explanatory and other material, including appendices. In practice, the distinction between essential procedures and the other material is unlikely to be important because an auditor who chooses not to apply a procedure that is recommended by the profession's standard setting body is still in danger of being accused of performing an inadequate investigation.

From an assessment point of view, it is important to be aware of the broad principles laid down by those standards that are relevant to the syllabus. However, there is no need to memorise the detailed content or formal definitions that they contain.

4 Features of an audit

4.1 Who is the external auditor?

The law defines who can be the statutory auditor and this is considered in Chapter 13. In this context, 'the auditor' can be a person or firm.

Practically, 'the auditor' includes all members of the audit team on a particular assignment.

The person who takes overall responsibility for the performance of the assignment and who signs the audit report is known as the reporting partner. He or she may delegate certain aspects of the audit work to other persons but the overall responsibility for the performance of the audit is the reporting partner's alone.

4.2 Audit team

A typical audit team for a large company audit might be made up as follows:

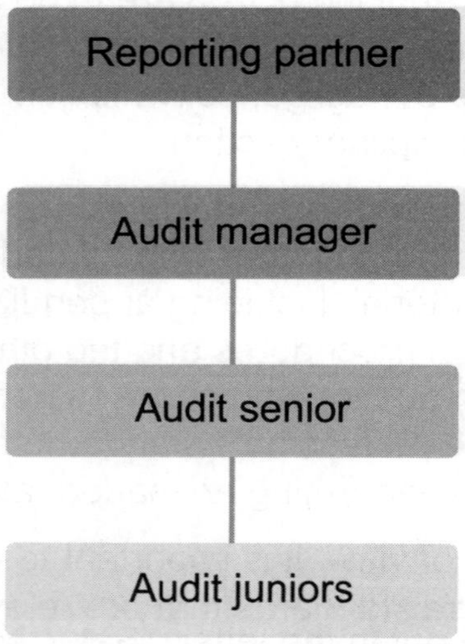

4.3 The process of auditing

The audit of a limited company consists of a cycle of activities which can be broken down into a number of distinct phases as shown below. Review the phases illustrated and discussed below to gain an overview only. This will all be developed in later chapters.

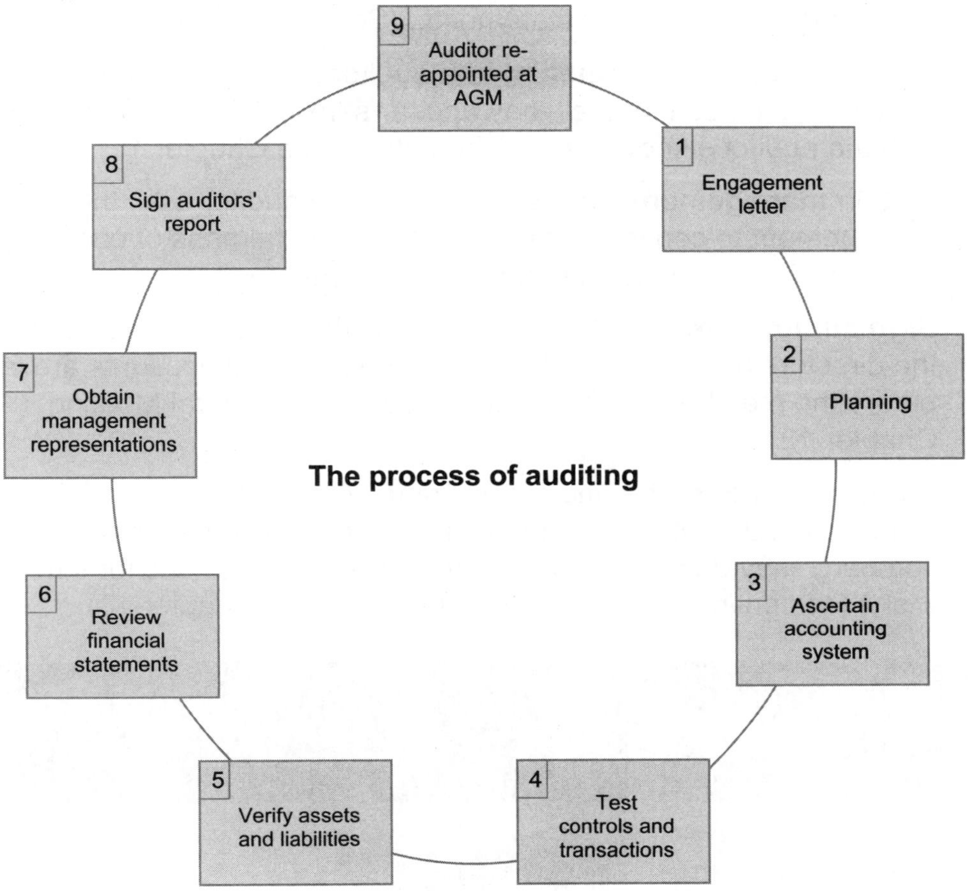

1 **Engagement letter.** Every auditor should send his client an engagement letter which sets out the auditor's duties and responsibilities. If the client requires other services the scope of these can also be set out in the letter. (See Chapter 3)

2 **Planning.** The auditor must plan and control the audit work if the work is to be done to a high standard of skill and care. (See Chapter 3)

3 **Ascertain accounting systems.** An auditor must enquire into and ascertain the client's system of accounting and internal control in order to understand how accounting data is prepared and to gain an impression as to whether systems are reliable, as it is the information generated from these systems which is summarised in the financial statements. (See Chapter 4)

4 **Test controls and transactions.** The auditor should test the controls if he intends to rely on them and he must test the records in order to obtain evidence that they are a reliable basis for the preparation of accounts. If systems are weak or unreliable, a high level of detailed work is needed. (See Chapter 5)

5 **Verify assets and liabilities.** The auditor must verify the figures appearing in the financial statements. (See Chapters 6 to 10)

6 **Review financial statements.** The auditor reviews the financial statements to see if overall they appear sensible and are consistent with the auditor's knowledge of the entity. (See Chapter 11)

7 **Obtain management representations.** The auditor asks the management to confirm formally the truth and fairness of certain aspects of the financial statements. (See Chapter 11)

8 **Sign auditors' report.** The auditor signs the auditors' report once the directors have approved the accounts. Audited accounts are laid before the members at the company's Annual General Meeting. (See Chapter 12)

9 **Re-appointment.** The end of the Annual General Meeting (AGM) signifies the end of the auditor's term of office. The members of the company may decide by a majority to re-appoint the auditor if he wishes to continue to act for the company. (See Chapter 13)

5 Summary

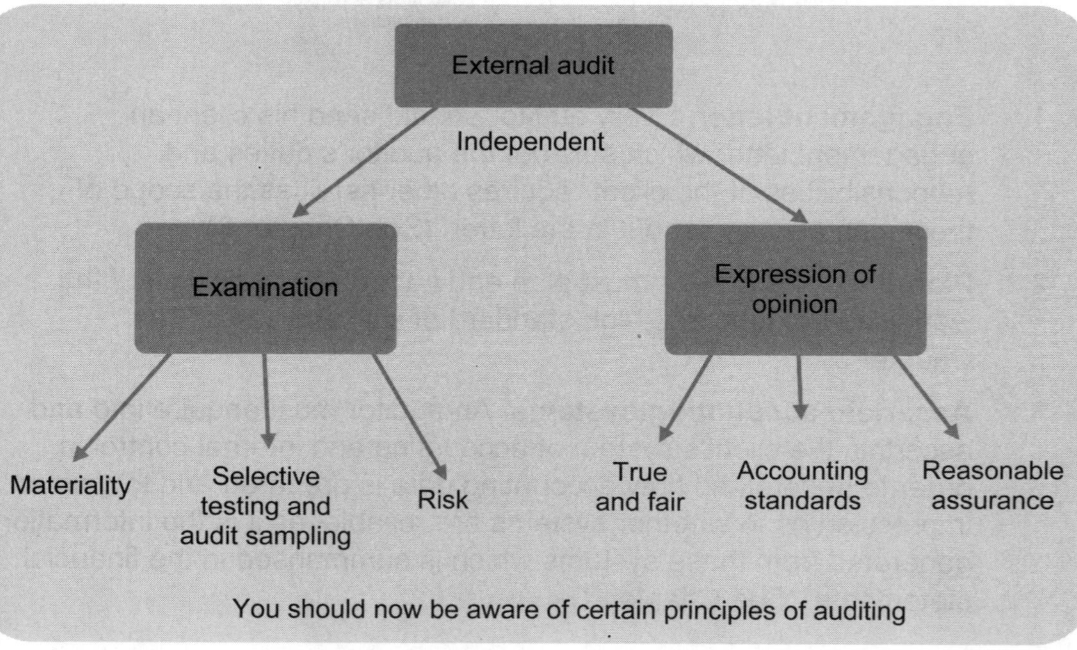

You should now be aware of certain principles of auditing

Answers to chapter activities

Activity 1

(a) The directors are responsible for the preparation of the annual financial statements of a company. The external auditor's responsibility is to report to the shareholders on whether the financial statements show a true and fair view.

(b) A true and fair view has no legal or formal definition. However, 'true' indicates that the figures are based upon fact and correctness while 'fair' indicates that the figures in the financial statements are presented so as to give an accurate impression of the position of the company.

6 Test your knowledge

Workbook Activity 2

1 What do the financial statements that the external auditor issues an opinion on comprise of?

2 Who is responsible for the preparation of the financial statements?

3 What is meant by qualitative materiality?

Business systems

2

Introduction

In this chapter we will consider the various cycles within a business and the key controls within each cycle. From this we can start to think about the risks surrounding the business and how these risks can be dealt with. This will enable us to start the building blocks of our risk based approach to an audit.

SYLLABUS AREA

1.1 Describe accounting systems relevant to the external audit.

1.2 Describe the features of an accounting system.

1.3 Identify these principles of control and when they should be used: Separation of functions, authorisation, recording custody, vouching and verification.

CONTENTS

1 Business systems in general

2 Sales cycle

3 Purchases cycle

4 Payroll cycle

5 Cash system

6 Inventory system

1 Business systems in general

1.1 Introduction

In virtually all businesses, both large and small, simple and complex, management will establish some form of formalised business system. Such a system will be designed largely to ensure that all day-to-day transactions are accurately recorded and thus management have up to-date information at their disposal to help them to control the business and its assets.

Although such systems may differ in complexity, many of the basic procedures remain very much the same.

1.2 Areas of business systems

In order that you are familiar with such procedures, you will find detailed descriptions of the major areas of a typical business system set out in this chapter. These descriptions concentrate upon the procedures involved in the processing of sales, purchases, payroll, cash payments and receipts and inventory. If you already have a good understanding of such procedures from your practical work to date, then this chapter need only be reviewed briefly rather than read in detail, to ensure that there are no 'gaps' in your knowledge.

2 Sales cycle

2.1 Introduction

The purpose of most business organisations is to make sales of either goods or services to its customers at a profit. In order that management may retain some degree of control over this process, a formalised sales system is usually developed. This system will ensure that the procedures adopted in respect of each individual sale will be the same.

2.2 Controls

Commonly such systems will incorporate controls. These controls are essentially checks which will help to ensure that every transaction is dealt with in the accepted way and, ultimately, that management receives complete and accurate information about sales made.

2.3 Overview of the sales cycle

Given below is an overview of the main stages involved in the sales cycle, together with a detailed narrative explanation of a typical system.

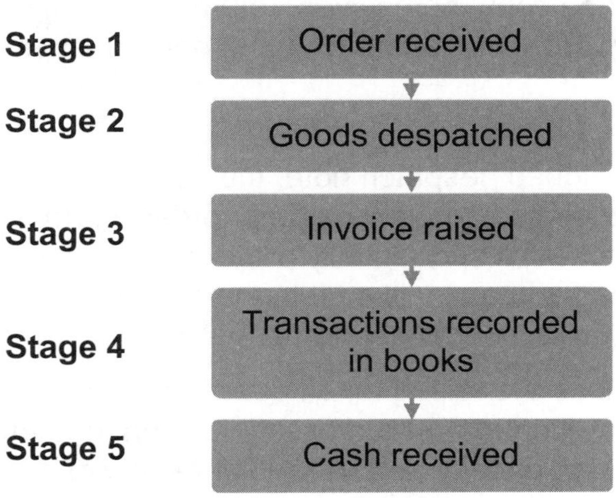

Each stage is examined in detail below.

2.4 Receiving an order

- The company receives an order from a new or existing customer. The order details are recorded immediately on an internal sales order form (usually a sequentially pre-numbered multi-part document).
- The sales order clerk checks the order against the customer's account to ensure that any credit limit allowed to that customer will not be exceeded as a result of this order.
- If the customer is within their credit limit, the order is priced (using the company's customer price list). One copy of the order remains in the sales department, one copy is passed to accounts and one copy is passed to the warehouse.

2.5 Despatch of goods

- When the warehouse receives the details, the information is used to prepare the order for despatch.
- A sequentially pre-numbered multi-part despatch note is generated in the warehouse, showing the descriptions and quantities of goods to be despatched and the order to which the despatch relates. Note that sequentially numbered documentation within any system permits checking of completeness of processing data.

- If any items required are not available (e.g. due to inventory shortages) the warehouse supervisor notes this on the despatch note. When the goods have been delivered and the customer's signature has been obtained on the multi-part despatch note, the warehouse retains one copy themselves, returns one to the sales department and forwards one to the accounts department.

2.6 Invoicing

- Upon receipt of the signed despatch note, the accounts clerk matches it against their copy of the customer order. From the details of the goods despatched, a sequentially pre-numbered two-part sales invoice is raised; one copy is sent to the customer, the other copy is retained by the accounts department.
- To ensure that invoices are raised for all goods sent to customers, the despatch notes will normally be crossed through, and the invoice number noted on them, once raised. A regular review of despatch notes is undertaken to ensure that they have all been dealt with in this manner.

2.7 Recording the information

- The details of each invoice will usually be recorded individually in the correct customer's account in the subsidiary sales ledger. An invoice listing (e.g. the sales day book) is usually used to record each month's sales in the main ledger accounts (i.e. sales account and receivables ledger control account). If the financial statements are to be accurate, there must be procedures to ensure that the details of every sale are properly recorded. A 'grid stamp' may be put on each invoice, to give a space for various individuals to sign (or initial) once certain procedures have been carried out (e.g. input of the invoice details, checking the calculations and checking the customer account number).
- Only when invoice details are properly recorded is the company able to generate regular customer statements and carry out adequate credit control procedures.

2.8 Receiving amounts due

- When customers' payments are received, the details are recorded initially by the cashier on a daily cash received sheet, or in the receipts side of the cash book (depending upon the number of transactions).
- Receipt details are passed to the sales ledger clerk and the amounts input into the individual sales ledger accounts.

- It is usual for payments received (especially those through the post) to be accompanied by a remittance advice. This shows the total amount of the cheque which it accompanies and may also show how the payment is broken down (into specific invoices). A remittance advice is often prepared with the statement sent to the customers. However, some customers will disregard them and/or send their own.

2.9 Controls

The above system also contains a number of controls to help ensure that only valid items are recorded, and that they are recorded completely and accurately.

Set out below are examples of:

- the objectives which a company might meet by incorporating controls
- the actual controls which could be implemented.

Control objectives for sales	Examples of sales controls
Stage 1 – Ordering	
To ensure that the company only sells goods to customers with a good credit rating and from whom it is likely to receive full and prompt payment. To ensure that all orders are dealt with promptly.	All orders received are checked against the customer's credit limit (to ensure it is not exceeded). Credit checks are carried out on all new customers before an account is opened. Sequentially pre-numbered order forms to identify if a particular order has gone astray.
Stage 2 – Despatch	
To ensure that all inventory is physically secure and all movements of inventory are valid and adequately recorded. (If the system does not achieve these objectives inventory pilferage could become a problem and management will have little or no idea about what levels of inventory are currently maintained, making efficient reordering virtually impossible).	Inventory is kept in physically secure locations, with restricted access to staff. Movements of inventory out of the warehouse require that a valid customer order has been received from the sales department. Such movements are accurately recorded, using sequentially pre-numbered despatch notes (as in the above system) or a goods despatched register.

Control objectives for sales	**Examples of sales controls**
	The customer's signature is obtained for all deliveries. (Proof of delivery can be used in any subsequent disputes with customers).
Stage 3 – Invoicing	
To ensure that customers pay for the goods they have received by ensuring that: • goods cannot be despatched without an invoice being raised shortly afterwards, and • invoices are accurate in the description, quantity and prices of items despatched. (If these objectives are not met, the company may never receive payment).	Copies of all sequentially pre-numbered despatch notes are sent to the accounts department which checks (at regular intervals) that all despatch notes have been received (by looking for any 'gaps' in the sequences). If any are missing, the accounts clerk can obtain a copy from the warehouse to ensure that the despatch is appropriately invoiced. The accounts department can distinguish despatch notes which have already given rise to an invoice and those which have not yet been dealt with (e.g. by crossing through the despatch note and making a note of the corresponding invoice number). A second accounts clerk staff checks the calculations on the invoice (including prices and discounts given) and evidences this check by initialling a grid stamp on the invoice.

Control objectives for sales	Examples of sales controls
Stage 4 – Recording	
To ensure that the information generated by the system is complete, accurate and as up to date as possible. This means ensuring that every invoice raised is recorded in both the sales and receivables control accounts (within the main ledger), as well as the customer's individual account (within the subsidiary sales ledger).	A signature is required as evidence, on the grid stamp, once the invoice details are input. A regular review of the invoices is undertaken to ensure that all parts of the grid stamp have been signed-off.
(It is only if individual account details are correct that adequate credit control procedures may be implemented (and the risk of bad debts reduced).	Producing customer statements and aged debtor listings is essential to maintaining adequate control over receivables.
Stage 5 – Receiving money	
To ensure that: • all receipts are recorded in the cash book and banked promptly and intact, and • receipts from particular customers are recorded in the correct individual account within the receivables ledger. (If such objectives are not met, the receipts are vulnerable to misappropriation).	Two members of staff having co-responsibility for opening the daily post and listing down the details of any receipts. (One of these individuals would normally be the cashier, but the other should be someone completely independent of the cashier function). (This information would then be used to write up the cash receipts side of the cash book and to prepare the paying-in slip for the daily bankings).
To ensure completeness of posting of both invoices and cash receipts to the sales, cash and receivables control accounts in the main ledger, as well as individual customer accounts.	A copy of the daily receipts sheet is passed to the sales ledger clerk, who crosses through each individual receipt as the details are entered onto the individual sales ledger accounts. A control account reconciliation is prepared and reviewed on a regular (e.g. monthly) basis.

Activity 1

(a) Why is it important that all documents within the business system are sequentially numbered?

(b) Why is it important to check the credit limit and account balance of a customer when an order is placed by a customer?

(c) How are sales invoices sent to customers recorded in the accounts?

(d) What is the control objective regarding the despatch of goods to customers?

3 Purchases cycle

3.1 Introduction

In its day-to-day operations, a business requires goods or services from outside suppliers. Management needs a reliable purchases system to ensure that all liabilities arising from such transactions are completely and accurately recorded and, at the same time, that such items represent only valid (i.e. bona fide) business expenditure.

3.2 Overview of the purchases cycle

Given below is an overview of the main stages involved in the purchases cycle. As you read through, see if you can think of some of the control objectives which management may require together with examples of specific controls – then check your thoughts against those given at the end.

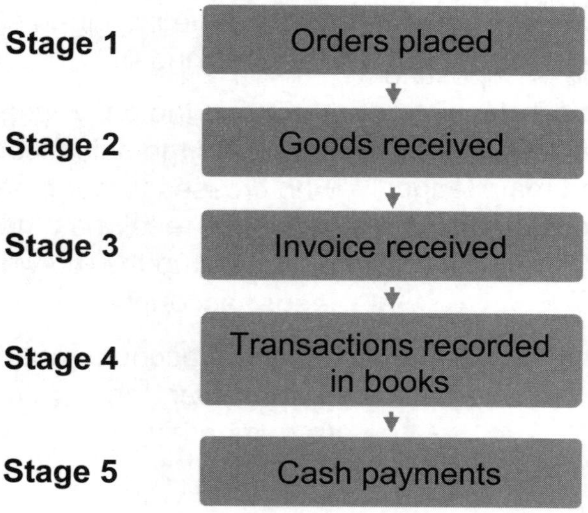

Each stage is examined in more detail below.

3.3 Ordering goods

- When an individual or department within the organisation recognises the need for goods or services from an outside supplier, a purchase requisition will be raised. The purchase requisition gives details of the items required. The requisition will then be passed to the purchasing (or buying) department, where it will be scrutinised to ensure the item represents valid business expenditure. If approved, the requisition form will be signed (usually by the manager of the purchasing department) to indicate that this is the case. Only when a purchase requisition has been signed can an order be placed.
- When placing the order, the purchasing clerk completes a purchase order form. This gives details of the goods ordered and their price (if such information is available from suppliers' catalogues/price lists, etc). The order is sent to the supplier, and a copy retained by the purchasing department.

3.4 Receiving goods

- When goods are delivered by a supplier, the warehouseman (or storeman) enters the details (inventory references/quantities, quality and supplier's name and reference number) on an internally generated, sequentially pre-numbered goods received note (GRN). A copy of the supplier's delivery note (DN) is attached to the copies of the GRN sent to the accounts department and purchasing department. A further copy of the GRN is retained in the warehouse, filed in numerical order.
- The purchasing department compares the details of the GRN against those ordered. If the order has not been fulfilled, the purchasing department may need to reorder some of the items.
- If a supplier delivers more than the quantities required, the purchasing clerk completes a goods returned note. Once this note is approved by the purchasing department manager, a copy is sent to the warehouse from where the goods are despatched back to the supplier. Details of all goods returned are recorded by the warehouseman in a separate returns ledger. A copy of the goods returned note will also be sent to the accounts department.

3.5 Receiving invoices

- When the supplier submits a purchase invoice to the company, the details are recorded in the purchase day book and the invoice given an internal, sequential reference number. The accounts clerk must then ensure that the company is only being billed for the goods received by comparing the details on the invoice (i.e. quantity and inventory reference) against the GRN, supplier's DN and any goods returned note. Check any prices on the original order against those on the invoice to ensure that they are correct.
- Check the numerical calculations of the invoice, including VAT.
- Once these procedures have been performed, the accounts clerk indicates as such by signing the purchase invoice.

3.6 Recording the transactions

- The details of all suppliers' invoices must be accurately recorded in the purchases account and payables ledger control account in the main ledger. The weekly or monthly totals of the purchase day book are normally used to record the main ledger transactions.
- In addition, each invoice must be recorded individually in the correct supplier's account in the subsidiary purchases ledger. This can be achieved, quite simply, by indicating on the invoice by means of a stamp or signature that the details have been so recorded.
- The purchase invoices may be filed in their internal reference number order. They can then be reviewed regularly to ensure that there are no gaps in the sequence and that each invoice carries the necessary stamp or signature which signifies that it has been entered. Alternatively, they may be filed by supplier in alphabetical order (as the cross-referencing in the purchase day book should ensure completeness).
- The details entered on an individual supplier's account will usually be checked against the supplier's statement at the end of each month. The supplier's statement reconciliation that is produced will normally be signed by the chief accountant as evidence of his review.

3.7 Making payment

- Payments to suppliers, particularly those of a large monetary value, should only be made by authorised signatories, once they are satisfied that the amount outstanding to a particular supplier represents a valid business expense. It is usual for cheques over a specified monetary value to require two signatures from senior personnel. Such cheques should only be signed after a review of the supplier's account and the most recent reconciliation have taken place.

3.8 Controls

The control objectives and examples of such controls are given below.

Control objectives for purchases	Examples of purchase controls
Stage 1 – Ordering	
To ensure that the ability to make orders in the company's name is restricted (to prevent individual members of staff ordering items which are not for use in the business).	All requisitions need the approval of the purchasing department manager before the order can be placed. (This gives management a greater control over the whole process).
To ensure that ordering from suppliers is done in the most efficient manner possible. (If ordering is centralised, this reduces the possibility of the same order being placed twice, or a vital order being forgotten altogether).	Pricing the original order by reference to suppliers' price lists increases control over costs. (When the purchase invoice is compared against this document, any significant overcharge will be noticed).
Stage 2 – Receiving	
To maintain control over the company's physical inventory levels by quickly and accurately recording goods coming into inventory. (Only by accurately recording all movements, both in and out of inventory, can useful information about inventory levels be available to management).	Receipts of inventory are recorded on delivery, using sequentially numbered GRNs. GRNs are reviewed regularly to ensure that the sequence is complete, and that the details recorded correspond to the supplier's delivery note.
To ensure that the company does not accept poor quality or damaged items.	The warehouseman inspects the delivery before signing the supplier's delivery note.
To ensure that goods delivered by a supplier which have not been ordered are highlighted. (The company will therefore not find itself paying for goods which are of no use to it).	The purchasing department compares delivery notes against orders to prevent the possibility of 'stock-outs' occurring due to insufficient goods being delivered by the supplier. (If deliveries are short, further orders may be placed as necessary). This comparison will also prevent the company from accepting unnecessary goods.

Control objectives for purchases	Examples of purchase controls
	The purchasing department manager reviews orders and delivery notes the above comparison is being carried out for all deliveries.
Stage 3 – Invoices	
To ensure that payments can only be made to suppliers for valid deliveries. To prevent suppliers being able to overcharge for deliveries (e.g. through simple errors of calculation or by failing to recognise discounts negotiated with the supplier at the time the order was placed). (If the system fails to meet these objectives, the company will be incurring unnecessary costs and may find it difficult to continue in business).	Suppliers' invoices are compared with their delivery notes and the check is evidenced (e.g. the purchase clerk signs the invoice, or the invoice is stamped 'checked'). Once the invoices and delivery notes have been 'matched' in this way, the relevant invoice number should be noted on the delivery note. The matching process should include a comparison of physical quantities and inventory descriptions. More comprehensive controls would also include a comparison of the unit price per the invoice against price lists etc. for that supplier. Simple checks on the arithmetical accuracy of invoices.

Control objectives for purchases	Examples of purchase controls
Stage 4 – Recording	
To ensure that management have an accurate and up-to-date record of the company's liabilities to suppliers (i.e. to ensure that all valid business expenses are recorded completely and accurately in the main ledger, purchases and payables control accounts and the supplier's individual account).	The accounts clerk should deal with invoices in their reference number order (to ensure completeness). The clerk signs or stamps the invoice 'entered' as it is processed (to ensure it is not entered twice). An accounts supervisor reviews the purchase invoices (to ensure that the sequence is complete and that all invoices have been processed).
To ensure that all relevant invoices are received. To ensure completeness of recording the details on the supplier's individual account.	One of the accounts clerks regularly reviews the copies of delivery notes retained by the accounts department. (Those deliveries for which an invoice has been received will carry the invoice number.) Any deliveries which have not therefore been invoiced within, say, two months of delivery should be investigated. If necessary, copy invoices should be requested from the supplier. Comparison of the statements sent by the supplier at the end of each month with the individual account balance. A formal reconciliation should be produced for all accounts, with any differences between the two being investigated and explained. The accountant reviews such reconciliations and signs them as evidence of this review.

Control objectives for purchases	Examples of purchase controls
Stage 5 – Payment	
To ensure that payments are made only by personnel authorised to do so. To ensure that payments are made only to valid suppliers. To ensure that payments made represent amounts outstanding in respect of valid business expenditure.	Cheques signed by a small number of relatively senior personnel. (If anyone else within the organisation attempts to sign business cheques, they will not be honoured by the bank. It is usual for one signature only to be required for payments of a small value, but two for any larger payments). Before signing any cheque, the authorised signatory reviews some documentation (to ensure that the recipient and amount are valid). This could be in the form of a single supplier's invoice, or reconciled account balance.

3.9 Illustration

The following brief case study illustrates some of the audit techniques that have just been studied. You should pay particular attention to the strengths and weaknesses of the internal controls that are present in the system.

Miller Ltd is a company engaged in pharmaceutical manufacturing. The purchasing department is managed by Mr Wurm, the buyer, and his assistant Walter Green. The value of purchases annually is about £3 million. When goods are required the inventory records clerk (Frederica) sends a purchase requisition to Mr Wurm, who gets Walter to type out an order form. Walter enters a serial number sequentially numbered after the last purchase order and photocopies the order. The original is sent to the supplier, and the copy is kept in a file.

When the goods arrive, they are taken into inventory, and the supplier's despatch note is sent to Walter from the goods inwards supervisor. Walter then marks off the items received on the order and sends the despatch note to the inventory records section, who use it to write up the inventory ledger and file it in chronological sequence.

Task 1: Identify deficiencies in the system and their implications.

Task 2: Make recommendations to improve the system. (These need to be set out in outline only – detailed systems notes are not required). You may assume that the company has sufficient resources to implement suitable recommendations.

3.10 Solution

Deficiency (Task 1)	Implication (Task 1)	Recommendation (Task 2)
Purchase orders are numbered manually.	Unauthorised orders could be placed.	Use pre-numbered multi-part order documents.
Purchase orders are not multi-part.	Copies may not be made, or may be subsequently altered.	Maintain sequential controls by recording spoiled and unused copies.
Orders are not priced.	Incorrect prices charged by suppliers may go unnoticed and be paid.	Price orders before despatch by reference to supplier's catalogues.
Mr Wurm does not check or sign orders before they are sent to suppliers.	Unauthorised purchases could be made.	Mr Wurm should check and sign orders as evidence of authorisation.
There is no goods inwards note system to evidence the arrival of goods.	Goods may be received but not accounted for.	Use a pre-numbered three part Goods Received Note (GRN): • Part 1 – to update order file, so that outstanding orders can be identified by Mr Wurm. • Part 2 – to write up the inventory ledger. • Part 3 – to maintain sequential control.

Deficiency (Task 1)	**Implication (Task 1)**	**Recommendation (Task 2)**
Goods are accepted without reference to purchase orders.	Unwanted goods may be accepted.	Send a copy of the purchase order to goods inwards department. Delivery notes should be matched with an order before goods are accepted.

Activity 2

(a) Which document is the goods received note compared to and why?

(b) Which documents is the purchase invoice compared to when received and why?

(c) What is the purpose of a purchase requisition in terms of control objectives?

4 Payroll cycle

4.1 Introduction

Payroll costs in most businesses represent a significant expense and the administrative procedures involved can be quite complicated. As a result, a formalised payroll system is vital if the business is to record its payroll costs accurately, employees are to be paid the correct amounts, and the liability to HM Revenue and Customs in respect of deductions is to be correctly reflected.

4.2 Overview of the payroll system

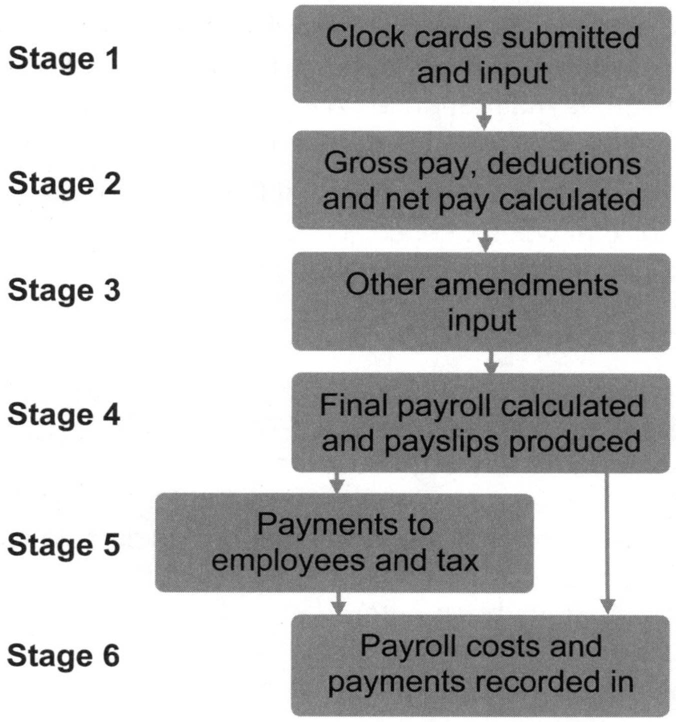

A typical system to deal with the processing of wages paid to weekly paid employees is set out above. Although the procedures in respect of monthly paid salaries differ slightly, the basic aims remain the same. At the end of the detailed description below you will find these main differences between wages and salaries highlighted.

4.3 Clock cards

Clock cards are collected from each employee at the end of each week. These show the hours worked during that period. The factory supervisor signs each clockcard as evidence that it has been reviewed and that the hours worked appear reasonable. This review also ensures that any overtime worked by an employee is controlled. The clockcards are passed by the supervisor to the wages clerk, and new cards collected for the following week.

The wages clerk checks the clock cards against a list of employees, ensuring that there is a card for each one. The details of the hours worked are recorded for each employee and the card stamped once it has been processed.

4.4 Wages calculations

The wages clerk calculates the gross pay for each employee using the rates of pay (basic and overtime) from the employees' wages file. PAYE and NI are calculated with any sundry deductions applicable to that employee (such as maintenance payments, loan repayments, details of which will also be found on the wages file).

The payroll supervisor reviews the total figures for gross pay, net pay, and deductions for that week to ensure that they appear reasonable. The supervisor signs the report as evidence of this review.

4.5 Other amendments

Before the payroll can be produced, there may be other amendments which need to be processed, for example, if an employee is due holiday pay, sick pay or maternity pay. Such amendments should be authorised by the supervisor before being processed by the payroll clerk. A standard, sequentially pre-numbered amendments form is completed and signed by the supervisor before being passed to the payroll clerk. Once the details of the amendments have been entered onto the system, the clerk stamps the form to indicate that it has been processed. There are sundry other amendments which are also dealt with at this stage. For example, a new employee may start work, an employee leaves or one of the workers be given a pay increase. The payroll supervisor should be given written notification by a senior member of staff, such as the chief accountant, before completing the necessary amendments form. Any documentation relating to starters, leavers and pay increases should be attached to the amendments form or otherwise rejected by the payroll clerk. If the amendment relates to a new employee, a new wages file is created for that individual by the payroll clerk.

The accountant reviews the amendment forms on a regular basis, ensuring that the sequence is complete, that all forms have been signed by the supervisor and relevant documentation is attached for amendments relating to starters, leavers and pay increases.

4.6 Payslips

Once all the necessary information has been entered, the final payroll can be calculated and individual payslips for all employees for that week can be produced together with a payroll summary of gross pay, net pay and PAYE and NI. The summary is reviewed by the accountant, to ensure that it appears reasonable, and the payroll report signed. The supervisor checks the payslips against the employee list to ensure that one has been produced for each employee. The payslips are then passed to the factory manager for distribution to the staff.

4.7 Payments

The payroll clerk prepares a bank transfer form for each employee and enters the wages figure from the payslip. Once such information is notified to the company's bank, transfers of funds to employees' accounts take place automatically.

The accountant compares the total net pay figure on the payroll summary each week to the total transferred from the company's bank account in respect of wages. If these amounts are different, immediate investigations should be made.

Where employees are paid by cash (which is often the case for hourly-paid and part-time workers) the payroll is passed to the accountant who draws a cheque for the net total. This is then processed and signed following the procedure set out in the section of this chapter covering the cash system. The total deductions due to HM Revenue and Customs for that week are recorded in a special Revenue payments book, using the figures on the weekly payroll summary for PAYE and NI. At the end of each month, the amount due is paid to Revenue and Customs and the date and amount of the payment is entered.

4.8 Recording

The payroll clerk passes a copy of the payroll summary to the accounts department each week. The accounts clerk credits the net pay to the wages control account in the main ledger, the statutory deductions to the deductions control account and the total debits to the payroll expense account. The accounts clerk writes the account number beside the relevant figure on the payroll summary to ensure that everything is posted. The payments made (net pay or payments to Revenue and Customs) are also recorded in the wages control and deductions control accounts respectively. The accountant should review these two control accounts on a regular basis to ensure they are showing a nil balance.

4.9 Controls

The main control objectives and types of controls for the payroll system are given below.

Control objectives for payroll	Examples of payroll controls
Stage 1 – Clock cards	
To ensure that only bona fide employees can be paid for work which they have done. (Otherwise regular overpayments will be made which could even affect the business's own cash flow).	Restrictions on issue of clock cards (for example by payroll clerk to factory supervisor). Authorisation of clock cards by factory supervisor before processing. Comparison of returned clockcards against employee list.
Stage 2 – Calculation	
To ensure that the calculations for gross and net pay and all deductions are accurate. (Otherwise employees may receive the wrong amount and the total wage expense may be wrongly recorded).	Comparison of total gross, net and deductions with previous amounts by payroll supervisor. Review of week's starters and leavers to consider impact on payroll figures. Check that each amendment in the week is correctly reflected on an individual and total basis.
Stage 3 – Other amendments	
To ensure that any amendments to standing data (such as starters and leavers, pay rises etc.) are valid and authorised. (Otherwise invalid changes could occur, leading to the creation of fictitious employees, keeping employees on the payroll who had left and paying inflated rates to existing employees.)	Standardised, pre-numbered amendment forms. Signature of wages supervisor on all amendments before acceptance for input. Supporting documentation for starters, leavers and pay rises to be attached to amendment forms.

Control objectives for payroll	Examples of payroll controls
Stage 4 – Payslips	
To ensure the accuracy of the payroll report. (Otherwise the wrong amounts will be posted to the wages expense and control accounts and the wrong amounts paid).	Review of the payroll by the chief accountant to ensure totals seem reasonable. Signature on report. Check individual payslips against an employee list to ensure completeness of processed information.
To ensure that all deductions for PAYE and NI and payments for statutory sick pay and maternity pay are accurately recorded. (If the amounts are wrongly stated, the company may incur serious penalties).	Accountant should check total deductions figure and maintain a deductions control account.
Stage 5 – Payments	
To prevent payments being made to staff who are not entitled to that pay.	Use of a credit transfer facility to avoid need for cash controls. Authorisation and documentation of amendments to employees' bank account details. Comparison of the total net pay figure for the week against the total funds transferred from the company's bank account.
Stage 6 – Recording	
To ensure that all payroll details for each week are posted correctly to the wages expense account and the wages and deductions control accounts in the main ledger.	Entry of the main ledger account code beside the relevant figure as posting occurs. Use of wages and deductions control accounts (which should carry nil balances after wage payments and payments to HM Revenue and Customs have been made). Review of wages and deductions control accounts by the chief accountant.

4.10 Stages 1 and 2

As mentioned in the payroll cycle section, the system outlined above concentrates on weekly paid employees paid at an hourly rate. Although the objectives and controls would be very similar if the system were to process monthly salaries instead, some aspects of the operation of the system would differ slightly.

4.11 Stages 1 and 2

Rather than calculating the gross pay with reference to hours worked detailed on clockcards, the monthly salary is calculated by reference to the employee's annual salary, recorded on their employee file. Once deductions and net pay have been calculated, a summary is produced and reviewed by the payroll supervisor in the normal manner. Any overtime for which the employee is entitled to payment is noted on an overtime form and authorised by that employee's department manager before being passed to the payroll clerk for processing. The payroll clerk stamps the overtime forms once they have been processed and files them in numerical order.

4.12 Stages 3 and 4

Amendments relating to salaried employees are dealt with in the same manner as outlined in the wages system. A separate salaries report is produced which will be reviewed by the accountant.

4.13 Stages 5 and 6

The posting of the salaries is largely identical to that for wages, the only difference being that the net cost of salaries is credited to the salaries control account rather than the wages control account. The deductions are credited to the deductions control account in the normal manner and total costs relating to salaries debited to the payroll expense account.

Example

Philip plc is a manufacturing company employing a total of 300 people, 200 of these being workers who are paid weekly in cash. All workers are required to record their times of arrival and departure using a clock card which is inserted in a time recording clock.

At weekly intervals the cards are collected and passed to the works office where the clerks total up the hours worked on each card and list the total hours worked (a 'hash' total). The cards and the add list are then passed to Elizabeth in the wages department who enters the names and hours worked on the payroll sheet, and agrees the add list total.

The payroll sheets are then passed to Roderick who keeps the payroll records. He enters the rate of pay and calculates the gross pay. He also computes the PAYE deduction, NIC deduction and employer's NIC, which he enters on the payroll. He passes the payrolls back to Elizabeth who calculates the net amount and totals all the columns on the payroll.

The completed payroll is then passed to Charles, the accountant, who scans the payroll, compares the totals with the previous week, and initials the payroll. Charles raises a cheque requisition which is sent to the cashier's department.

The cashier draws a cheque for the net amount of the payroll which is then signed by two directors. The cheque is given to a representative of Crypto Nat Security Services plc who draw the money from the bank and deliver it under guard to Elizabeth. The cashier, Theobald, then puts the money into pay envelopes along with a pay slip.

The sealed envelopes and relevant clock cards are then used for payouts. Each worker obtains his money once he has identified himself and signed his clock card. Unclaimed wages are held for three weeks before being re-banked.

5 Cash system

5.1 Introduction

Your study of the sales and purchases cycles earlier in this chapter, and the payroll cycle above, has indicated some of the typical processes involved in cash payments and receipts.

There will however be controls over and above those already discussed, because cash is a significant asset for many businesses, and is also at a higher risk of potential misappropriation.

5.2 Overview of the cash system

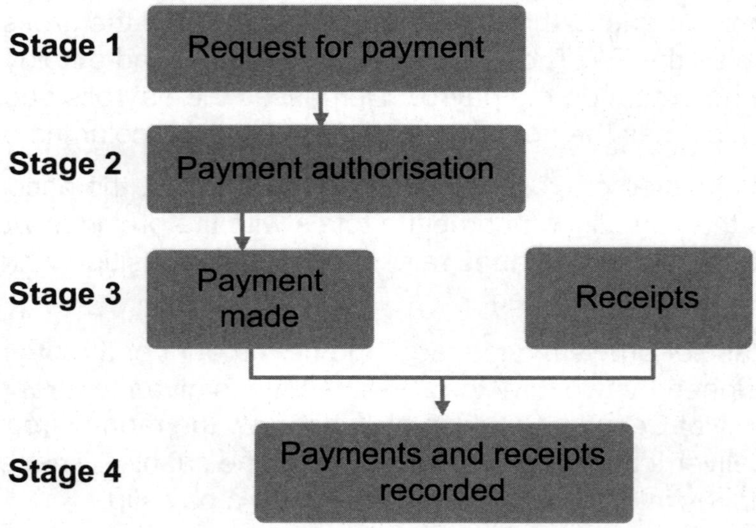

Each stage of this system is covered in more detail below.

5.3 Request for payment

- Any payment, whatever its nature and whether it is large or small, can only be made in response to a request, which is in the form of an invoice or a bill, or a cheque requisition supported by an invoice.
- The cashier completes a cheque for the relevant amount but should not be able to sign the cheque.

5.4 Authorisation

- The cashier passes the cheque to the accountant (who normally is the main authorised cheque signatory). The cheque is accompanied by some form of supporting documentation, so that the accountant can satisfy himself that the payment is in respect of a valid business expense. The documentation is usually the relevant invoice or a copy of the supplier's statement.

5.5 Making payments and receiving money

- Cheque payments which are over a predetermined value require a second signature. If this is the case, the accountant passes the cheque to the additional signatory. The cheque books should be kept secure at all times by the cashier.
- All post received by the company should be opened by two members of staff. Any receipts from customers, or in respect of sundry income (such as dividends), are recorded immediately on a cash received sheet. The source and amount of the payment is recorded and the sheet totalled and signed by the two members of staff. Cash received sheets are sequentially pre-numbered documents.

5.6 Recording receipts and payments

- The cashier records all payments as they are made in the payments side of the cash book, noting the date, the name of the payee and the amount. The cashier receives the cash received sheets on a daily basis and records the details in the receipts side of the cash book. Both payments and receipts are analysed under the appropriate cash book headings, depending upon their nature. The cashier also completes a paying-in slip from the cash received sheet details. All receipts are paid into the bank on a daily basis.
- At the end of each day the cashier totals the cash book and completes a posting form. The posting form contains the totals from each of the cash book columns, and the relevant main ledger account codes. The posting form is dated and passed to the accounts clerk.
- The accounts clerk makes the postings to the appropriate main ledger accounts, stamping the form as processed once all items have been dealt with. The posting forms are filed in date order.
- At the end of each month, the cashier performs a bank reconciliation. The reconciliation is passed to the accountant who reviews it and then signs it. The approved reconciliations are returned to the cashier, and filed in date order.

5.7 Controls

The main control objectives and types of controls in the cash system are given below.

Control objectives for cash	Examples of cash controls
Stages 1 and 2 – Request and authorisation	
To ensure that payments are only made in respect of valid business expenses. (Otherwise the business will be operating inefficiently and may be making unnecessary payments).	The cheque signatory is a senior member of staff, independent of the day-to-day recording of business transactions. Cheques are only signed after appropriate supporting documentation has been submitted. Cheques in respect of large amounts require a second signatory.
Stages 3 and 4 – Payments, receipts and recording	
To ensure that all receipts and payments are recorded accurately and promptly. (Otherwise, management will find it difficult to run the business as it will not have up-to-date information about the cash position). To ensure that the risk of misappropriation of cash from the business is minimised.	The initial recording of receipts is carried out by two independent members of staff. (This should largely prevent the possible misappropriation of receipts or accidental non-recording.) Stamping of posting forms once all the figures have been posted to the relevant main ledger accounts. (This helps to ensure completeness of information). The performance and review of monthly bank reconciliations.

Note that this section assumes payment is by cheque. If settlement is by other means, such as bank transfer, then similar authorisation controls should apply over the payment method used.

6 Inventory system

6.1 Introduction

Inventory is usually one of a business's larger value assets and one, like cash, which is particularly susceptible to misappropriation. Adequate systems must be installed to control movements in and out of inventory and to prevent damage or misappropriation. This will help to safeguard inventory and assist in the effective management of inventory levels. Although a number of elements of a typical inventory system have already been mentioned in the outlines of sales and purchases systems, a more detailed description is given below.

6.2 Overview of the inventory system

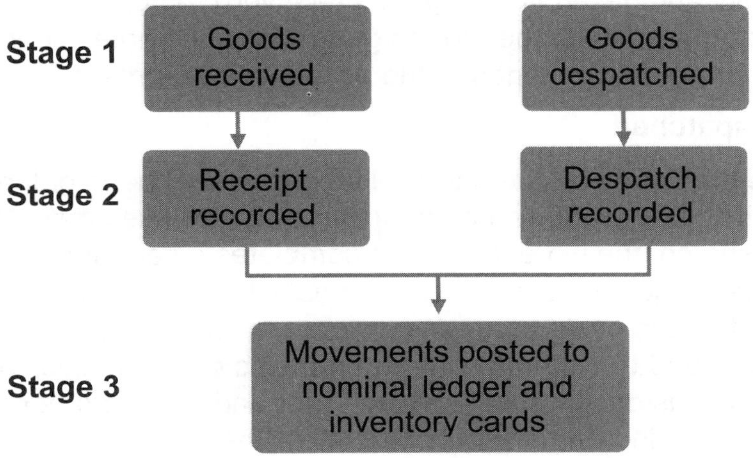

Each stage is covered in more detail below.

6.3 Goods received and despatched

Goods received

- When a delivery is made by a supplier, the warehouseman physically checks the delivery to ensure that damaged goods are not accepted. The inventory is stored carefully so that it cannot be damaged or misappropriated and it is stored with similar items.

Goods despatched

- Details of the order are required from the sales department before goods can be despatched to customers. Two of the warehousemen should prepare the goods for despatch together; one counting out the items whilst the other marks the goods off against the order. If any of the required goods are out of inventory, the warehouse manager places the order in an 'open orders' file. At the same time, he completes an 'incomplete order sheet' with details of the unavailable inventory and returns this to the sales department. The sales department informs the customer. So that customers are dealt with as efficiently as possible, the warehouse manager reviews the 'open orders' file on a regular basis to ensure that orders are despatched as soon as the goods become available.

6.4 Recording

Goods received

- The warehouseman signs the supplier's delivery note once he has inspected the goods. A copy of this note is retained by the warehouseman. Details of the delivery are recorded immediately on a 3-part sequentially pre-numbered goods received note (GRN) (i.e. the date of delivery, supplier's name and reference number, quantity and description of goods received). A copy of the supplier's delivery note is attached to the goods received notes sent to the purchasing department and the accounts department.

Goods despatched

- Once the goods required to fulfil an order have been gathered together, the goods can be despatched to the customer. At the time of despatch, the warehouseman completes a sequentially pre-numbered goods despatched note (GDN). This shows the date of despatch, the customer name, reference number and delivery address and the quantity and descriptions of goods despatched. This document is despatched with the order and the customer's signature acknowledging delivery will be obtained before it is returned to the warehouse. One copy is retained in the warehouse (filed in number order) whilst the other two copies are sent to the sales department and accounts department respectively.
- If a customer rejects or returns goods, the warehouse staff must ensure that the receipt is correctly recorded. The details of the goods returned, and the customer's details, are recorded on a sequentially pre-numbered goods returned note. One copy of the note is retained by the warehouse in number order and the other two copies sent to the sales and accounts department. Returned inventory must be stored in an appropriate location immediately to ensure that it is not damaged or misappropriated.

6.5 Accounting

Goods received

- Goods received will not be input to the main ledger until the supplier raises an invoice in respect of the delivery. However, the goods received note details are used by the warehouse manager to update his inventory cards. An Inventory card is maintained for each category of inventory and shows the current balance in hand for that line. Thus the balance is increased each time a delivery of that Inventory line is received. The warehouse manager stamps his copy of the goods received note as processed once all lines have been posted to the appropriate inventory cards.

Goods despatched

- Similarly, the information detailed in the goods despatched notes is used in two ways. First, the accounts department uses the details to raise sales invoices and secondly, the inventory card balances are reduced in respect of any inventory despatched to customers.

6.6 Inventory cards

By operating the inventory card system outlined above, the warehouse manager knows the balance on hand for every inventory line at any time. These records of inventory quantities are then used for comparison against the physical inventory counted at the year-end. If there are any differences between book inventory quantities and physical quantities these should be investigated and the inventory cards amended, if necessary.

6.7 Controls

The main control objectives and types of controls are given below.

Control objectives for inventory	**Examples of inventory controls**
Stage 1 – Goods received	
To ensure that damaged goods are not accepted from a supplier.	Physical inspection of all deliveries before acceptance of goods.
To ensure that all inventory is stored securely so as to prevent misappropriation and/or damage.	Storage of inventory in secure locations on receipt.

Control objectives for inventory	**Examples of inventory controls**
Stage 1 – Goods despatched	
To ensure that all orders are dealt with accurately and promptly. To ensure that any goods returned by customers are correctly recorded and controlled. (Otherwise customer goodwill may be lost).	Two of the warehouse staff work together to compile orders. (The possibility of customers inadvertently being sent the wrong items will be significantly reduced). Maintain an open orders file which is reviewed regularly (so that customers whose orders cannot be fulfilled immediately should not be kept waiting any longer than necessary). Send details of out of inventory items to the sales department, so the customer is kept informed.
Stage 2 – Goods received	
To ensure that the details of all goods received are accurately recorded.	Sequentially pre-numbered GRNs. Copies of GRNs sent to the sales department for comparison against orders. Investigate any orders for which a delivery is not received.
Stage 2 – Goods despatched	
To ensure that the details of all goods despatched to customers, together with any returns by customers, are accurately recorded.	Sequentially pre-numbered GDNs. Customer's signature to be obtained on despatch note (reduces risk of disputes). Accounts department checks sequence of GDNs for completeness. Sales department despatches against customer orders Sequential pre-numbered goods returned notes.

Control objectives for inventory	Examples of inventory controls
Stage 3 – Accounting	
To ensure complete control over all inventory movements and the recording of such on inventory cards. (Otherwise, management may not have accurate information regarding inventory quantities).	Use GDNs and GRNs to update inventory cards. Stamp GDNs and GRNs as processed and file in numerical order (enables warehouse manager to be aware of physical quantities at any one time). Regular inventory counts and comparison of book to actual quantities and investigation of variances.

7 Summary

You should now understand the following aspects of typical sales and purchases systems:

- How information is processed.
- The typical documents involved in processing.
- The controls which may be included.
- Management's reasons for adopting these controls.

This chapter has also covered payroll, cash and inventory. For each of these, you should now understand:

- the stages involved in the system
- the key documents which are processed
- management's control objectives and the various controls which may be implemented.

Before leaving this chapter, quickly review the last few pages and note the style of writing which has been adopted to describe the control objectives as compared with the controls themselves.

This management objective is of less relevance to the external auditor.

Answers to chapter activities

Activity 1

(a) If the documents are sequentially numbered then it is easy to check for completeness, i.e. to check that no documents are missing or have not been processed.

(b) Selling on credit always involves an element of risk. In order to minimise the risk of non-payment by a receivable, each customer is given a credit limit which must not be exceeded. Therefore, when an order is placed, it is important to ensure that by accepting that order the customer's credit limit is not exceeded. Therefore, the current balance on the customer's account plus the amount of the order must be compared to the credit limit.

(c) In the main ledger the totals of the sales day book are debited to the receivables control account and credited to the sales account. Each individual invoice must also be recorded as a debit in the receivables own account in the subsidiary sales ledger.

(d) The control objective regarding the despatch of goods to customers is that all movements of inventory are valid and adequately recorded.

Activity 2

(a) The goods received note is compared to the purchase order to ensure that all that was ordered has in fact been received. At a later date the goods received note will also be compared to the invoice to ensure that the business is only paying for goods that have actually been received.

(b) In order to ensure that the business only pays for goods that were actually received in good condition, the purchase invoice is compared to the goods received note, the supplier's despatch note and any goods returned note.

(c) The control objective of an approved purchase requisition is to ensure that only goods and services that are required and have been approved are ordered.

8 Test your knowledge

Workbook Activity 3

An entity uses internal control procedures in order to mitigate the risks to which the entity is exposed. Listed below are two internal control procedures which are applicable to an entity's inventory procurement system.

Required:

For each internal control procedure, match the procedure with the risk mitigated.

1 Purchase invoices matched to goods received records prior to posting to the ledger.

2 Physical counts of inventory and reconciliation with recorded amounts.

Picklist:

Purchasing goods from unauthorised suppliers.

Theft of inventory.

Purchasing unnecessary goods.

Paying for goods not received.

Workbook Activity 4

Cleanco Ltd is a company which undertakes commercial and domestic cleaning work. The company provides labour and cleaning materials. All purchases of cleaning materials are paid for at time of purchase and Cleanco Ltd's employees collect the fee as soon as each job is completed.

In addition to cash handling activities, which of the following combinations of accounting systems are likely to be subject to external audit?

1 Sales, trade receivables and trade payables.

2 Purchases, trade payables and trade receivables.

3 Sales, purchases and payroll.

4 Purchases, trade receivables and trade payables.

Planning, controlling and recording

3

Introduction

Planning an audit is essential to the effective running of the assignment. There are a number of factors to consider when planning an audit which we will see in this chapter. These factors will shape the entire assignment as you will see in the chapters that follow.

SYLLABUS AREA

2.1 Identify the accounting systems under review and accurately record them on appropriate working papers.

2.2 Identify the control framework.

2.3 Assess risks associated with the accounting system and its controls.

2.7 Explain tests of control and substantive procedures and their links to the audit objective.

2.9 Provide clear information and recommendations for the proposed audit plan for submission to the appropriate person for consideration.

3.2 Recognise the importance of audit files and working papers and their role in the audit process.

5.4 Explain audit risk and how it applies to external auditing.

5.5 Explain materiality and how it applies to external auditing.

CONTENTS

1 Planning

2 The client/auditor relationship

3 The engagement letter

4 Planning the assignment

5 Audit planning memorandum

6 Quality control

7 Audit risk

8 Materiality

9 Analytical procedures

10 The audit approach

11 Recording audit work

1 Planning

1.1 Introduction

ISA 300 *Planning an Audit of Financial Statements* states:

The auditor should plan the audit so that the engagement will be performed in an effective manner.

Planning entails developing a general strategy and a detailed approach for the expected nature, timing and extent of the audit.

1.2 Audit plan and audit programme

Auditors formulate the general audit strategy in an overall audit plan, which sets the direction for the audit and provides guidance for the development of the audit programme. The audit programme sets out the detailed procedures required to implement the strategy.

1.3 Objectives

Planning is necessary for audits of entities of all types and sizes. The objectives of planning the audit work, which takes place before the detailed audit work begins, include:

- ensuring that appropriate attention is devoted to the different areas of the audit
- ensuring that potential problems are identified, and
- facilitating review.

Planning also assists in the proper assignment of work to members of the audit team and their briefing, and in the co-ordination of work done by other auditors and experts, so that the audit may be performed in an efficient and timely manner.

1.4 Procedures

An understanding of the entity's business and, as far as practicable, of the nature and scope of the work they are to carry out is necessary for all members of the audit team before the audit field work starts.

The auditors' experience with the entity and knowledge of its business assist in the identification of events, transactions and practices which may have a material effect on the financial statements.

Auditors may need to discuss elements of the overall audit plan and certain audit procedures with the entity's management and staff to improve the effectiveness of the audit and to co-ordinate audit procedures with the work of the entity's personnel, including internal auditors. The overall audit plan and the detailed audit procedures to be performed, however, remain the auditors' responsibility.

2 The client/auditor relationship

2.1 Knowing the client

An auditor has a duty of care to carry out his work with a reasonable standard of skill and care and therefore should not take on engagements which he cannot properly fulfil. (See Chapter 14)

Consequently the auditor must:

- understand how the business operates, its strengths and its weaknesses, the markets served, the products it supplies
- have a good working relationship with the key members of the management team
- have a clear understanding of the nature of the services provided by the auditor to his client
- be aware of what can be regarded as 'best practice' and be able to implement the latest professional developments.

In the case of companies audited in prior years, most of the information required for planning will be available in the permanent file, working papers and other files.

2.2 New audits

On being asked to accept appointment as auditor to a new client, there are various matters that the auditor should consider before accepting such an appointment (see Chapter 13 for details of appointment).

- Does the auditor have the capability and resources to carry out the audit? The auditor will need to determine the following:
  - size, location and nature of business of the prospective client
  - timing of the audit
  - number and degree of experience of the staff required
  - current commitments of the firm
  - firm's experience in the audit of such a business.
- Is the auditor independent of the client? The auditor must establish the independence of the firm.
- Are there any other reasons for not accepting appointment?

Communication with the existing auditor may reveal professional reasons why the audit should not be accepted. (See Chapter 13 for changes in professional appointment).

3 The engagement letter

Definition

An **engagement letter** is a letter from the auditor to the client setting out the terms of the assignment.

3.1 Introduction

The purpose of the engagement letter is:

- to set out the terms under which the assignment is to be carried out; and hence
- to minimise the chances of misunderstanding between client and external auditor.

3.2 Procedures

Auditors should:

- agree the terms of their engagement with new clients in writing
- thereafter, regularly review the terms of engagement and if appropriate agree any changes in writing.

3.3 New audits

The agreement of an engagement letter is in the interests of both auditors and client. It is therefore desirable that the contents be agreed prior to the audit appointment (and the letter sent soon after) and, in any event, before the commencement of the first audit assignment. Subsequently, the regular review of the engagement letter helps the auditors and the client avoid misunderstandings with respect to the engagement.

3.4 Recurring audits

As part of the annual planning process, auditors consider whether a new engagement letter is required. The following factors may make the agreement of a new letter appropriate:

- any indication that the client misunderstands the objective and scope of the audit
- a recent change of management, board of directors or audit committee

- a significant change in ownership, such as a new holding company
- a significant change in the nature or size of the client's business
- any relevant change in legal or professional requirements.

It may be appropriate to remind the client of the original letter when the auditors decide a new engagement letter is unnecessary for any period.

3.5 Principal contents of the engagement letter

The engagement letter should:

- document and confirm acceptance of the appointment; and
- include a summary of the responsibilities of the directors and of the auditors, the scope of the engagement and the form of any reports.

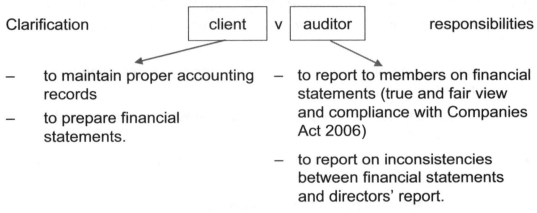

Clarification **client** v **auditor** responsibilities

client	auditor
– to maintain proper accounting records – to prepare financial statements.	– to report to members on financial statements (true and fair view and compliance with Companies Act 2006) – to report on inconsistencies between financial statements and directors' report.

The letter should outline the main stages in the audit. The remaining content hinges around areas where particular misunderstandings may occur, including the following:

- fees and billing arrangements
- procedures where the client has a complaint about the service
- where appropriate, arrangements concerning the involvement of:
  - other auditors and experts in some aspect of the audit
  - internal auditors and other staff of the entity
- arrangements, if any, to be made with the predecessor auditors, where the audit is being performed by a new auditor
- where appropriate, the country by whose laws the engagement is to be governed
- a reference to any further agreements between the auditors and the client
- a proposed timetable for the engagement.

Representations by management may be requested in writing. If the auditor does not clarify this 'up front', the directors may be reluctant to provide written representations. (See Chapter 11 for more detail.)

Accounting and taxation services should be distinguished from audit.

Fees are (usually) based on time spent and level of staff involved (i.e. variable not fixed).

4 Planning the assignment

4.1 Audit approach

An important aspect of the auditor's judgement is to determine the most appropriate audit approach for the individual client. This will be based on the following:

- general economic factors and industry conditions affecting the entity's business
- the operating style and control consciousness of directors and management
- the auditors' cumulative knowledge of the accounting and internal control systems and any expected changes in the period
- the scale and size of the organisation
- the volumes and value of transactions
- the geographical spread of business operations.

The auditor must thoroughly familiarise himself with the affairs of the business and its recent financial history. This is done by reviewing files of working papers, and regular contact with the client.

4.2 Obtaining the knowledge

In the first audit the necessary information must be collected before planning can commence. A starting point is to consider the industry in which the business operates in broad terms. The following matters should be noted:

- typical kinds of business within the industry (e.g. large international)
- the broad functions involved (e.g. manufacturing, distribution, wholesaling)
- any particular features of the business important to management (e.g. long-term contracts)

- typical sources of income (e.g. room lettings in a hotel)
- typical kinds of expenditure (e.g. food in a restaurant)
- the kinds of records kept (e.g. day books, registers)
- management's information needs.

Such information is vital if the auditor is to discuss the industry, its problems and solutions with management in a credible manner.

4.3 Client liaison

The auditor should obviously pay attention to the client's requirements in carrying out the audit. The client will wish to avoid audit visits at critical times of the year (e.g. when quarterly accounts are being prepared). The auditor should consult with his client in order to ascertain the following dates:

- to which accounts are to be made up for the period under review
- by which final accounts will be prepared together with supporting schedules
- on which the directors intend to meet in order to approve the financial statements
- of the AGM when audited accounts must be laid before the members
- by which accounts must be filed at the Companies Registry.

4.4 Time and fee budgets

The auditor should aim to provide his client with an efficient and cost effective service. Budgetary planning is an important part of the overall audit plan in order to ensure that:

- the work is completed efficiently
- the costs of carrying out the audit are monitored
- the client's fee can be negotiated on a reasonable basis (this is now often a sensitive issue in good client/auditor relationships)
- forward planning for staff requirements is facilitated.

4.5 Staffing

The audit budget will also assist the auditor to determine the manpower requirements. It is important to select the right 'mix' of skills so that the audit work is competently performed. Other factors to consider:

- staff members' prior experience of the client, and
- personal qualities of staff (e.g. potential personality clashes with client or other audit staff).

4.6 The planning meeting

Once staff have been selected they should be briefed at a planning meeting. The matters discussed at the meeting must be documented in the form of a minute and should cover the following:

a description of key features of the client and the names of contacts any special features that may be encountered on the audit the general instructions to staff on their responsibilities any issues of confidentiality and security.

Many firms use a planning memorandum, see overleaf.

4.7 Timing of audit visits

The timing of the audit visits varies according to the type of enterprise. When dealing with a large public company audit there is a need to ensure that the work is reasonably spread that undue pressure is not placed upon the auditor in the critical period between the date of the statement of financial position and the date of the directors' meeting to finalise the accounts. Instead work will be spread over the period prior to the year-end date.

4.8 First interim visit

- To review accounting systems.
- To document any new systems or changes that have occurred.
- To ascertain and evaluate internal controls using standard checklists, questionnaires, etc.
- To confirm the system by means of 'walk-through' tests on one or two transactions.

4.9 Second interim visit

- To test processing systems of the major transaction cycles of purchases, sales and payroll to ensure that the controls are sound.
- To test the records (on the basis of the above) in order to form an opinion as to whether the processing is accurate and the records are reliable.

4.10 Year-end inventory count

To witness the physical ascertainment of inventory (see Chapter 7).

4.11 Final audit visit

After the year-end date the auditor can devote himself to verifying assets and liabilities and carrying out a review of the financial statements so as to be in a position to sign the audit report.

It is common, however, to find that the audits of small companies (whose control systems are limited) are performed in a single phase commencing after the year-end date.

5 Audit planning memorandum

5.1 Introduction

Most audit firms prepare an audit planning memorandum which sets out factors to be taken into account, the methods by which the audit objectives will be achieved and the organisational matters which need to be considered.

5.2 Typical contents

Terms of the engagement

The work to be done (i.e. audit work, accounting work to be done for the client, tax work, letters to be sent). Including reports required and client expectations.

The client and its background

History, products, locations, especially noting factors like a new managing director, a new computer, a new product.

Important figures and ratios

From previous years audit working papers and, if available, from management and draft accounts.

Audit risk areas

These might include inventory and work in progress or dealings with a fellow group company (see later in this chapter). This may include the requirement for involvement of specialists.

Preliminary estimate of materiality

(See later in this chapter).

Client assistance

Assistance from the client may be required in providing documents and analyses, providing computer time, arranging visits to branches. Also the extent to which internal audit may be involved.

The audit approach

Extent of reliance on internal control, the use of tests of control and substantive procedures (see later in this chapter).

Timetable

Key audit dates e.g. of interim, year-end and final audits and of deadlines to meet (e.g. AGM of the company).

Staffing requirement

Time budget and audit fee estimate. This may be included in a separate memorandum.

5.3 Confidentiality matters

The following matters illustrate the nature of confidential information which may be encountered in the planning process.

- **Risk assessment** – some factors which increase the auditor's perception of risk may appear to cast aspersions on the integrity of the client's staff and/or management (see later in this chapter for more detail).
- **Sensitive issues re client** – for example, new product development, plans for business acquisitions etc. These must be kept confidential within the client-auditor relationship.
- **Audit approach** – where locations are to be visited on a surprise basis (e.g. to attend the inventory count or count cash) it is inappropriate to warn the client in advance by incorporating details in an audit planning memorandum which is shown to the client.
- **Nature and scope of audit tests to be performed** – if there is suspicion of irregularities being perpetrated by the client's staff, their detection by the auditor may be thwarted.
- **Budgets and fees** – although the audit fee is negotiated with the client, it is usually inappropriate to disclose budgeted hours and charge-out rates of the audit team. Pressure from an audit client to curtail audit work and reduce fees would impair objectivity (see Chapter 13).

Example – AUDIT PLANNING MEMORANDUM

HASTINGS & WARWICK

Client: Peppers Ltd	Prepared by: K.E.D.	Date: 5.6.X6
Period: Y/e 31 July 20X6	Reviewed by:	Date:

Audit plan

1	Terms of engagement including reports required and client expectations	Normal Companies Act audit; we write up nominal ledger and prepare draft statutory accounts from client records.
2	The company and its business	New company set up in 20X4 to retail PCs and related software packages – provides some consultancy services. Financed mainly by proprietors and overdraft until £100,000 new capital injected by Capital Venture Ltd in January 20X6. Turnover about £1,200,000 (£650,000 last year).
3	Special audit problems	Possible obsolete inventory due to changes in technology; NX50 software may be unsaleable. Billing of sales is likely to give rise to errors – new systems are invoiced in advance of delivery; consultancy work is billed retrospectively and there is little by way of 'work in progress' records.

4	Results of analytical procedures	Client produces management accounts comprising sales analysis and cash flows (not reproduced); these are in line with the forecasts done in the report to Capital Venture Ltd.
5	Evaluation of audit risk	In view of the rapid growth of the business, the importance placed on the accounts by Capital Venture Ltd and the problems in recording sales, this audit should be treated as higher than normal risk. No reliance can be placed on the accounting systems nor on any analytical procedures.
6	Preliminary estimate of materiality	£7,000 based on estimate of turnover of £1.2m and likely profit of around £120,000–£250,000.
7	Audit approach	No attempt to rely on internal controls or analytical procedures. The following specific procedures should be carried out: • Reconcile purchases and sales of computer systems and check that cut off is correct, bearing in mind that it is the company's practice to invoice before delivery. • Review consultants' diaries for the last 3 months to check that all assignments are included in WIP or billings. For other procedures and objectives, see the audit programme which has already been prepared (not reproduced).

8	Other matters	The company moved to new leasehold premises in April; we need to take particular care that leasehold improvements are treated as tax efficiently as possible (see attached letter – not reproduced).
9	Budget and fee	Budget £15,500, excluding VAT
10	Timetable and staffing	G. Smith and J. Taylor to complete by 2.10.X6.

Audit plan approved	Date
Manager ______________	________
Partner ______________	________

5.4 Matters of security

All audit staff should be briefed in the observance of the client's security procedures. For example:

- presenting temporary passes for door security
- no smoking
- completing log books (e.g. for photocopier/computer utilisation).

Audit staff should take precautions to protect themselves when handling cash or other valuables. For example, when counting cash:

- a responsible member of the client's staff must be in attendance throughout so the auditor is never left unattended with client monies
- if possible, the room should be locked to prevent interruption
- it is advisable that the auditor does not have any cash in his possession
- the responsible official should sign a declaration that the cash has been returned intact into their custody.

6 Quality control

6.1 Methods of control

Direction, supervision and review are the principal methods for controlling the audit.

6.2 Procedures for controlling the audit

- Audit assistants are informed of their responsibilities and the objectives of the procedures they are to perform.
- Audit directions are communicated via briefing meetings, internal oral communications, audit manuals and checklists and the audit planning memorandum.
- Work should be done by staff with suitable skill and experience.
- The audit partner should be in constant contact with team members, ensuring that supervision is carried out by himself or his manager.
- The audit plan should be monitored by regular reports on work done so that the partner or manager is alerted to any changes from the agreed sequence of tasks.
- The procedures for carrying out audit field work should be documented in a manual of instruction and followed by audit staff.
- The work carried out by audit staff should be properly documented and reviewed by a more senior person.
- Troublesome points should be brought to the attention of partners, and staff should be sufficiently skilled to be alerted to unusual matters so that they are followed up.
- There should be written evidence that audit work has been reviewed.

7 Audit risk

7.1 Introduction

Most audit firms adopt a 'risk-based' approach to auditing.

Auditors should:

(a) obtain an understanding of the accounting and internal control systems sufficient to plan the audit and develop an effective audit approach, and

(b) use professional judgement to assess the components of audit risk and to design audit procedures to ensure it is reduced to an acceptably low level.

7.2 Risk-based audit approach

A risk-based approach to auditing:

- encourages a rational and systematic approach (which is essential to performing a high quality audit in the current climate of litigation)
- gives a plausible reason for keeping the level of audit testing to a minimum in certain cases (as commercial pressure on audit fees has forced firms to perform more cost-effective audits).

7.3 Audit risk

Definition

Audit risk is the risk that the auditor will form an inappropriate opinion, either on the financial statements as a whole, or in relation to a particular account balance or area.

This means that the auditor would issue a modified opinion where, in fact, an unmodified opinion was appropriate, or the converse (which is highlighted more frequently in litigation) an unmodified opinion when modification was required.

Some firms quantify their overall acceptable level of audit risk as a matter of practice policy and as the basis for mathematical derivation of detection risk and sample sizes (see Chapter 5).

Audit risk is made up of inherent risk, control risk and detection risk.

7.4 Inherent risk

> **Definition**
>
> **Inherent risk** is the risk that derives from the characteristics of the company or entity which is to be audited, or the circumstances of the audit or assignment.

- A company which operates in a high technology industry could be regarded as risky due to the impact of specialist technical advances on inventory values and trading base.
- A new client could be perceived as high risk owing to the auditor's lack of experience of the company and its management.
- An audit which is performed to a tight reporting deadline is performed without the same reliance on hindsight in the form of post year-end events which confirm the statement of financial position picture.

7.5 Control risk

> **Definition**
>
> **Control risk** is the risk that the client's internal controls will fail to prevent or detect and correct on a timely basis material misstatements.

Any initial assessment of control risk will be confirmed (or otherwise) by the results of adequate tests of control.

If it is believed that such testing is unlikely to be cost effective, then control risk must be assumed to be 100%, and the emphasis returns to inherent risk as the essential determinant of detection risk (see below) and therefore audit work.

7.6 Detection risk

> **Definition**
>
> **Detection risk** can be formally defined as the risk that the auditor's substantive procedures will fail to detect any remaining errors or omissions. This could be due to the inappropriate nature, extent or timing of audit procedures.

Having assessed IR and CR, detection risk is then the balancing figure set to achieve an acceptable total audit risk.

7.7 The audit risk model

Inherent risk and control risk exist independently of the audit and must be assessed by the auditor in order that detection risk (which is under the auditor's control) can be 'managed' to achieve an acceptable level of overall (i.e. audit) risk.

Where inherent risk and control risk together are high, detection risk must be minimised (rendered low) by the audit procedures performed. The auditor can respond by varying the nature, extent and/or timing of audit work.

7.8 Minimising detection risk

Methods of varying detection risk		Examples of audit work where inherent/control risk are high
1	Change the nature of audit work.	Obtain third party confirmation in preference to relying on internal documentation.
2	Change the extent of audit work.	Submit more items to scrutiny in audit test.
3	Change the timing of audit work.	Perform a circularisation closer to the year-end rather than at the interim.

7.9 Recognising risk

Audit risk can be assessed at two levels: the overall financial statement (or 'entity') level and the individual account balance and class of transactions level.

7.10 Entity level

An assignment would be judged risky if the circumstances of the client or of the assignment as a whole meant that the financial statements as a whole were more prone to material error. Examples have been suggested in the previous section in relation to inherent risk.

Control risk could be judged to be high at the overall financial statement level, for example in a company with poor general controls over its computer environment.

The consequence is that more (or more reliable) audit work will be required in respect of account balances generally, in order that audit evidence is sufficient.

7.11 Account balance and class of transactions level

This means that on a generally low risk assignment (e.g. the recurring audit of an established company in a stable industry) areas with high inherent risk can be identified. These could include the audit of inventory, especially if these are manufactured by the client. These are high risk due to judgements involved in attributing overheads.

Inventory is also high risk where they do not form part of the day to day accounting records and where physical count and subsequent valuation form the basis of the inventory figure in the accounts. The direct profit impact of the valuation increases the possibility of deliberate management bias. The area of provisions would also be judged risky due to the degree of subjectivity involved.

Poorly programmed procedures relating to a specific computer application (e.g. sales ledger processing) would increase control risk at the individual account balance level. Here, audit procedures can be extended, or more reliable sources of evidence sought, in respect of the particular account balance identified.

7.12 High inherent risk factors

Factors contributing to high inherent risk	
At overall financial statement level	**At individual account balance level**
1 Tight reporting deadline.	1 Items which are not part of the accounting records on a day to day basis (e.g. inventory).
2 Non-audit assignment.	2 Items which are essentially judgmental (e.g. provisions).
3 Newly formed company.	3 Items which are complex in calculation.
4 New client.	4 Cash-based transactions.
5 Client in financial services sector.	5 Transactions with related parties.
6 Client in high-tech industry.	
7 Existence of a large number of business locations.	

8 Poor quality management.	
9 Strained financial circumstances.	
10 Dominant influence by proprietor or a director.	
11 Impending change of ownership.	
12 Need for additional capital.	

Activity 1

Outline the 3 components of audit risk and give an example of each.

8 Materiality

Definition

Materiality is an expression of the relative significance or importance of a particular matter in the context of financial statements as a whole. A matter is material if its omission or misstatement would reasonably influence the decisions of an addressee of the auditors' report. Materiality may also be considered in the context of any individual primary statement within the financial statements or of individual items included in them. Materiality is not capable of general mathematical definition as it has both qualitative and quantitative aspects.

Performance Materiality is the amount or amounts set by the auditor at less than materiality for the financial statements as a whole to reduce to an acceptably low level the probability that the aggregate of uncorrected and undetected misstatements exceeds materiality for the financial statements as a whole.

8.1 Why is materiality important?

Materiality is important both to the auditor who expresses an opinion on the financial statements and to the preparer of the accounts.

- The auditor must direct his attention to material items as any errors or omissions will have an impact on the truth and fairness of the financial statements and therefore on the audit opinion.
- For the accountant the Companies Act 2006 does not define materiality. However, it states that: 'amounts which are not material in the context of any requirements of the Act may be disregarded for that purpose'.

Clearly it is important that the auditor and accountant are able to calculate materiality given its importance to both the profession and the law.

8.2 When is something material?

There are essentially three considerations:

- the size of the item
- the nature of the item
- the likely influence on a user of financial statements.

8.3 Size of the item

ISA 320 recognises, and permits the use of benchmark calculations of materiality. However, it must be stressed, that these should be used in the initial assessment of materiality. The auditor must then use judgement to modify materiality so that it is relevant to the unique circumstances of the client.

A traditional calculation basis is as follows:

	Value	**Comments**
Pre tax profit	5 – 10%	Users usually interested in profitability of the company.
Turnover	0.5 – 1%	Materiality relates to the size of the business, which can be measured in terms of revenue.
Total assets	1 – 2%	Size can also be measured in terms of the asset base.

When deciding on an appropriate benchmark the auditor must consider:

- the elements of the financial statements
- whether particular items tend to be the focus of users
- the nature of the entity, its life cycle and its environment
- the ownership of the financing structure, and
- the relative volatility of the benchmark.

8.4 Nature of the items

Again it is necessary to consider the impact on the user. Certain items in the accounts are capable of 'precise determination', for example 'directors' emoluments' and 'share capital'. Any error (however small) in respect of these items would be considered material and must be adjusted.

Other items are not capable of precise determination, for example, the inventory provision. With regard to such items some degree of latitude is acceptable. Auditors are also alert to the nature of misstatements relating to qualitative aspects of a matter. Examples of qualitative misstatements are the inadequate or inaccurate description of an accounting policy when it is likely that a user of the financial statements could be misled by the description.

8.5 Likely influence on a user

The definition of materiality is 'user-orientated'. Different users will base their assessment of materiality on different criteria; for example, a bank considering a loan application will consider matters to be material if they affect the company's:

- profit before interest (affects interest cover), and
- net assets (affects solvency).

The auditor is reporting to the shareholders and therefore this group of users are of primary importance when setting materiality levels.

8.6 Materiality at the overall financial statement level

'Calculations' of materiality are not usually appropriate at this stage. Consideration about materiality will usually come down to the auditor's judgement. In exercising this judgement, the partner may dismiss, as immaterial at the entity level, audit adjustments proposed by the audit staff as exceeding materiality thresholds at the account balance level. This does not mean that the audit staff were wrong to propose the adjustments; it reflects that a different level of materiality is relevant to forming an opinion on the financial statements as a whole.

8.7 Evaluating the effect of misstatements

The auditor will:

- aggregate the effect of misstatements noted during audit work
- consider their impact on critical points (e.g. profit/loss)
- use his experience to assess whether or not the financial statements can still give a true and fair view if the misstatements remain uncorrected.

The aggregate of uncorrected misstatements comprises:

- specific misstatements identified by the auditors, including uncorrected misstatements identified during the audit of the previous period if they affect the current period's financial statements, and
- their best estimate of other misstatements which cannot be quantified specifically.

If the audit partner concludes that the misstatements may be material he considers:

- reducing audit risk by extending audit procedures, or
- requesting the directors to adjust the financial statements.

In any event, the directors may want to adjust the financial statements for the misstatements identified. If the directors refuse to adjust the financial statements and the results of extended audit procedures do not enable the partner to conclude that the aggregate of uncorrected misstatements is not material, he must consider the implications for the auditors' report.

9 Analytical procedures

9.1 Introduction

Definition

'Analytical procedures' means the analysis of relationships:

- between items of financial data, or between items of financial and non-financial data, deriving from the same period, or
- between comparable financial information deriving from different periods or different entities

to identify consistencies and predicted patterns or significant fluctuations and unexpected relationships, and the results of investigations thereof.

Analytical procedures involve the case of ratios, percentages and trend information which may allow the auditor to assess whether the figures subject to audit make sense.

Auditors should apply analytical procedures at the planning stage to assist in understanding the entity's business, in identifying areas of potential audit risk and in planning the nature, timing and extent of other audit procedures.

9.2 Information for analytical procedures

Analytical procedures at this stage are usually based on interim financial information, budgets and management accounts. However, for those entities with less formal means of controlling and monitoring performance, it may be possible to extract relevant financial information from the accounting system (perhaps when preparing the draft financial statements), VAT returns and bank statements. Discussions with management, focused on identifying significant changes in the business since the prior financial period, may also be useful.

Application of analytical procedures may indicate aspects of the entity's business of which the auditors were previously unaware and assist in determining the nature, timing and extent of other audit procedures.

Analytical procedures as substantive procedures are considered in detail in Chapter 5.

10 The audit approach

10.1 Introduction

The audit approach is a plan of action (general strategy) to tackle the critical aspects and meet the audit objective in a cost effective manner.

Where the auditor believes that the client's internal controls are strong, or relevant to the audit (e.g. because they address certain inherent risks identified by the auditor), tests on controls (also called compliance tests) may be performed. If these indicate that controls are operating satisfactorily, the amount of detailed checking may be reduced.

10.2 Alternative audit approaches

The general audit approaches, outlined below, reflect the alternatives:

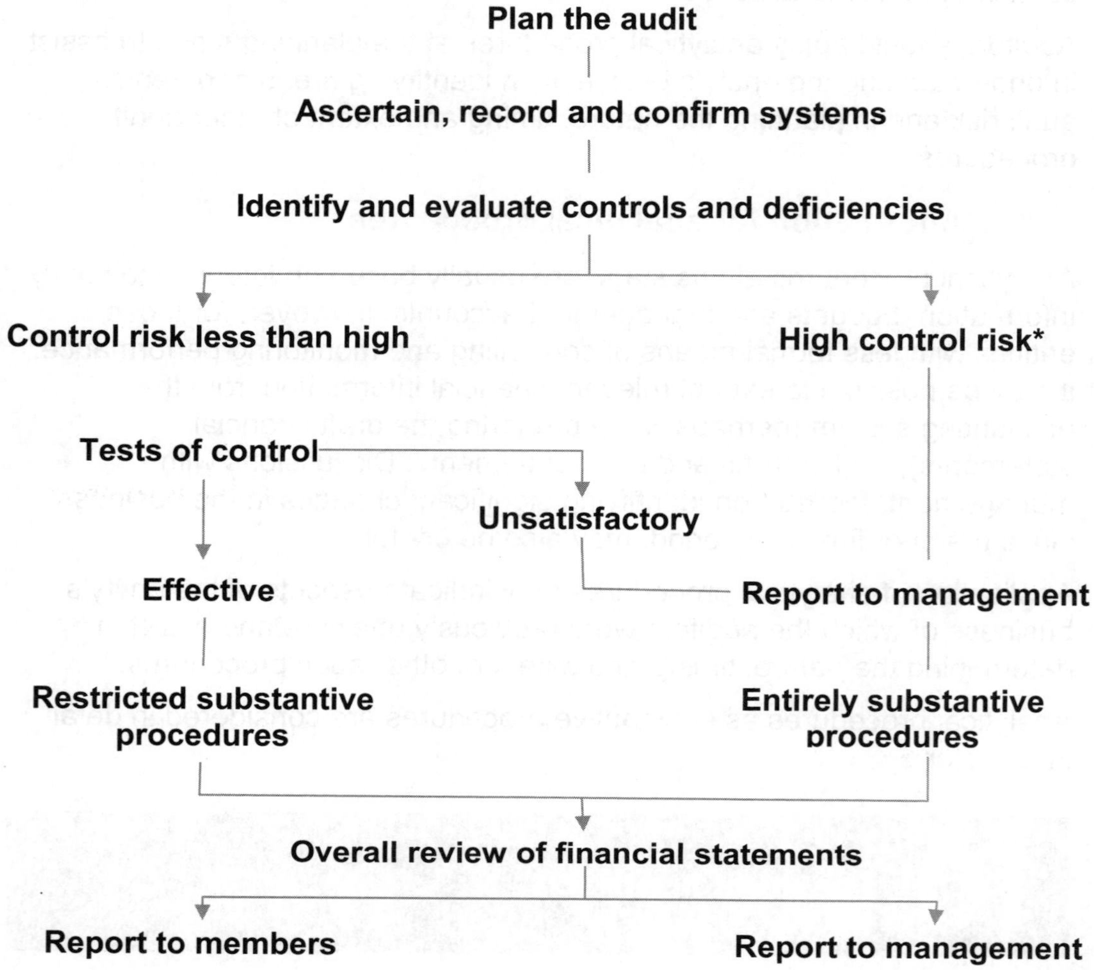

* Remember, high control risk does not mean that controls are necessarily weak. If an entirely substantive approach is considered more cost-effective (i.e. no reliance is sought to be placed on internal controls), then control risk is assessed as high in the audit risk model.

10.3 Substantive or compliance tests?

Compliance tests are tests of controls substantive tests are tests of the accuracy of the recording of transactions and balances.

In some cases (e.g. the audit of a small business where controls are known to be weak or poorly evidenced) the evaluation of controls may be very superficial and the auditor may proceed very quickly with entirely substantive procedures.

In other cases, the identification and (preliminary) evaluation of internal controls may be more thorough, as the decision whether to test controls becomes more critical (e.g. due to cost savings where substantive procedures can be restricted because less staff time is required).

The choice of audit approach (i.e. tests of control with some substantive procedures v wholly substantive procedures) is an important commercial decision. If reliance on controls is sought but tests of control reveal that controls are not operating effectively, full substantive procedures must be performed in that area – an expensive 'mistake'.

10.4 Choosing the audit approach

In choosing between the two main alternative approaches, the audit partner and manager will consider the following:

- previous experience with this (or for a new client, similar) client(s)
- the extent of any limitations on the effectiveness of internal controls for example, human error (see Chapter 4 for more detail)
- the relative efficiency of the two main types of test which are classified as 'substantive procedures' or 'tests of control' according to their primary purpose.

10.5 Tests of controls (compliance tests)

Tests to obtain audit evidence about the effective operation of the accounting and internal control systems – that is, that properly designed controls identified in the preliminary assessment of control risk exist in fact and have operated effectively throughout the relevant period.

This form of testing is usually regarded as more efficient where an account balance is made up of a high volume of individually low value transactions.

10.6 Substantive procedures

Tests to obtain audit evidence to detect material misstatements in the financial statements. They are generally of two types:

(a) analytical procedures, and

(b) other substantive procedures, such as tests of details of transactions and balances, review of minutes of directors' meetings and enquiry.

This type of testing is usually regarded as more efficient where an account balance is made up of a low volume of individually high value transactions. The nature and extent of these tests are indicated in Chapter 5. Numerous examples are to be found in Chapters 6 and 7 which follow.

Where the auditor examines internal controls the quality of the report to management is often improved (see Chapter 12).

11 Recording audit work

11.1 Working papers

Working papers are the material that auditors prepare or obtain, and retain in connection with the performance of the audit. Working papers may be in the form of data stored on paper, film, electronic media or other media. Working papers support, amongst other things, the statement in the auditors' report as to the auditors' compliance or otherwise with Auditing Standards, and thus record compliance with Auditing Standards to the extent that this is important in supporting their report.

Working papers record:

- the planning and performance of the audit
- the supervision and review of the audit work, and
- the audit evidence resulting from the audit work performed which the auditors consider necessary and on which they have relied to support their report.

As such, they are important evidence of the quality of work performed if disputes later emerge.

ISA 230 *Audit Documentation* states that 'the auditor should document matters which are important in providing audit evidence to support the auditor's opinion and evidence that the audit was carried out in accordance with ISAs'.

11.2 Features of working papers

- They should be clearly labelled with the name of the client.
- The objective and purpose of all work should be clearly stated.
- The accounting period under review should be shown.
- The date the working paper was prepared and the name of the person who prepared it should be stated.
- The date the working paper was reviewed and the name of the person who reviewed it should be stated.
- All working papers should be prepared in a permanent form.
- Where the firm's audit manual prescribes any standard form of documentation the working papers should be prepared on a basis which is consistent with the standards laid down.

Working papers should be of a standard which allows any person who is unconnected with the audit to follow the objectives of and results obtained from the tests.

11.3 Permanent audit file

Matters of continuing importance affecting the company or the audit should be kept in a separate permanent file, suitably indexed.

Typically this will include:

- Copies of the Memorandum and Articles of Association appropriate statutory or legal regulations.
- Copies of other documents of continuing importance:
  - the letter of engagement
  - minutes of important board or general meetings
  - debenture deeds
  - mortgages and charges
  - title deeds of freehold and leasehold properties
  - trade agreements
  - agreements for licences and royalties.
- Descriptions of the nature and history of the client's business, its locations and products.
- Organisation charts, with extra details for the finance department.
- A list of the main accounting records, showing where they are kept and of what type (e.g. handwritten, mechanised or computerised).
- Copies of previous financial statements.
- Copies of previous reports to management (reports from auditors to the client detailing the deficiencies found in the accounting system).
- A list of the client's investments (if any).
- A list of the client's other professional advisers.
- Details of the client's insurance cover.
- Tables of significant ratios.
- Descriptions of accounting systems in flow chart and narrative form.
- Internal control evaluation data: questionnaires and checklists.
- Details of principal accounting policies.
- Accounts completion checklist.

11.4 Current audit file

The current year's file will relate primarily to the set of accounts or statements being audited.

Typically, this will include:

- A copy of the **accounts or statements** on which the auditors are reporting, authenticated by directors' signatures or otherwise.
- An **index** covering all the working papers.
- A **schedule for each item** in the statement of financial position, preferably including comparative figures, showing its make-up and how existence, ownership and value or liability have been verified. These schedules should be cross referenced to documents arising from external verification such as bank letters and the results of circularisation of receivables and attendance at physical inventory count.
- A **schedule supporting each item** in the statutory profit and loss account, preferably including comparative figures, and such other items in the trading or subsidiary accounts as may be necessary.
- A **checklist** concerning compliance with statutory disclosure provisions.
- A **record showing queries raised** during the audit and their clearance, with notes where appropriate for attention the following year. Queries not cleared at the time should be entered on to a further schedule for the attention of the person reviewing the audit and for reference to the client if necessary. Material queries which cannot be settled satisfactorily by immediate reference to the client may require a qualification of the auditor's report, and should be fully documented and supported by a note of all discussions with the client and any explanations given.
- A **record of extracts** of minutes of meetings of the directors and shareholders. These should be cross-referenced where relevant to the auditors' working schedules.
- Copies of **letters to the client** setting out any material deficiencies or matters with which the auditors are dissatisfied in respect of the accounts or control procedures. Such letters should be sent even where the particular matter has been discussed informally with one or more of the company's officials. (See extracts in Chapter 12.)

Letters of representation, (i.e. written confirmation by the client of the information and opinions expressed in respect of certain matters such as, inventory values and amounts of current and contingent liabilities). (See Chapter 11 for a sample letter.)

- **Job administration** data which includes:
  - details of partner and staff employed
  - dates when phases of audit were completed
  - time summaries of work carried out by the audit staff
  - details of performance monitored against budget.
- The **audit planning memorandum**.
- **Working papers** created to show the results of tests and evaluation of systems, records of control weakness and the action taken. (See Chapter 4 for extracts.)
- **Schedules showing the result of audit tests** carried out on transactions and balances. An important aspect of the current file is careful indexing and cross-referencing between items in the accounts and items in the schedules so that the collected working papers demonstrate that there is sufficient audit evidence. (See Chapters 6 and 7 for examples). The completed audit programme.

12 Summary

In this chapter we have examined the client/auditor relationship and considered planning, controlling and recording in more detail. You should have noted the following points in particular:

- features of a good auditor/client relationship
- purposes of the interim and final visits to the client
- contents of a planning memorandum
- contents of working papers and the permanent and current files.

You should also understand the impact on the audit approach of:

- the level of risk (both inherent and control) present
- materiality of different areas of the financial statements
- the auditor's previous knowledge of the client
- the type and extent of internal controls within the client's system.
- relative costs involved when choosing between the two main approaches of reliance on controls and substantive procedures.

Answers to chapter activities

Activity 1

Inherent risk – the risk that derives from the characteristics of the company or entity which is to be audited.

e.g. company operating in a hi-tech industry.

Control risk – the risk that the client's internal controls will fail to prevent or detect and correct on a timely basis material misstatements.

e.g. company employs temporary staff on a rolling basis who are not fully trained in how the systems work.

Detection risk – the risk that the auditor's substantive procedures will fail to detect any remaining errors or omissions.

e.g. sample sizes chosen to test were too small or not representative of the population.

13 Test your knowledge

Workbook Activity 2

Select whether the following statements in respect of an external auditor's working papers are true or false.

1 Working papers are prepared by the external auditor because there is a legal requirement to do so.

2 The objective of working papers is to provide evidence that the audit was planned and performed in accordance with International Standards on Auditing.

3 Working papers should contain the name of who performed the audit work and the date it was performed.

Workbook Activity 3

When planning an audit of financial statements, the auditor is required to consider how factors such as the entity's operating environment and its system of internal control affect the risk of misstatement in the financial statements.

Select whether the following factors are likely to increase or reduce the risk of misstatement or have no effect.

1 The entity is committed to employing personnel with appropriate accounting and financial reporting skills.

2 The entity is to be sold and the purchase consideration will be determined as a multiple of reported profit.

3 The entity's management does not intend to remedy deficiencies in internal controls identified by the external auditor.

Workbook Activity 4

"Mr Ice" is a private limited company which owns a number of ice-cream shops in seaside resorts on the southeast coast. The two directors of the company are also 50% owners of the company and they are called Wayne Falco and Mark Hunt.

Wayne is responsible for the financial side of the business. He is thinking of selling his stake in the company but wants to wait until the audited accounts are available.

The trade is very seasonal with high turnover and profits in the summer. However, the restaurants remain open through the year as they make sales to weekend and Christmas holidaymakers.

All sales are made on a cash basis. Purchases are made on credit from a number of suppliers. Inventories are kept in freezers on the premises and have to be used within 4 weeks of purchase. During the summer months a large number of casual workers are employed, and usually paid cash in hand. During the rest of the year, there are around 30 people on the payroll. This element of the workforce is fairly stable.

The company owns some of the premises from which the business is run. Others are leased.

Required

Consider the scenario above and list the risks you can identify.

Accounting systems and internal controls

4

Introduction

This chapter introduces the accounting systems and the methods used to gain an understanding of how these systems work. We will spend a while on flowcharting and its use within an audit. The chapter then goes on to discuss internal controls in further detail.

SYLLABUS AREA

- 2.10 Describe these verification techniques and their uses; physical examination, reperformance, third party confirmation, vouching, documentary evidence and identification of unusual items.
- 2.11 Explain the auditing techniques that could be used in an IT environment.
- 2.2 Identify the control framework.
- 2.3 Assess risks associated with the accounting system and its controls.
- 3.1 Explain these features of recording and evaluating systems including the use of conventional symbols, flowcharts, internal control questionnaires (ICQs) and checklists.
- 3.4 Establish the existence, completeness, ownership, valuation and description of assets and liabilities and gather appropriate evidence to support these findings.
- 5.6 Explain how interview and listening skills can be used by the auditor.

CONTENTS

1 Accounting systems
2 Flowcharting
3 Internal controls
4 Preliminary evaluation of internal controls
5 Reliance on internal controls
6 Management and supervision

1 Accounting systems

1.1 Overview of the audit approach

The audit approach will usually depend on the perceived strength of internal controls and has four main stages.

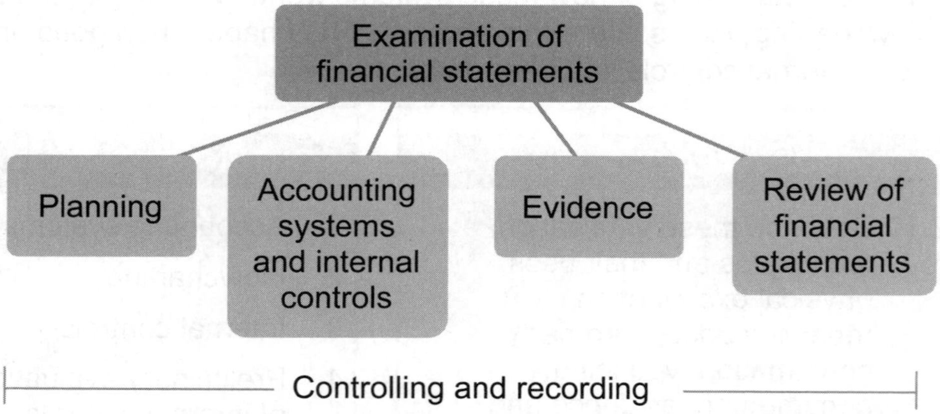

Ascertaining the accounting systems and control environment is one aspect of planning necessary to determining the audit approach.

If auditors, after obtaining an understanding of the accounting system and control environment, expect to be able to rely on their assessment of control risk to reduce the extent of their substantive procedures, they should make a preliminary assessment of control risk, and should plan and perform tests of control to support that assessment.

Note that tests of control are optional because a wholly substantive audit (where no reliance is placed on internal controls) can be performed if the auditor regards it as a more cost-effective approach.

1.2 External auditor's responsibility

To assess the adequacy of the accounting system as a basis for the preparation of financial statements (S237 Companies Act 2006).

1.3 Management's responsibility

To maintain an accounting system adequate to provide proper accounting records (S221 Companies Act 2006).

1.4 What is an 'adequate' accounting system?

An adequate accounting system provides assurance that:

- all transactions have been recorded
- errors in processing become apparent, and
- assets and liabilities exist and are recorded at the correct amounts.

To achieve these objectives, the system may or may not need to incorporate internal controls. The adequacy of the system will be assessed with reference to the size, nature and complexity of the enterprise.

1.5 Examples of 'adequacy'

Type of business	Adequate accounting system
Small mainly cash sales, small number of suppliers.	Analysed cash book and list of unpaid invoices.
Large manufacturing company with several products and a number of separate locations.	Complex accounting system, in order to collate and process information from numerous sources.

1.6 Recording the systems

If the auditor is to be able to assess the accounting system effectively, it must be recorded (including any internal controls). This could be done using either:

- narrative notes (e.g. those used to describe the systems in Chapter 2)
- flowcharts (see below)
- internal control questionnaires/evaluations (see later in this chapter)
- a combination of these methods.

2 Flowcharting

2.1 The purpose of flowcharting

The purpose of flowcharting is to reduce a procedure to its basic components and to emphasise their logical relationships, so that a connected pattern of activity can be traced from the beginning to the end.

The technique is simple but unfortunately flowcharting in practice lacks a uniform terminology, both in the descriptions of types of flowchart and in the symbols to be used.

The flowcharts dealt with in this chapter are called 'system flowcharts' or 'document flowcharts'. System flowcharts or document flowcharts depict, in outline, the sequence of events in a system showing document flow and the department or function responsible for each event.

It is important to distinguish between various copies of the same document particularly if they are to be separated and processed independently. With the following convention it is possible to use separate flow lines for separate copies.

2.2 Flowcharting conventions

Example

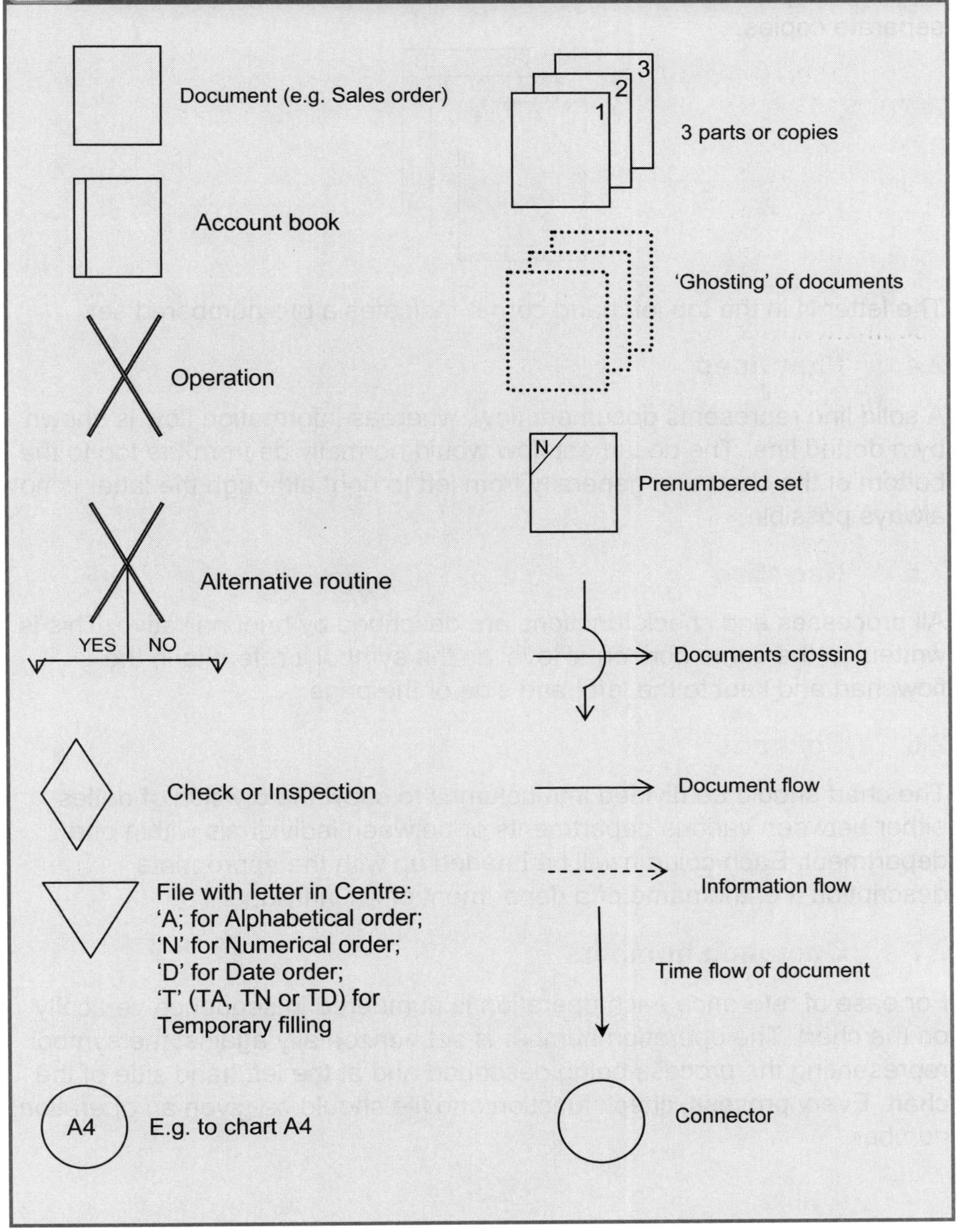
Document (e.g. Sales order)
3
2
1
3 parts or copies
Account book
'Ghosting' of documents
Operation
N
Prenumbered set
Alternative routine
YES
NO
Documents crossing
Check or Inspection
Document flow
Information flow
File with letter in Centre:
'A; for Alphabetical order;
'N' for Numerical order;
'D' for Date order;
'T' (TA, TN or TD) for
Temporary filling
Time flow of document
A4
E.g. to chart A4
Connector

2.3 Multiple copies

It is important to distinguish between various copies of the same document particularly if they are to be separated and processed independently. With the following convention it is possible to use separate flow lines for separate copies.

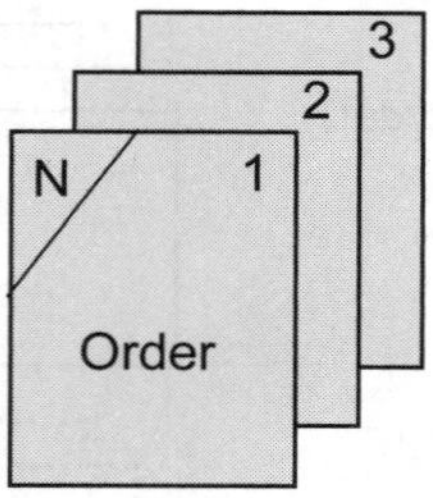

The letter N in the top left hand corner indicates a pre-numbered set.

2.4 Flow lines

A solid line represents document flow, whereas information flow is shown by a dotted line. The document flow would normally be from the top to the bottom of the chart and generally from left to right although the latter is not always possible.

2.5 Narrative

All processes and check functions are described by brief narrative. This is written on the same horizontal level as the symbol it refers to in the flowchart and kept to the left hand side of the page.

2.6 Columns

The chart should be divided into columns to show the division of duties either between various departments or between individuals within one department. Each column will be headed up with the appropriate description, i.e. the name of a department or an individual.

2.7 Operation numbers

For ease of reference each operation is numbered in sequence vertically on the chart. The operation number is set horizontally against the symbol representing the process being described and at the left hand side of the chart. Every process, check function and file should be given an operation number.

2.8 Annotation

To distinguish between permanent and temporary files it is possible to mark a temporary file with the letter 'T' as follows:

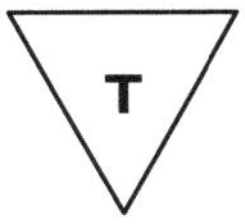

Even more information concerning the structure of the file can be added by coding.

A – alphabetical order

N – numerical order

D – date order

Thus 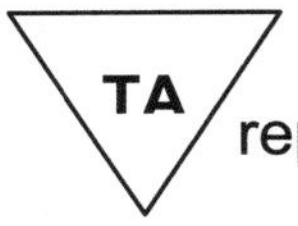

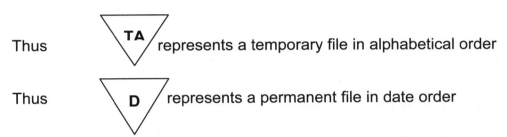

represents a temporary file in alphabetical order

Thus 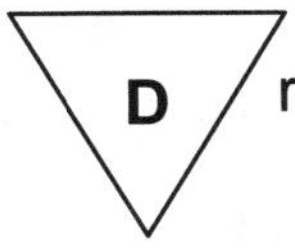

represents a permanent file in date order

2.9 'Ghosting'

When a document appears in the system for the first time it will be shown as a solid square symbol with the name of the document printed inside. Normally there is no need to show the document again, its progress can be seen by following the document flow line, but where the document is carried forward to another chart or when copies that have previously been processed together are split up, it is useful to repeat the document symbol with dotted lines as

2.10 Internal control procedures

Checks are denoted by  These usually indicate internal control procedures which may be tested by the auditor later.

2.11 Rules for clarity

- No diagonal lines. Avoid intersecting lines. If this is impossible show a 'bridge' as follows:

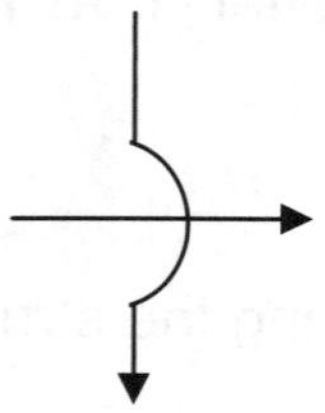

- Remember vertical lines represent the passage of time horizontal solid lines the transfer of documents between departments or individuals and horizontal broken lines the transfer of information. Documents can therefore only be processed on a vertical line.
- There should only be one operation number at a given horizontal level.
- Avoid excessive detail and narrative on the face of the chart. Keep in a column on the left hand side and be as brief as possible.
- Avoid unusual abbreviations (but can use a 'key' or symbols.)
- Avoid too many columns. Split a large system into smaller logical sections and draw a separate chart for each section.
- If a document may be processed in alternative ways according to some predetermined criteria the line of flow may be split as follows:

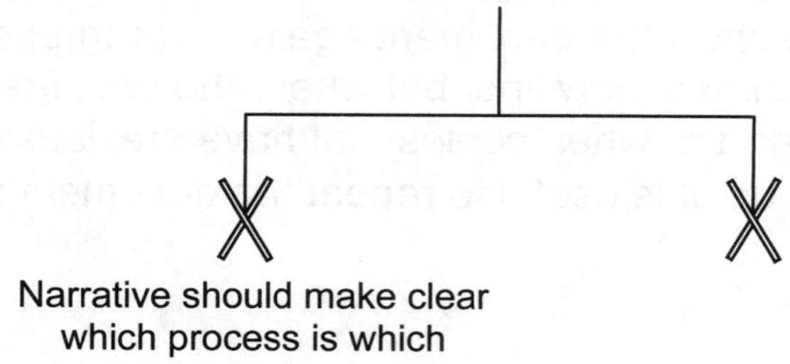
Narrative should make clear
which process is which

2.12 Illustration of a flowchart

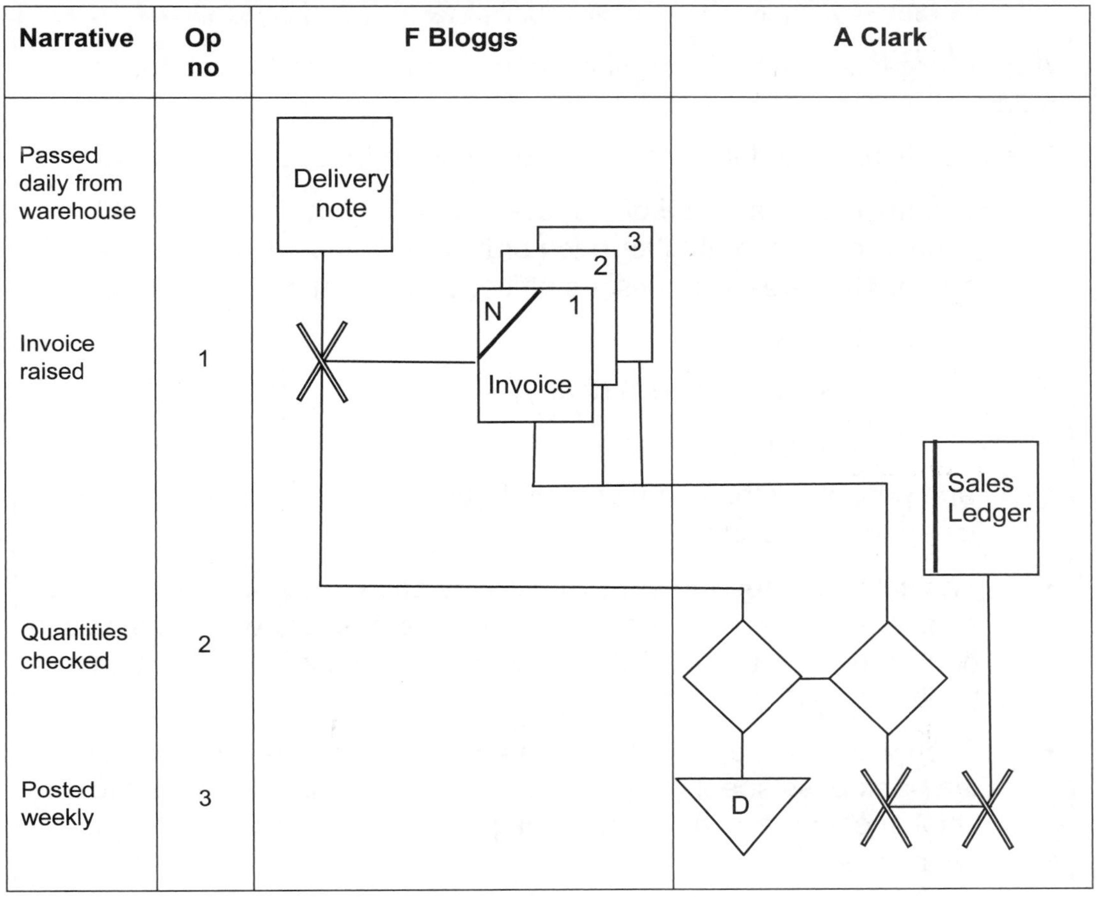

We will now interpret this simple flowchart.

When goods are delivered a delivery note is completed and is passed daily to F Bloggs. F Bloggs, on receipt of the delivery note, raises a three part pre-numbered invoice.

The delivery note and all three copies of the invoice are sent to A Clark for the quantities to be checked. One copy of the invoice will be sent to the customer, the delivery note and second copy of the invoice will be filed in date order and the remaining copy will be posted on a weekly basis by A Clark to the sales ledger.

Example

A retail organisation has a number of branches, each of which make sales.

The cash is banked daily and then the following takes place:

- The mail room at head office receives a daily cash report and supporting documents for each branch and passes them to the appropriate area supervisor's office. Supervisor's office checks:
  - additions
  - petty cash vouchers (if any)
  - bank paying-in slips

  and passes all these documents to the cashier's department after clearing any queries.
- The cashier's department summarises each day's cash report into a cash analysis book, which is a subsidiary record of the main cash book; weekly totals from this book are entered into the main cash book.
- Each week the cashier's department reconciles the cash book with the bank pass sheets and submits a reconciliation statement to the chief accountant. The cash reports are sent to the accounts department.

We must now produce a flowchart illustrating this system.

Solution

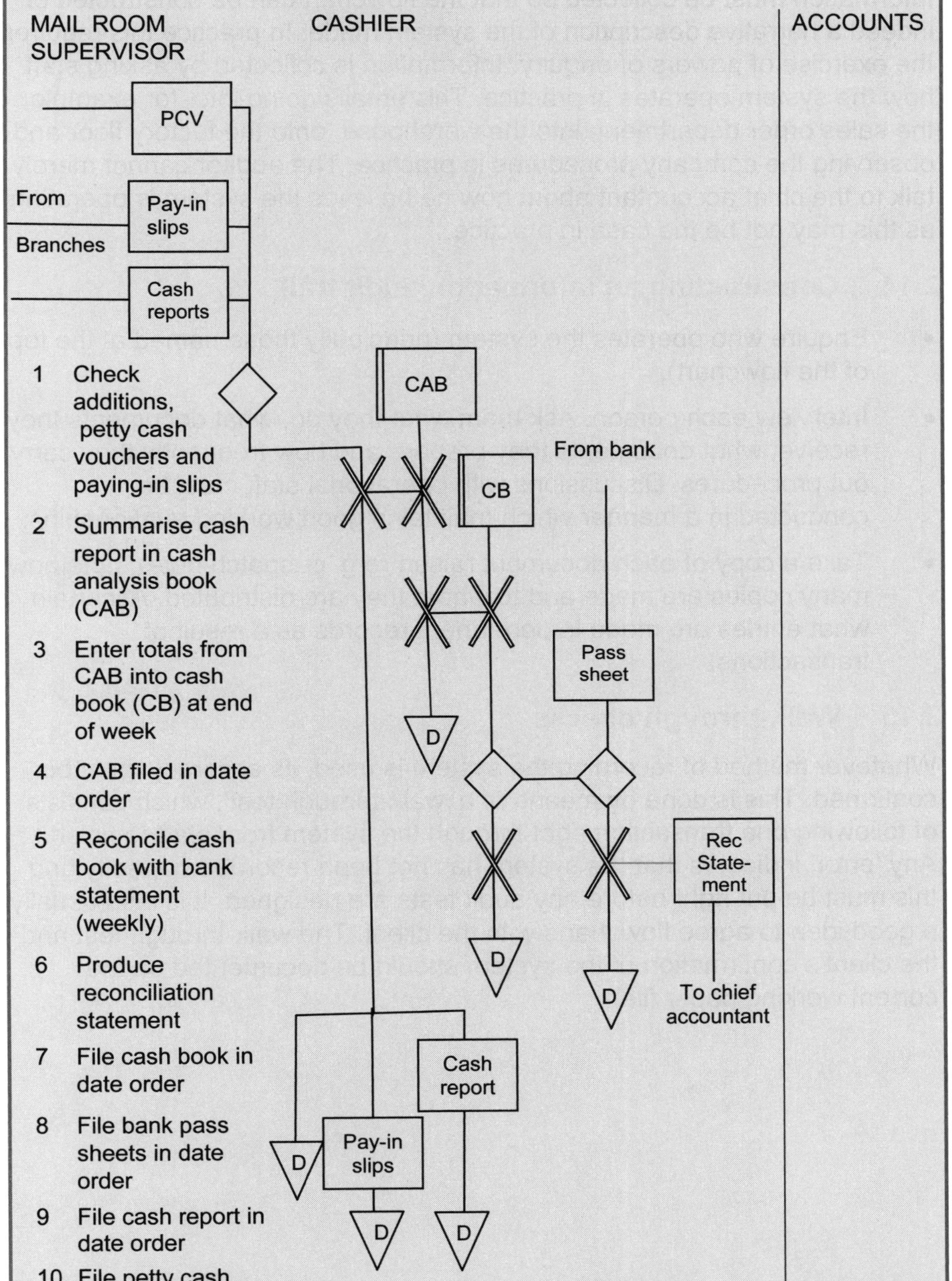

1. Check additions, petty cash vouchers and paying-in slips
2. Summarise cash report in cash analysis book (CAB)
3. Enter totals from CAB into cash book (CB) at end of week
4. CAB filed in date order
5. Reconcile cash book with bank statement (weekly)
6. Produce reconciliation statement
7. File cash book in date order
8. File bank pass sheets in date order
9. File cash report in date order
10. File petty cash vouchers in date order
11. File pay-in slips in date order

2.13 Collecting information

Information must be collected so that the flowchart can be constructed or indeed a narrative description of the system made. In practice this requires the exercise of powers of enquiry. Information is collected by asking staff how the system operates in practice. This entails going into, for example, the sales order department, into the warehouse, onto the factory floor and observing the company procedures in practice. The auditor cannot merely talk to the chief accountant about how he believes the system is operating as this may not be the case in practice.

2.14 Constructing an information/audit trail

- Enquire who operates the system (principally those named at the top of the flowchart).
- Interview each person. Ask them what they do, what documents they receive, what documents they prepare and how frequently they carry out procedures. Discussions with operational staff must be conducted in a manner which maintains good working relationships.
- Take a copy of each document raised (e.g. despatch note), note how many copies are made and to whom they are distributed. Ascertain what entries are made in permanent records as a result of transactions.

2.15 Walk-through checks

Whatever method of recording the system is used, its accuracy must be confirmed. This is done by means of a 'walk-through test', which consists of following one transaction right through the system from start to finish. Any 'error' indicates that the system has not been recorded correctly and this must be put right before any audit tests are designed. It is also usually a good idea to agree flowcharts with the client. The walk-through test and the client's confirmation of the system should be documented on the current working paper file.

Example

Walk-through test

Client:	Noel Ltd	**Prepared by:**	ABC
Year end:	31 December 20X6	**Date:**	17.5.X6
Subject:	Sales walk through test		

Customer order	
Date:	3.4.X6
No:	12345
Goods description:	Product x
Quantity:	3 boxes
Agreed price:	£15
Despatch note	
Date:	4.4.X6
No:	23456
Goods agreed to order:	✓
Quantity agreed to order:	✓
Evidence of check by gate staff:	✓
Invoice	
Date:	4.4.X6
No:	34567
Goods agreed to order and despatch note:	✓
Quantity agreed to order and despatch note:	✓
Price agreed to price on order:	✓
Checked	
Invoice correctly entered in	
Sales day book	✓
Sales ledger	✓

Conclusion

The system is correctly recorded on the flowchart

3 Internal controls

3.1 Definition of an internal control system

Definition

An **internal control system** comprises the control environment (the general attitude to control taken by the organisation) and control procedures. It includes all the policies and procedures (internal controls) adopted by the directors and management of an entity to assist in achieving their objective of ensuring, as far as practicable, the orderly and efficient conduct of its business, including adherence to internal policies, the safeguarding of assets, the prevention and detection of fraud and error, the accuracy and completeness of the accounting records, and the timely preparation of reliable financial information. Internal controls may be incorporated within computerised accounting systems. However, the internal control system extends beyond those matters which relate directly to the accounting system.

According to ISA 315, there are 5 components of an internal control system:

1 Control environment.

- This is the attitude and awareness of the directors.

2 Risk assessment procedures.

3 Information system.

- This refers to the controls over the software and hardware.

4 Control activities.

5 Monitoring of controls.

- Are the controls still appropriate and effective?

3.2 Control activities

'Control procedures' are those policies and procedures in addition to the control environment which are established to achieve the entity's specific objectives. They include in particular procedures designed to prevent or to detect and correct errors. The latter may be a particular focus of high level controls in small or owner-managed entities. Specific control procedures include the following:

Supervision	–	There should be adequate supervision of work to ensure controls are being complied with.
Organisation	–	Enterprises should have a formal, documented organisation structure with clear lines of responsibility.
Arithmetic and **A**ccounting	–	The company should ensure that there are adequate controls to ensure the completeness and accuracy of its financial records, such as reconciliations of key control accounts.
Physical	–	There should be adequate physical control to ensure the security and safe keeping of the company's assets such as inventory and cash, like banking cash immediately.
Management	–	There should be good controls in place to ensure management can effectively run the business, like using budgets, implementing an internal audit department.
Authorisation	–	All transactions should be authorised.
Personnel	–	Employees should be appropriately qualified and of suitable calibre to perform the required tasks.
Segregation of duties	–	There should be an appropriate division of responsibility to reduce the opportunity for fraud and manipulation. It is a fundamental control procedure that one person should not have sole charge of a transaction from beginning to end; if this were the case it would be very easy for the individual to defraud the company if they desired. Unless two or more members of staff decide to work together!

Remember the mnemonic '**SOAPMAPS**'.

ISA 315 refers to the following category of control activities:

- Authorisation
- Vouching
- Verification
- Recording custody
- Separation of functions.

3.3 Auditing in a computer environment

The use of computers in accounting functions has increased greatly over the last few years, and so auditors will regularly have to consider accounting systems which are based on a computer.

In order to be able to conclude whether accounting records produced by a computer form a reliable basis for the preparation of the financial statements, the auditor must understand and be able to audit the system.

Planning implications – additional factors to consider

- Controls in the computerised system.
- Potential loss of 'audit trail'.
- Likely weaknesses and breakdowns in computer systems.
- The timing of audit work to ensure data is available in readily useable format.

Controls

In addition to manual controls (user controls), computer systems should include

Programmed controls (in the software) over the data being processed.	Information technology controls (in the IT dept) over the implementation, security and use of programs and data.

Some user controls and programmed controls are known as 'application controls'.

Application controls are aimed at ensuring the completeness and accuracy of the accounting records and the validity of the entries processed.

Some examples of 'application controls' could include:

- processing invoices by batch rather than individually, and a manual check being performed to ensure the batch of invoices has been processed completely
- manual calculations and recording of the total of the batch of invoices before inputting to the system, and subsequent check to the total value of items recorded per the system.

Example of a batch control sheet

ABC

Batch N°	421
Date	1 March 20X6
Total value of batch	£28,541.40
N° of invoices in batch	24
Invoice numbers included	10072–10095

This batch control sheet would be attached to the invoices it relates to (i.e. those numbered 10072–10095) and checks should be performed to ensure:

1 the sequence of invoices in the batch is complete

2 the total value of invoices is correct

3 ensure processed accurately to the computer system, both that the sequence of invoices is complete and the total per batch agrees to system.

Other examples of application controls

- Random checks being performed on a one to one basis of input with output.
- Periodic printouts of data for manual review for reasonableness (e.g. a bank reconciliation, aged receivables report).
- Monthly agreement of the computer's closing balances with the balances on the control accounts in the nominal ledger.

Information Technology controls

These include controls over:

- the design and implementation of new systems and systems maintenance
- program and data file security
- computer operations and systems software.

Examples of such controls could include:

- password protection – a programmed recognition of a valid identification to activate a terminal. The same technique could be used to restrict user's access to certain files.
- physical access controls:
  - over the computer room (e.g. security coded locks)
  - over terminals (e.g. keys)
- adequate training of all users
- up-to-date user manuals
- adequate supervision of staff using the systems
- regular maintenance of the computer, perhaps under a service agreement from the software supplier
- regular backing-up of copies of data files, and their secure storage away from the PC
- virus checkers being installed and regularly updated for terminals that have internet access.

Loss of 'audit trail'

The results of computer processing may not be printed out in detail. Difficulties arising include:

- totals and analyses being printed without supporting details
- it not being apparent whether reports of 'exceptions' (e.g. customer accounts in excess of credit limits) or rejected data are complete
- control procedures being carried out without visible evidence of it having taken place (e.g. if input data is corrected on a visual display by an operator).

The phrase **'loss of audit trail'** does not necessarily constitute a weakness in the system (e.g. 'reporting by exception' should assist management in controlling the business). The term 'loss of visible evidence' is therefore preferred.

Overcoming loss of visible evidence

Techniques which the auditor can plan to use to overcome the problems include the following:

- Requesting printouts of complete information to check makeup of totals and analyses.
- Manually checking data before it is processed to test a programmed procedure.
- Simulating a report condition (e.g. withholding an input document to create a 'no data' report), with the client's permission.
- Clerical recreation of totals from source documents (this may be time consuming and expensive).
- Testing totals rather than tracing individual items (e.g. comparing analyses with previous periods and budgets).
- Using alternative tests (e.g. testing inventory count procedures when movements making up inventory balances cannot be tested).

Computer assisted audit techniques (CAATS)

In addition to reviewing the controls surrounding computer systems, auditors might use CAATS throughout the audit. These tend to fall in to two categories:

- **Audit software:** This is the use of software to help with various audit procedures. For example, the selection of a sample, extraction of inventory balances over £5,000 in order to carry out further testing.
- **Test data/Integrated Test Facilities:** This is the use of a 'dummy' system which is an exact replica of the client's accounting system. The auditor can, for example, input data with false inventory codes to check that the system would reject such data.

Activity 1

Two types of computer-assisted audit techniques (CAATs) are test data and audit software. For each of the procedures listed below, select the type of CAAT which would be used to perform that procedure.

1 Comparison of the cost and net realisable value of inventory items to determine the lower value.

2 Input of data with false inventory code numbers to check that the system rejects such data.

3 Extraction of inventory balances over £5,000 in order to carry out further testing.

3.4 Preliminary assessment

One of the external auditor's objectives in ascertaining and recording the accounting system is to make a preliminary evaluation of the internal control system.

The degree of reliance which the external auditor feels can be placed on the internal controls will determine the sorts of test to be carried out on the system (to determine its adequacy as a basis for preparing financial statements).

3.5 Extent of internal controls

The extent of the internal control system will depend on what is appropriate to the enterprise. Factors which may have an influence include:

- the nature, size and volume of transactions
- the degree of personal control by management
- the geographical distribution of the enterprise, and
- the cost effectiveness of operating certain controls, with respect to the benefits expected to be derived from them.

Thus the external auditor's approach to evaluating the internal control system will depend on the type of business.

3.6 Small businesses

Auditors obtain an appropriate level of audit evidence to support their audit opinion regardless of the size of the entity. However, many internal controls relevant to large entities are not practical in the small business; for example, in small businesses accounting procedures may be performed by few persons who may have both operating and custodial responsibilities and, consequently, segregation of duties may be severely limited. Inadequate segregation of duties may, in some cases, be offset by other control procedures and close involvement of an owner or manager in strong supervisory controls where they have direct personal knowledge of the entity and involvement in transactions – though this in itself may introduce other risks. In circumstances where segregation of duties is limited and evidence of supervisory controls is lacking, the audit evidence necessary to support the auditors' opinion on the financial statements may have to be obtained entirely through the performance of substantive procedures and any audit work carried out in the course of preparing the financial statements.

3.7 Larger businesses

Procedures are likely to be more formalised than for a smaller business, and the internal controls in operation much more extensive and sophisticated. However, even where this is the case, the auditor may choose not to rely on such controls if, for example, his preliminary evaluation shows that they are ineffective.

4 Preliminary evaluation of internal controls

4.1 Introduction

In order to make the decision about whether or not to place reliance on the internal controls of the business, the auditor makes a preliminary evaluation of their operation. This may be carried out using internal control questionnaires (ICQs) and/or evaluations (ICEs).

4.2 Internal control questionnaires (ICQs)

Definition

Internal control questionnaires (ICQs) are checklists of questions designed to:

- discover the existence of internal controls, and
- identify possible areas of weakness.

The questions are framed in order to highlight situations where:

- there is no subdivision of duties between essential functions
- controls do not exist, or
- essential aspects of management supervision of controls do not exist.

The questionnaire is phrased consistently so that, for example, a 'yes' answer indicates a strength, and a 'no' answer a weakness. This makes it easier to evaluate the completed questionnaire. Weaknesses can then be cross referenced to the relevant part of the audit programme.

Example

We will work through the steps required for drafting appropriate questions for an ICQ.

Step 1 – Identify the cycle e.g. sales

What do we start with?	Opening receivables
What do we do to change it?	Transactions
What do we end up with?	Closing receivables

Step 2 – Consider overall audit approach

Opening balances – Agree to prior year working papers.

Transactions – Controls help ensure completeness and accuracy.

Therefore:

Closing balances – Auditor can obtain comfort as to completeness and accuracy.

Step 3 – Break down the transaction types into components

Customer order → sales order → despatch note → invoice → receivables ledger → statement

Step 4 – Ask 'what could go wrong?'

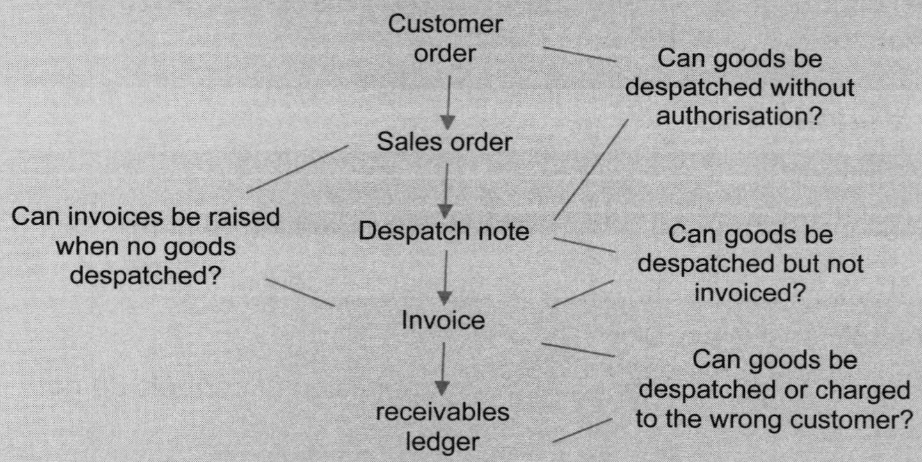

Step 5 – Formulate internal control questions

Internal control questions should be phrased consistently, e.g. so that a 'yes' answer always indicates a strength and a 'no' answer always indicates a weakness.

Examples:

- Are invoices pre-numbered and issued in strict numerical sequence?

4.3 Example of an internal control questionnaire

The following is an example of an internal control questionnaire.

Example

Sales and trade receivables

Client:	Normanton Ltd		
Year end:	30 September 20X6	**Prepared by:**	B.E. Mignano
Cycle:	Sales	**Date:**	7.9.X6

		Yes/No or N/A	**Flowchart reference**
1	**To ensure that all orders received are processed in such a way that keeps errors to a minimum.**		
	Are persons responsible for preparation of sales orders independent of credit control, custody of inventory and recording sales transactions?		
	Are standard forms used to record orders?		
	Are sales orders pre-numbered?		
	Do sales order clerks check the goods ordered are available in quantity and quality required?		
	Are standard prices, delivery and payment terms in written form for the use of sales order clerks? Are special orders (special qualities, quantities, prices) authorised by a responsible official?		

2 **To ensure that sales orders are not accepted in respect of a bad credit risk.**

Is the credit controller independent of the sales order clerks?

Are new credit customers vetted for creditworthiness by reference to independent persons or organisations?

Are orders from existing customers checked for payment record, sales ledger balance and credit limit?

Are credit limits set by responsible officials for all credit customers?

Is the credit approval evidenced on the sales order by the signature of a responsible official?

Is the work of a credit control clerk independently checked?

3 **To ensure that goods are only despatched to customers after proper authorisation.**

Is warehouse/despatch department independent of sales order preparation, credit control and invoicing?

Do warehouse personnel release goods from the warehouse on the basis of sales orders signed by authorised sales order and credit control personnel?

Is the despatch of goods evidenced by the preparation of a goods despatch note?

Are goods despatch notes pre-numbered?

Are two copies of the goods despatch notes sent to the customer for one to be returned as evidence of receipt? Is a copy of the despatch note sent to the inventory control department to update inventory records?

Is inventory counted periodically and compared with inventory records?

4 **To ensure that all goods despatched are invoiced at authorised prices and terms.**

Is sales invoicing independent of sales order preparation, credit control, warehouse and despatch departments? Are copies of sales orders received by sales invoicing?

Is a sequence check carried out on sales orders?

Is a sequence check carried out on goods despatch notes?

Are goods despatch notes matched with sales orders and unmatched orders followed up?

Do invoicing clerks have details of current prices, terms and conditions, including special agreements with particular customers? Are sales invoices independently checked before despatch?

5 **To ensure that all sales invoices are properly recorded in individual customers' accounts in the sales ledger.**

Is the sales ledger clerk independent of sales order preparation, credit control, warehouse, despatch and sales invoicing?

Is a sales ledger control account maintained independent of the sales ledger clerk?

Are differences between extracted list of sales ledger balances and control account balances investigated by a responsible official?

> Are monthly statements of amounts outstanding prepared and despatched to customers?
>
> Is an aged receivable listing prepared and reviewed by a responsible official?
>
> Are sales ledger balances made up of identifiable sales invoices and other items?
>
> Are bad debt write-offs and discounts authorised by a responsible official other than the sales ledger clerk?

4.4 Internal control evaluations (ICEs)

An ICE may be used as well as or instead of an ICQ. See the specimen on the next page.

In practice, many audit firms make no distinction between an ICQ and an ICE (even to the extent of calling one an ICEQ!). However, an ICE is usually more detailed than an ICQ as it links the control to the effect this will have on the audit and the resulting substantive work.

4.5 Principal features of an ICE

- Contains only those key control questions on which reliance is to be sought. Records the key control which satisfies the key control question (an ICQ may well be required to distinguish the key control from the non-key controls).
- Describes the nature and extent of the tests of controls.
- Records the test conclusion and how substantive procedures are affected.

Definition

An **Internal Control Evaluation** contains the key control questions, the key control which satisfies this question and details of the audit to test the key control.

Example of internal control evaluation

Client:	Albany Ltd
Year end:	30.5.X6

	Initials	**Date**
Prepared by	WANV	27/7/X6
Reviewed by		

Key control question	Key control	System ref	Tests of controls	WP ref	Substantive procedures	WP ref	Conclusions
Can goods be ordered without authorisation? Can goods be received without authorisation?	All orders are authorised before being placed. All GRNs are matched with purchase orders before goods are accepted.		Select a sample of GRNs and confirm that the PO is: – attached/ cross-referenced; – signed by the buyer; and – supported by a signed purchase requisition.		For the same sample: – agree quantities received to quantities ordered; and – confirm part of short deliveries (e.g. to credit note).		

5 Reliance on internal controls

5.1 Introduction

Where the preliminary assessment has indicated that there are internal controls upon which the auditor wishes to rely, the auditor will design and carry out tests of controls.

Definition

Tests of controls seek to provide audit evidence about the effective operation of the accounting and internal control systems – that is, that properly designed controls identified in the preliminary assessment exist in fact and have operated effectively throughout the relevant period.

The auditor seeks assurance from these tests that the controls have been operating effectively throughout the period and consequently that:

- the accounting records are complete and accurate, and
- all entries are valid.

5.2 If favourable

The auditor may restrict substantive procedures to be carried out.

(***Note:*** Substantive procedures may never be eliminated completely – see below).

5.3 If unfavourable

The auditor may extend tests of controls to determine whether the breakdowns in controls which have been recorded are only isolated incidents. If the original results are particularly unfavourable, or the additional tests of control in this area reveal further breakdowns, a wholly substantive approach must then be adopted.

5.4 Limitations on the effectiveness of internal controls

As mentioned above, even where the internal control system is extensive, and tests of control have revealed that such controls have operated effectively throughout the period, some substantive procedures must still be carried out. This requirement stems from the fact that no internal control system can guarantee the completeness and accuracy of the records by itself, due to inherent limitations on their effectiveness such as the following:

- The usual requirement that the cost of an internal control is not disproportionate to the potential loss which may result from its absence.
- Most systematic internal controls tend to be directed at routine transactions rather than non-routine transactions.
- The potential for human error due to carelessness, distraction, mistakes of judgement and the misunderstanding of instructions.
- The possibility of circumvention of internal controls through collusion with parties outside or inside the entity.
- The possibility that a person responsible for exercising an internal control could abuse that responsibility, for example by overriding an internal control.
- The possibility that procedures may become inadequate due to changes in conditions or that compliance with procedures may deteriorate over time.

Activity 2

The external auditor may seek to place reliance on internal controls in order to restrict substantive testing. In each of the following circumstances select whether the external auditor is likely to place reliance or place no reliance on internal controls.

1 A company where the processing of accounting transactions is undertaken by one person.

2 A company which has an internal audit function which monitors operational and financial controls.

3 A company which has internal controls with a history of management override.

6 Management and supervision

6.1 Professional Scepticism

During the course of an audit, the auditor will hold a number of discussions with the client. It is very important that throughout these discussions, the auditor maintains their professional scepticism.

Definition

Professional scepticism is an attitude that includes a questioning mind, being alert to conditions which may indicate possible misstatement due to error or fraud, and a critical assessment of audit evidence.

Professional scepticism does not mean that auditors should disbelieve everything they are told; however they must have a questioning attitude.

All the discussions held with the client must be documented by the auditor to ensure there is evidence that these discussions took place and the information and explanations received.

7 Summary

The following are the key points arising in this chapter which you should have noted.

Accounting systems

- Factors affecting adequacy of accounting systems.

Internal control

- Considerations affecting the extent of internal controls.
- Factors affecting the auditor's reliance on internal controls.
- Limitations of internal controls

Flowcharting

- How to draft and interpret a flowchart.

Walk-through tests

- How to confirm the accuracy of the system recorded.

ICQs and ICEs

- Purpose and principal features.

Professional scepticism

Differences to old syllabus

The section on management and supervision has been added in the current year.

Answers to chapter activities

Activity 1

1 Audit software.

2 Test data.

3 Audit software.

Activity 2

1 No reliance.

2 Reliance.

3 No reliance.

8 Test your knowledge

Workbook Activity 3

External auditors use a variety of methods for documenting systems of control, including flowcharts internal control questionnaires and internal control checklists. For each of the following descriptions select whether it represents a flowchart, internal control questionnaire or internal control checklist.

1 A listing of controls necessary to provide reasonable assurance of effective internal control within a given transaction cycle.

2 A pictorial presentation of the processing steps within a given transaction cycle.

Workbook Activity 4

For each of the following statements, select whether they are true or false.

1 If the controls of a company are considered to be very strong, the auditor can avoid doing any substantive testing.

2 A walk through test is a type of substantive test.

Audit evidence, techniques and procedures

5

Introduction

In this chapter, we will consider gathering sufficient and appropriate audit evidence and methods with which we can calculate our audit samples. We will move on to discussing how we can evaluate the results from our chosen samples and examine the use of analytical procedures within an audit assignment.

SYLLABUS AREA

2.6 Explain these different sampling techniques selecting a sample for a specific situation; confidence levels, random numbers, interval sampling and stratified sampling.

2.9 Provide clear information and recommendations for the proposed audit plan for submission to the appropriate person for consideration.

3.3 Conduct tests, record test results and draw valid conclusions as specified in the audit plan.

CONTENTS

1 Audit evidence

2 Audit sampling

3 Evaluation of sample results

4 Analytical procedures

1 Audit evidence

Definition

Audit evidence is the information used by the auditor in arriving at the conclusions on which the audit opinion is based.

1.1 Introduction

Auditors should obtain sufficient, appropriate audit evidence to draw reasonable conclusions on which to base the audit opinion.

Audit evidence is obtained in a number of ways, including from an appropriate mix of tests of control and substantive procedures (see below). In some circumstances, evidence may be obtained entirely from substantive procedures and enquiries made to ascertain the adequacy of the accounting system as a basis for the preparation of the financial statements.

1.2 Sufficient, appropriate audit evidence

Sufficiency and appropriateness are interrelated and apply to audit evidence obtained from both tests of control and substantive procedures.

- Sufficiency is the measure of the quantity of audit evidence.
- Appropriateness is the measure of the quality or reliability of audit evidence and its relevance to a particular assertion (e.g. 'inventory exists at the year-end date').

Usually, audit evidence is persuasive rather than conclusive, and auditors therefore often seek audit evidence from different sources or of a different nature to support the same assertion.

Auditors seek to provide reasonable, not absolute, assurance that the financial statements are free from material misstatement. In forming their audit opinion, therefore, auditors do not normally examine all of the information available. Appropriate conclusions can be reached about a financial statement assertion using a variety of means of obtaining evidence, including sampling (see below).

1.3 Auditors' judgement

The auditors' judgement as to what is sufficient appropriate audit evidence is influenced by such factors as the following:

- assessment of the nature and degree of risk of misstatement at both the financial statement level and the account balance or class of transactions level
- nature of the accounting and internal control systems, including the control environment
- the materiality of the item being examined
- experience gained during previous audits and the auditors' knowledge of the business and industry
- the findings from audit procedures, and from any audit work carried out in the course of preparing the financial statements, including indications of fraud or error (fraud is considered in Chapter 14)
- the source and reliability of information available.

1.4 Tests of control ('compliance tests')

In obtaining audit evidence from tests of control, auditors should consider the sufficiency and appropriateness of audit evidence to support the assessed level of control risk. Aspects of the relevant parts of accounting and internal control systems about which auditors seek to obtain audit evidence are:

(a) **Design:** the accounting and internal control systems are capable of preventing or detecting material misstatements, and

(b) **Operation:** the systems exist and have operated effectively throughout the relevant period.

1.5 Substantive procedures

In obtaining audit evidence from substantive procedures, auditors should consider the extent to which that evidence together with any evidence from tests of controls supports the relevant 'financial statement assertions'. These are the representations of the directors that are embodied in the financial statements, for example:

- **Completeness:** there are no unrecorded assets, liabilities, transactions or events, or undisclosed items.
- **Occurrence:** a transaction or event took place which pertains to the entity during the relevant period.
- **Valuation and allocation:** an asset or liability is recorded at an appropriate carrying value.

- **Existence:** an asset or a liability exists at a given date.
- **Rights and obligations:** an asset or a liability pertains to the entity at a given date.
- **Accuracy:** a transaction or event is recorded at the proper amount.
- **Cut-off:** transactions and events are recorded in the correct accounting period.
- **Classification and understandability:** transactions and events have been recorded in the proper accounts and described and disclosed clearly.

Audit evidence is usually obtained to support each financial statement assertion. Audit evidence regarding one assertion (e.g. existence of inventory) does not compensate for failure to obtain audit evidence regarding another (e.g. its valuation). Tests may, however, provide audit evidence about more than one assertion (e.g. testing subsequent receipts from receivables may provide some audit evidence regarding both their existence and valuation).

1.6 Directional testing

If an item in the financial statements is misstated, it may be overstated or understated. When testing for overstatement (existence) a different approach is used from testing for understatement (completeness).

When testing for overstatement, the auditor would begin by looking at the balance in the accounts and then work backwards towards the supporting evidence. This can be explained by way of an example.

Example

Invoice 1 is a fraudulent purchase invoice for £5,000 and should not have been posted. As a result, purchases are overstated by £5,000. To find this misstatement, the auditor can either:

- examine every purchase invoice and try to identify the fraudulent one; or
- look at the figure in the financial statements and find supporting evidence.

If the fraudulent invoice had been hidden by the client in some way, it would not be possible to find it by examining every purchase invoice and so the auditor should start from the financial statements and work backwards.

When testing for understatement, the auditor will start by looking at the supporting evidence and agree this to the figure in the financial statements. Again, let's look through an example:

> **Example**
>
> Invoice 2, a sales invoice for £5,000, has been omitted and therefore revenue is understated by £5,000. If the auditor were to select a sample from the financial statements, this will be of no use as the item is not there to test. Therefore, the auditor will select items from the population and agree this to the financial statements.

1.7 Audit objectives

Programmes of detailed audit procedures are sometimes drawn up by auditors by reference to 'audit objectives'. Such objectives may provide a satisfactory way of enabling auditors to satisfy themselves that the planned work will result in appropriate evidence being obtained, provided that the objectives cover all the relevant financial statement assertions made by the directors.

1.8 Nature, timing and extent

The nature, timing and extent of substantive procedures depends on:

- the auditors' assessment of the control environment and accounting systems generally and of the inherent and control risks
- any evidence obtained from audit work performed during the preparation of the financial statements.

Where tests of control provide satisfactory evidence as to the effectiveness of accounting and internal control systems, the extent of relevant substantive procedures may be reduced, but not entirely eliminated.

Substantive procedures may be incorporated within other procedures. For example, tests of control may be designed as dual purpose tests to provide evidence of a substantive nature, and such evidence may also be obtained as part of the work carried out to make preliminary assessments of risks of error.

1.9 Reliability of evidence

The reliability of audit evidence is influenced by its source: internal or external, and by its nature: visual, documentary or oral.

The following generalisations may help in assessing reliability:

- Audit evidence from external sources (e.g. confirmation received from a third party) is more reliable than that obtained from the entity's records.
- Audit evidence obtained from the entity's records is more reliable when the related accounting and internal control system operates effectively.
- Evidence obtained directly by auditors is more reliable than that obtained by or from the entity.
- Evidence in the form of documents and written representations is more reliable than oral representations.
- Original documents are more reliable than photocopies, telexes, faxes or email.

Audit evidence is more persuasive when items of evidence from different sources or of a different nature are consistent. When audit evidence from one source is inconsistent with that from another, auditors determine what additional procedures are necessary to resolve the inconsistency.

Auditors consider the relationship between the cost of obtaining audit evidence and the usefulness of the information obtained. However, the existence of difficulty or expense is not in itself a valid basis for omitting a necessary procedure.

1.10 Procedures for obtaining audit evidence

Audit evidence is obtained by one or more of the following procedures: inspection, observation, enquiry and third party confirmation, computation/reperformance and analytical procedures. The choice of which procedures is partly dependent upon the periods of time during which the audit evidence sought is available and the form in which the accounting records are maintained (e.g. manual, computer printout, etc).

1.11 Inspection

Inspection consists of examining records, documents or tangible assets. Inspection of records and documents provides audit evidence of varying degrees of reliability depending on their nature and source (see above) and the effectiveness of internal controls over their processing. Three major categories of documentary audit evidence, listed in descending degree of reliability as audit evidence, are evidence:

- created and provided to auditors by third parties (e.g. a bank loan confirmation)
- created by third parties and held by the entity (e.g. suppliers' statements),
- created and held by the entity (e.g. monthly statements for customers).

Inspection of tangible assets provides reliable audit evidence about their existence but not necessarily as to their ownership or value. Further procedures will be needed to gather evidence on these matters.

1.12 Observation

Observation consists of looking at a process or procedure being performed by others (e.g. the observation by auditors of the counting of inventory by the entity's staff or the performance of internal control procedures, in particular those that leave no 'audit trail' (i.e. visible evidence)).

1.13 Enquiry and confirmation

Enquiry consists of seeking information of knowledgeable persons inside or outside the entity. Enquiries may range from formal written enquiries addressed to third parties (e.g. a letter to the entity's solicitor) to informal oral enquiries addressed to persons inside the entity. Responses to enquiries may provide auditors with information not previously possessed or with corroborative audit evidence.

Confirmation consists of the response to an enquiry to corroborate information contained in the accounting records (e.g. obtaining direct confirmation of debts by communication with receivables).

1.14 Computation

Computation consists of checking the arithmetical accuracy of source documents and accounting records or performing independent calculations.

1.15 Analytical procedures

Analytical procedures consist of the analysis of relationships between items of financial data, or between items of financial and non-financial data, deriving from the same period, or between comparable financial information deriving from different periods or different entities, to identify consistencies and predicted patterns or significant fluctuations and unexpected relationships, and the results of investigations thereof. (For details see later in this chapter.)

Activity 1

State whether the following statements are true or false:

1 A controls test is a type of substantive test.

2 Substantive testing must always be performed during an audit.

3 Testing for completeness is an example of a substantive test.

2 Audit sampling

2.1 Introduction

The auditor is not required to carry out a complete check of all the transactions and balances of a business because:

- the cost in terms of expensive audit resources would be uneconomical
- the complete check would take so long that accounts would be ancient history before users saw them
- users of accounts do not require 100% accuracy
- a complete check would be so tedious that the audit staff would become ineffective and errors would be missed
- a complete check would not add much to the worth of figures if, as would be normal, few errors were discovered (the emphasis in auditing should be on the completeness of records and the true and fair view).

In most areas a 100% check is not necessary and a test check is made by the examination of a sample of items taken from the whole class of transactions or balances.

In the following areas a 100% check is still necessary:

- unusual, one-off, or exceptional items
- high risk areas
- categories which are few in number but of great importance (e.g. land and buildings)
- categories with special importance where normal materiality levels do not apply (e.g. directors' emoluments and loans).

Definition

'Audit sampling' means the application of audit procedures to less than 100% of the items within an account balance or class of transactions to enable auditors to obtain and evaluate audit evidence about some characteristic of the items selected in order to form or assist in forming a conclusion concerning the population which makes up the account balance or class of transactions.

2.2 Benefits of audit sampling

These include:

- developing a consistent approach to audit areas
- providing a framework within which sufficient appropriate audit evidence is obtained
- forcing clarification of audit thinking to determine how the audit objectives will be met
- minimising the risk of 'over-auditing'
- facilitating quicker review of working papers.

2.3 The decision to sample

When planning the audit procedures to be adopted, the decision to sample account balances and transactions is influenced by:

- materiality and number of items in the population
- inherent risk (of errors arising)
- relevance and reliability of evidence available through non-sampling procedures
- costs and time involved.

To obtain the overall level of assurance required, a cost-effective combination of sampling and non-sampling procedures should be determined.

2.4 Stages in sampling

If the auditor chooses to use sampling then the following stages will be required:

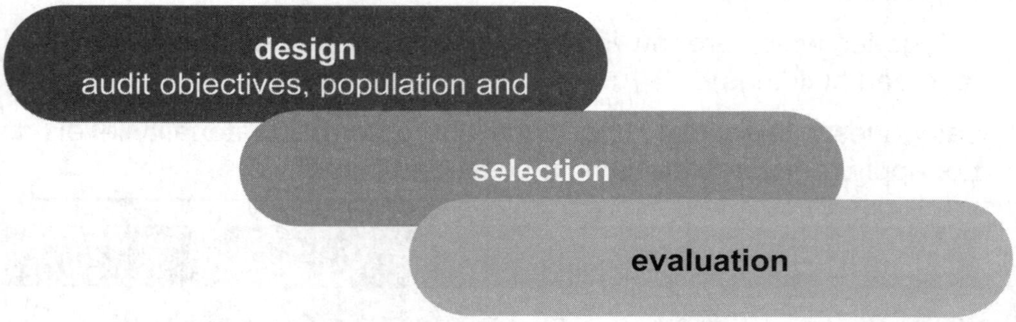

2.5 Design of the sample

When designing the size and structure of an audit sample, auditors should consider the specific audit objectives, the nature of the population from which they wish to sample, and the sampling and selection methods.

2.6 Audit objectives

Auditors first consider the specific audit objectives to be achieved and the audit procedures which are most likely to achieve those objectives. In addition, when audit sampling is appropriate, consideration of the nature of the audit evidence sought and possible error conditions or other characteristics relating to that evidence assists auditors in defining what constitutes an error and what population to use for sampling.

For example, when performing tests of control over purchasing procedures, auditors may be concerned with matters such as whether an invoice was clerically checked and properly approved.

Alternatively, when performing substantive procedures on invoices processed during the period, auditors are concerned with matters such as the proper reflection of the creditor and of the monetary amounts of such invoices in the financial statements.

2.7 Population

The population is the entire set of data from which auditors wish to sample in order to reach a conclusion. Therefore the population from which the sample is drawn has to be appropriate and complete for the specific audit objective.

If the audit objective is to test for overstatement of receivables, the population may be defined as the receivables listing.

When testing for understatement of payables, the population is not the payables listing but rather subsequent disbursements, unpaid invoices, suppliers' statements, unmatched goods received notes or other populations that can provide evidence of understatement of payables.

2.8 Sampling units

The individual items that make up the population may be described as sampling units. The population can be divided into sampling units in a variety of ways. For example, if the audit objective is to test the validity of receivables, the sampling unit may be defined as customer balances or individual customer invoices. In monetary unit sampling each £1 of, for example, a receivables balance listing is the sampling unit. Auditors define the sampling unit in order to obtain an efficient and effective sample to achieve the particular audit objectives.

2.9 Sample size

When determining sample sizes, auditors consider sampling risk, the amount of error that would be acceptable (tolerable misstatement) and the extent to which they expect to find errors (expected error).

2.10 Factors influencing sample size for tests of controls

Factor	**Impact on sample size**
Sampling risk	• The greater the reliance on the results of a test of control using audit sampling, the lower the sampling risk auditors are willing to accept and, consequently, the larger the sample size. • The lower the assessment of control risk, the more likely auditors are to place reliance on audit evidence from tests of control. • A high control risk assessment may result in a decision not to perform tests of control.
Tolerable misstatement	• The higher the tolerable misstatement rate the lower the sample size and vice versa.
Expected error	• If errors are expected, a larger sample usually needs to be examined to confirm that the actual error rate is less than the tolerable misstatement rate. • High expected error rates may result in a decision not to perform tests of
Number of items in population	• Virtually no effect on sample size unless population is small.

2.11 Factors influencing sample size for substantive tests

Factor	Impact on sample size
Inherent risk	• The higher the assessment of inherent risk, the more audit evidence is required to support the auditors' conclusion.
Control risk	• The higher the assessment of control risk, the greater the reliance on audit evidence obtained from substantive procedures. • A high control risk assessment may result in the decision not to perform tests of control and reliance entirely on substantive procedures.
Detection risk	• Sampling risk for substantive tests is one form of detection risk. The lower the sampling risk auditors are willing to accept, the larger the sample size
Tolerable misstatement	• The higher the monetary value of the tolerable misstatement the smaller the sample size and vice versa.
Expected error	• If errors are expected, a larger sample usually needs to be examined to confirm that the actual error rate is less than the tolerable misstatement rate.
Population value	• The less material the monetary value of the population to the financial statements, the smaller the sample size that may be required.
Number of items in population	• Virtually no effect on sample size unless population is small.
Stratification	• If it is appropriate to stratify the population this may redirect the sample and lead to a smaller sample size.

2.12 Sampling risk

Fundamental to audit sampling is sampling risk. This may be regarded as a component of detection risk, the other component being non-sampling risk.

Sampling risk arises from the possibility that the auditors' conclusion, based on a sample, may be different from the conclusion that would be reached if the entire population were subjected to the same audit procedure.

Auditors are faced with sampling risk in tests of controls and in substantive procedures.

Sampling risk is essentially the risk that the auditor's sample from a population will not be representative. In other words it will, by chance, include too many or too few errors to give a realistic impression of the population as a whole. Sampling risk reduces as samples become larger.

2.13 Tests of control

Sampling risk can arise in tests of control. If the sample contains a disproportionately high number of errors then the auditor might get the false impression that a control has not operated and control risk will be evaluated as too high. Conversely, the auditor might attach too low a control risk if there are too few compliance errors in the sample.

2.14 Substantive procedures

There are two possible aspects to sampling risk when carrying out substantive procedures:

- The risk of concluding that a recorded account balance or class of transactions is materially misstated when it is not, because the error in the sample is greater than the error in the population as a whole.
- The risk of concluding that a recorded account balance or class of transactions is acceptable when it is materially misstated, because the error in the sample is less than the error in the population as a whole.

Sample size is affected by the degree of sampling risk that auditors are willing to accept from the results of the sample, which depends upon the importance of the results of the audit procedure involving sampling to the auditors' conclusions.

The greater their reliance on the results, the lower the sampling risk auditors are willing to accept and the larger the sample size needs to be.

2.15 Measuring sampling risk

When an audit sample is designed using a statistical sampling method (see later), it is possible to measure sampling risk. In practice, only the risk of accepting a population which does contain material errors is measured. The risk is expressed as a percentage; for example a risk of 5% means that there is a 1 in 20 chance of a material error going undetected. It is the policy of many auditors to accept a 5% risk of failure to detect a material error in any given test. This figure is a judgement based on experience.

2.16 Non-sampling risk

Non-sampling risk is the risk that auditors might use inappropriate procedures or might misinterpret evidence and thus fail to recognise an error.

Non-sampling risk arises because, for example, most audit evidence is persuasive rather than conclusive. Furthermore, inexperienced or over-stretched audit staff might make mistakes in the evaluation of evidence and reach invalid conclusions. Audit firms attempt to reduce non-sampling risk to a negligible level by appropriate planning, direction, supervision and review.

2.17 Tolerable misstatement

Tolerable misstatement is the maximum error in the population that auditors are willing to accept and still conclude that the audit objective has been achieved. Tolerable misstatement is considered during the planning stage and, for substantive procedures, is related to the auditors' judgement about materiality. The smaller the tolerable misstatement, the larger is the sample size as a proportion of the population.

- In **tests of control,** the tolerable misstatement is the maximum rate of deviation from a prescribed control procedure that auditors are willing to accept in the population and still conclude that the preliminary assessment of control risk is valid.
- In **substantive procedures,** the tolerable misstatement is the maximum monetary error in an account balance or class of transactions that auditors are willing to accept so that, when the results of all audit procedures are considered, they are able to conclude, with reasonable assurance, that the financial statements are not materially misstated.

2.18 Expected error

If auditors expect error to be present in the population, a larger sample than when no error is expected generally has to be examined to conclude that the actual error in the population is not greater than the planned tolerable misstatement. The size and frequency of errors is important in assessing the sample size. Larger sample sizes arise, for the same overall error, if there are a few large errors compared to where there are many small ones. Smaller sample sizes result when the population is expected to be error free. If the expected error rate is high then sampling may not be appropriate. In determining the expected error in a population, auditors consider such matters as the size and frequency of errors identified in previous audits, changes in the entity's procedures and evidence available from other procedures.

2.19 Selection of the sample

Auditors should select sample items in such a way that the sample can be expected to be representative of the population in respect of the characteristics being tested.

For a sample to be representative of the population, all items in the population are required to have an equal or known probability of being selected.

While there are a number of selection methods, the methods commonly used are random or systematic selection.

2.20 Random selection

This method ensures that all items in the population have an equal chance (i.e. same statistical probability) of selection (e.g. by use of random number tables or a computer program).

2.21 Systematic selection

This method (which is also called interval selection) involves selecting items using a constant interval between selections, the first interval having a random start.

This method is suitable for both tests of control and substantive procedures and is particularly useful for sampling from non-monetary populations.

Example

A systematic sample of 125 of the despatch notes issued during the year is to be made. The first despatch note raised in the year was 11,129 and the last was 18,671.

Solution

Sampling interval: $\frac{\text{Population}}{\text{Sample size}} = \frac{18{,}671 - 11{,}129}{125} = 60$

Random start: 36 (between 0 and 60)

Selection procedure	DN number	
	11,165	(11,129 + 36)
	11,225	(11,165 + 60)
	11,285	(11,225 + 60)
	:	:
	: etc	:

When using systematic selection, auditors must ensure that the population is not structured in such a manner that the sampling interval corresponds with a particular pattern in the population.

2.22 Stratified sampling

Stratified sampling can be used if the population naturally falls into strata or layers. So, for example, if a sample were to be taken for receivables balances, the population of debtor balances might be split into the following strata:

Up to £5,000

£5,000 to £30,000

Over £30,000

An appropriate size of sample would then be taken from each of these groups using random or systematic sampling.

Activity 2

A sample of sales invoices are to be tested to ensure that they agree to customer orders and despatch notes. A sample of 200 is required and is to be selected using the systematic sampling method with a random start number of 44. The first sales invoice in the year was number 110652 and the last sales invoice number in the year was 126435.

Task

Determine the invoice number of the first four invoices to be tested in the sample.

2.23 Haphazard selection

In haphazard selection, the auditors select the sample without following a structured technique. This may be an acceptable alternative to random selection provided auditors are satisfied that the sample is representative of the entire population. This method requires care to guard against making a selection which is biased (e.g. towards items which are easily located) as they may not be representative.

2.24 Block sampling

With block sampling, a number of adjacent transactions or items will be selected, e.g. all sales invoices in a particular week, or all receivables with a name beginning with a particular letter. The main disadvantage of this method is that it may not show characteristics that are representative of the whole population. However, block sampling can result in significant cost savings in audit time.

3 Evaluation of sample results

3.1 Introduction

Having carried out, on each sample item, those audit procedures which are appropriate to the particular audit objective, auditors should:

- analyse any errors detected in the sample, and
- draw inferences for the population as a whole.

3.2 Analysis of errors

In analysing the errors detected in the sample, auditors first confirm that an item in question is in fact an error. In designing the sample, auditors define those conditions which constitute an error by reference to the audit objectives.

For example, in a substantive procedure relating to the recording of receivables, a mis-posting between customer accounts does not affect the total receivables. Therefore, it may be inappropriate to consider this an error in evaluating the sample results of this particular procedure, even though it may have an effect on other areas of the audit such as the assessment of doubtful debts.

When the expected audit evidence regarding a specific sample item cannot be obtained, auditors may be able to obtain sufficient appropriate audit evidence through performing alternative procedures. For example, if a positive receivables confirmation has been requested but no reply received, auditors may be able to obtain sufficient appropriate audit evidence of the debt by reviewing subsequent payments from the customer. If they are able to perform satisfactory alternative procedures, the item is not treated as an error.

Auditors also consider the **qualitative aspects of the errors.** These include the nature and cause of the error and the possible effect of the error on other phases of the audit. In analysing the errors discovered, auditors may observe that many have a common feature, for example type of transaction, location, product line or period of time. In such circumstances, they may decide to identify all items in the population which possess the common feature, thereby producing a sub-population, and extend audit procedures in this area. They may then perform a separate analysis based on the items examined for each sub-population, so that they have sufficient appropriate audit evidence for each sub-population.

3.3 Inferences to be drawn for population as a whole

Auditors project the error results of the sample to the population from which the sample was selected, ensuring that the method of projection is consistent with the method used to select the sampling unit.

The projection of the sample involves estimating the probable error in the population (by extrapolating the errors found in the sample), and estimating any further error that might not have been detected because of the imprecision of the technique. This is in addition to the consideration of the qualitative aspects of any errors found.

Auditors consider whether errors in the population might exceed the tolerable misstatement. To accomplish this, they compare the projected population error to the tolerable misstatement taking into account the results of other audit procedures relevant to the specific control or financial statement assertion. The projected population error used for this comparison in the case of substantive procedures is net of adjustments made by the entity. When the projected population error exceeds the tolerable misstatement, they re-assess the sampling risk and, if that risk is unacceptable, consider extending the audit procedure or performing alternative audit procedures, either of which may result in them proposing an adjustment to the financial statements.

3.4 Statistical sampling

Statistical sampling involves:

- the use of random sample selection, and
- probability theory to:
  - determine the sample size
  - evaluate quantitatively the sample results, and
  - measure the sampling risk.

In practice, a high level of mathematical competence is required if valid conclusions are to be drawn from sample evidence. However, most firms that use statistical sampling have drawn up complex plans which can be operated by staff without statistical training. These involve the use of tables, graphs or computer methods.

The main advantages of using statistical sampling are as follows:

- It imposes a more formal discipline to planning the audit of a population.
- It objectively determines sample sizes.
- It evaluates test results more precisely.
- It quantifies the sampling risk.
- The use of judgement is not precluded, since it is required to set objectives and evaluate results.

3.5 Non-Statistical sampling

Non-statistical sampling is any approach which does not fulfil all the conditions set out above in the definition of statistical sampling. This includes not only non-random selection but choosing a sample size on a 'judgement' basis. This approach has the following advantages:

- The approach has been used for many years, it is well understood and refined by experience.
- The auditor can bring greater judgement and expertise into play.
- Non-random selection may be quicker and more cost effective. · No special knowledge of statistics is required.
- In tests of controls the qualitative aspects of error evaluation cannot be statistically analysed.

There are some potential disadvantages to non-statistical sampling:

- Sampling risk cannot be quantified.
- Sample sizes may be too small to satisfy stated objectives.
- Sample sizes may be larger than necessary.
- Personal bias in the selection of samples is unavoidable.

4 Analytical procedures

4.1 Nature of analytical procedures

Analytical procedures include the consideration of comparisons of the entity's financial information with, for example:

- comparable information for prior periods;
- anticipated results of the entity, from budgets or forecasts;
- predictive estimates prepared by the auditors, such as an estimation of the depreciation charge for the year; and
- similar industry information, such as a comparison of the entity's ratio of sales to trade receivables with industry averages, or with the ratios relating to other entities of comparable size in the same industry.

Analytical procedures also include consideration of relationships:

- between elements of financial information that are expected to conform to a predicted pattern based on the entity's experience, such as the relationship of gross profit to sales, and
- between financial information and relevant non-financial information, such as the relationship of payroll costs to number of employees.

Various methods may be used in performing the above procedures. These range from simple comparisons to complex analyses using advanced statistical techniques. Analytical procedures may be applied to consolidated financial statements, financial statements of components (such as subsidiary undertakings, divisions or branches) and individual elements of financial information.

4.2 Purpose of analytical procedures

Analytical procedures are used by auditors:

- to assist in planning the nature, timing and extent of other audit procedures
- as substantive procedures when their use can be more effective or efficient than other procedures in reducing detection risk for specific financial statement assertions, and
- as part of the overall review of the financial statements when completing the audit.

4.3 Analytical procedures at the planning stage

Auditors apply analytical procedures at the planning stage to assist in:

- understanding the entity's business
- identifying areas of potential audit risk, and
- planning the nature, timing and extent of other audit procedures.

Analytical procedures at this stage are usually based on interim financial information, budgets and management accounts. However, for those entities with less formal means of controlling and monitoring performance, it may be possible to extract relevant financial information from the accounting system (perhaps when preparing the draft financial statements), sales tax returns and bank statements. Discussions with management, focused on identifying significant changes in the business since the prior financial period, may also be useful.

Application of analytical procedures may indicate aspects of the entity's business of which the auditors were previously unaware and assist in determining the nature, timing and extent of other audit procedures.

Example

Albatross Ltd had 100 employees last year with total wages of £840,000 and 100 employees this year with a wage bill of £950,000, an increase of 13%. We know that the annual pay rise was 6% and the level of business has remained approximately constant.

Solution

At first sight, the figures do not appear to make sense because the increase is substantially greater than expected. There may, however, be satisfactory explanations. For example, there may have been a change in sales mix with previously bought-in goods being replaced by goods manufactured in house, resulting in substantial authorised overtime. This could be verified by looking at the sales figures for different products as well as the payroll. Alternatively there could have been a switch to more skilled, and hence more expensive, labour; this could be verified from payroll and production records.

If no such explanation is available, it is possible that the payroll has been inflated by an error or irregularity, for example:

- mis-posting in the nominal ledger
- 'dummy' employees on the payroll
- unauthorised overtime being paid
- employees being paid at higher rates of pay than authorised.

Substantive tests will therefore be directed towards finding any errors of this nature.

4.4 Types of analytical procedures

For a manufacturing company analytical procedures may include:

- **comparing sales** for each major product with budget and previous years actual, and assessing the reasonableness of explanations for variances shown in the monthly sales report
- **comparing monthly figures** for each major product to establish trends and seasonal fluctuations (This may help to verify explanations about the performance of individual products).
- **comparing sales quantities** for each major product, in relation to budgets and previous years

- **reconciling sales quantities to production schedules** and opening and closing inventory for each major product
- **comparing ratios** such as gross profit, inventory turnover, receivables collection period, with budget and previous years (Gross profit and inventory turnover may be calculated on an individual product basis.)
- **examining price lists** to establish the effect of changes in prices.

If the results of these procedures are satisfactory, sample sizes for sales and receivables may be reduced.

4.5 Analytical procedures at the detailed testing stage

The decision about whether to use analytical procedures as substantive procedures and the nature, timing and extent of their use is based on the auditors' judgement about the expected effectiveness and efficiency of the available procedures in reducing detection risk for specific financial statement assertions. Auditors usually enquire of management as to the availability and reliability of information needed to apply analytical procedures and the results of any such procedures performed by the entity. It may be efficient to use analytical data prepared by the entity, provided the auditors are satisfied that such data is properly prepared.

4.6 Factors affecting use

When intending to apply analytical procedures as substantive procedures, auditors consider a number of factors such as the following:

- The **plausibility** and **predictability** of the relationships identified for comparison and evaluation. For example, there is a strong relationship between certain selling expenses and turnover in businesses where the sales force is paid by commission.
- The **objectives** of the analytical procedures and the extent to which their results are reliable.
- The **degree to which information can be disaggregated,** for example analytical procedures may be more effective when applied to financial information on individual sections of an operation or to financial statements of components of a diversified entity, than when applied to financial information relating to the entity as a whole.
- The **availability of information,** both financial (such as budgets or forecasts) and non-financial (such as the number of units produced or sold). The relevance of the information available, for example whether budgets are established as results to be expected rather than as goals to be achieved.

- The **comparability** of the information available, for example broad industry data may need to be supplemented to be comparable with that of an entity that produces and sells specialised products.
- The **knowledge gained** during previous audits, together with the auditors' understanding of the effectiveness of the accounting and internal control systems and the types of problems that in prior periods have given rise to accounting adjustments.

4.7 Reliability of information

The reliability of the information used in analytical procedures is likely to be enhanced if it comes from sources independent of, rather than internal to, the entity. If the information is produced internally, its reliability is enhanced if it is produced independently of the accounting system or there are adequate controls over its preparation. The necessity for evidence on the reliability of such information depends on the results of other audit procedures and on the importance of the results of analytical procedures as a basis for the auditors' opinion.

4.8 Extent of reliance

The extent of reliance that auditors place on the results of analytical procedures when used as substantive procedures may also depend on the following factors.

- **Other audit procedures** directed towards the same financial statement assertions. For example, other procedures auditors undertake in reviewing the collectability of receivables, such as the review of subsequent cash receipts, may confirm or dispel questions arising from the application of analytical procedures to an aged profile of customers' accounts.
- The **accuracy** with which the expected results of analytical procedures can be predicted. For example, auditors normally expect greater consistency in comparing the relationship of gross profit to sales from one period to another than in comparing discretionary expenses, such as research or advertising.
- The **frequency** with which a relationship is observed (e.g. a pattern repeated monthly as opposed to annually).

The application of analytical procedures is based on the expectation that relationships between data exist and continue in the absence of known conditions to the contrary. The presence of these relationships provides audit evidence as to the financial statement assertions relating to the data produced by the accounting system. However, reliance on the results of analytical procedures depends on the auditors' assessment of the risk that the analytical procedures may identify relationships as expected whereas, in fact, a material misstatement exists.

4.9 Proof in total

Proof in total is where the value of one item can be verified directly by reference to another item of data, the validity of which has already been established. In some circumstances, this may by itself provide the required level of assurance.

- Commission expense = (audited) sales × known commission %
- Sales = (audited) opening inventory + purchases – closing inventory × known mark-up
- Interest expense = (confirmed) balance of loan outstanding × interest rate, per loan agreement

4.10 Reasonableness tests

Reasonableness tests may contribute to the sufficiency of evidence when used in conjunction with other substantive tests.

- Closing receivables = Opening receivables + credit sales – cash receipts
- Depreciation = Average cost (or NBV, if reducing balance) of non-current assets – fully depreciated assets + purchases – closing inventory × Average depreciation rate
- Payroll costs = Average no. of employees × average wage × (1 + employers NI rate)

4.11 Analytical procedures at the overall review stage

When completing the audit, auditors apply analytical procedures in forming an overall conclusion as to whether the financial statements as a whole are consistent with their knowledge of the entity's business.

The conclusions drawn from the results of such procedures are intended to corroborate conclusions formed during the audit regarding individual components or elements of the financial statements and to assist in arriving at the overall conclusion as to whether the financial statements as a whole are consistent with the auditors' knowledge of the entity's business. However, they may also identify areas requiring further procedures.

4.12 Investigating significant fluctuations or unexpected relationships

The investigation of significant fluctuations and unexpected relationships normally begins with enquiries of management, followed by corroboration of management's responses:

- by comparing them with the auditors' knowledge of the entity's business and with other evidence obtained during the course of the audit; or
- if the analytical procedures are being carried out as substantive procedures, by undertaking additional audit procedures where appropriate to confirm the explanations received.

If management is unable to provide an explanation or if the explanation is not considered adequate, auditors determine the audit procedures to be undertaken to obtain an explanation for the fluctuation or relationship noted.

Activity 3

Task 1

A manufacturing business operates at a gross profit margin of 33%. The audited figure for cost of sales (i.e. opening inventory + purchases – closing inventory) is £583,406. What would you expect the sales figure to be?

Task 2

A class of non-current asset had a cost of £380,700 at the start of the year and a total cost of £420,600 at the end of the year. Within those totals there were assets costing £68,400 which were fully depreciated at the start of the year. This class of non-current assets is depreciated at 25% straight line on cost.

Carry out a reasonableness test for the depreciation charge for the year.

5 Summary

Audit evidence

You should now be able to specify the nature and reliability of sources of audit evidence and apply the procedures by which audit evidence is obtained.

Audit sampling

You should appreciate what constitutes audit sampling and the factors which affect its use. In particular, you should be able to design, select and evaluate a sample for a specified audit objective.

Analytical procedures

You should understand how analytical procedures contribute to the planning, testing and review stages of the audit. You should be able to design proofs in total and reasonableness tests for specified audit areas.

Answers to chapter activities

Activity 1

1 False.

2 True.

3 True.

Activity 2

$$\text{Sampling interval} = \frac{\text{Population}}{\text{Sample size}} = \frac{126{,}435 - 110{,}652}{200}$$

$$= 79$$

Invoice 1 (110,652 + 44) Invoice no: 110696

Invoice 2 (110,696 + 79) Invoice no: 110775

Invoice 3 (110,775 + 79) Invoice no: 110854

Invoice 4 (110,854 + 79) Invoice no: 110933

Activity 3

Task 1

$$\text{Anticipated sales} = £583{,}406 \times \frac{100}{67}$$

$$= £870{,}755$$

Task 2

$$\text{Average cost} = \frac{380{,}700 + 420{,}600}{2} = £400{,}650$$

Consider: (Average cost – fully depreciated assets) × depreciation rate

= (£400,650 – £68,400) × 25%

= £83,062

6 Test your knowledge

Workbook Activity 4

The objective of a substantive test will determine the population from which the sample for testing is selected.

For each of the objectives set out below, select the population from which the sample should be selected.

1 Obtain evidence of the existence of a non-current asset.

2 Obtain evidence of the completeness of the trade payables balance.

Workbook Activity 5

For each of the following, select whether they are a test of control or a substantive procedure:

1 Vouching of an addition to the non-current assets to the purchase invoice.

2 Observation of the order process in respect of a new customer placing an order.

3 Comparison of this year's receivables figure with the previous year's figure.

Audit verification work 1 – General principles

6

Introduction

This chapter looks at how we can verify our evidence and how this evidence corresponds to our financial statement assertions. We will review the contents of financial statements and will finish with considering the impact of accounting estimates on our audit assignment.

SYLLABUS AREA

- 2.5 Identify account balances to be verified and the associated risks.
- 2.7 Explain tests of control and substantive procedures and their links to the audit objective.
- 2.8 Select or devise tests in accordance with the auditing principles and agree them with the audit supervisor.
- 2.10 Describe these verification techniques and their uses; physical examination, reperformance, third party confirmation, vouching, documentary evidence and identification of unusual items.
- 3.3 Conduct tests, record test results and draw valid conclusions as specified in the audit plan.
- 3.4 Establish the existence, completeness, ownership, valuation and description of assets and liabilities and gather appropriate evidence to support these findings.

CONTENTS

1 Audit verification techniques

2 Review of financial statements

3 Accounting estimates

1 Audit verification techniques

1.1 Introduction

At this, the verification stage of the audit, the auditor is typically presented with a set of draft financial statements prepared by the client. The role of the auditor is to generate evidence to allow a conclusion to be reached as to whether the information contained in those financial statements, and the way the information is presented and disclosed, give a true and fair view.

We know already that audit evidence is generated by the auditor performing audit tests. Here, in verification work, the auditor will use substantive testing procedures, designed to give evidence relating to the figures in the financial statements, rather than control tests, dealing with the systems that produced those figures. However, the testing procedures available to the auditor here are the same as those we saw earlier. As a reminder, audit-testing procedures available to the auditor are:

Inspection

This covers the physical review or examination of records, documents and tangible assets. An example in substantive testing is examining purchase invoices to ensure that they have been properly recorded and analysed in the financial statements.

Observation

This procedure is mainly applicable to tests of control, but may also be used in substantive testing, such as the auditor observing the client's inventory count to gain evidence that the inventory figure in the financial statements had been arrived at accurately.

Enquiry

Seeking relevant information from knowledgeable persons inside or outside the enterprise.

An example in substantive testing is asking management for an explanation as to why a debtor has, or has not, been treated as a bad debt.

Computation

Checking the arithmetical accuracy of records or performing independent calculations, for example computing or re-computing the depreciation expense for the year.

Analytical procedures

You should note that these procedures are mainly used in substantive testing rather than as a test of controls. They may help the auditor to understand relationships between figures in the financial statements. This is sometimes referred to as the business approach to auditing.

Reperformance

This involves reperforming client procedures e.g. test checking inventory counts.

Confirmation

- This refers to the auditor obtaining a direct response (usually written) from an external, third party.
- Examples include:
  - circularisation of receivables;
  - confirmation of bank balances in a bank letter;
  - confirmation of actual/potential penalties from legal advisers; and
  - confirmation of inventories held by third parties.
- May give good evidence of existence of balances, e.g. receivables confirmation.
- May not necessarily give reliable evidence of valuation, e.g. customers may confirm receivable amounts but, ultimately, be unable to pay in the future.

1.2 Choice of verification techniques

There are no specific rules that exist as to the type(s) of techniques that the auditor should use in a given set of circumstances.

This is principally a matter of audit judgement and the nature of the audit objective(s). The auditor has to look at each individual item in its own right, identify the audit objective(s) for that particular item and then decide the most reliable audit evidence available. The circumstances and evidence available will affect the type of technique(s) he uses.

1.3 Audit objectives and financial statement assertions

As just stated the type(s) of technique(s) used depend on the audit objectives that the auditor is seeking to achieve.

The general objective to be achieved by audit verification work is to establish whether the financial statements present a true and fair view.

We can identify a number of more detailed objectives which underlie this overall objective. These more detailed objectives allow the auditor to design a series of substantive tests on each audit area (inventory, receivables, etc) which will build up the overall bank of evidence necessary to support the overall audit opinion.

In carrying out substantive audit tests (verification work) the auditor will be looking for evidence on:

Completeness: there are no unrecorded assets or liabilities, transactions or events (i.e. the assets, liabilities, transactions and events are not understated).

Occurrence: a transaction or event occurred during the relevant accounting period (i.e. the transaction is recorded in the correct period – this is often referred to as cut-off).

Valuation: the asset or liability is recorded at an appropriate amount. The valuation principles will differ, between non-current assets and current assets.

Existence: an asset or liability exists at a given date (i.e. the assets and liabilities are not overstated). Auditors spend a great deal of time confirming the existence of assets such as tangible non-current assets, inventory, receivables and cash. Clearly this is fundamental to the true and fair view principle.

Rights and obligations. The entity has legal or other rights or obligations relating to the asset or liability.

Allocation: a transaction or event is recorded at the proper amount and revenue or expense is allocated to the proper period.

Classification and understandability: must be in accordance with relevant legislation and accounting standards (e.g. the CA 2006 and relevant IFRSs and IASs).

Cut-off: transactions and events have been recorded in the correct accounting period.

The above objectives link into a concept known as the financial statement assertions. This concept takes the view that draft accounts presented by the client to the auditor are making a number of statements, or assertions. The role of substantive testing is to verify these assertions.

The assertions made by the financial statements and the related objectives of the substantive testing objectives set out above can be shown as follows:

ASSERTION	TESTING OBJECTIVE
Assets shown include all rights under the control of the enterprise.	Completeness
Transactions arising during the period are reflected in the period's financial statements.	Occurrence
The amounts at which assets and liabilities are stated are correct.	Valuation
Assets and liabilities included on the statement of financial position actually exist.	Existence
Assets and liabilities are shown in the financial statements such that the user would have a clear understanding of the client's financial situation.	Classification and understandability

2 Review of financial statements

2.1 Content of financial statements

It is important that you are clear as to exactly what the financial statements consist of under modern accounting practice.

They comprise the following:

(a) The primary statements

- (i) statement of financial position
- (ii) statement of profit or loss
- (iii) statement of changes in equity
- (iv) cash flow statement

(b) The notes to the accounts

The main principles underlying the preparation and presentation of company financial statements are now set out by the International Accounting Standards Board's Framework for the Preparation and Presentation of Financial Statements.

The major points from this document are summarised below:

The elements of financial statements

The starting point here is definitions of assets and liabilities. The other elements are then defined in terms of these.

Assets are resources controlled by the entity as a result of past events and from which future economic benefits are expected to flow to the entity.

Liabilities are present obligations of the entity arising from past events, the settlement of which is expected to result in an outflow from the entity of resources embodying economic benefits.

Owners' equity is arrived at by deducting liabilities from assets (capital = assets – liabilities).

Revenue is determined in terms of increases in owners' equity.

Expenditure is determined in terms of decreases in owners' equity.

Recognition in financial statements

Recognition essentially means the recording process. The principles here address such questions as when is it acceptable to recognise (record) an asset or liability and when should assets and liabilities be de-recognised (no longer recorded in financial statements).The main points to note are:

Assets and liabilities should be recognised when there is evidence of their existence AND they can be reliably measured.

They should be derecognised when the right (assets) or obligations (liabilities) no longer exist.

2.2 The timing of audit procedures

Whereas tests of control can be (and usually are) performed by the auditor before the client's year end – at the so called interim audit stage – substantive audit procedures and verification work will be performed primarily at or very soon after the client's year end, as these procedures normally rely on the availability of draft financial statements.

Verification of the individual assets and liabilities by the auditor extends into the post year-end period (i.e. the period between the year-end date and the date of approval of the financial statements). The auditors will use this to their advantage when seeking to verify amounts stated for contingent liabilities, and for post year-end events (these are explained in a later chapter).

3 Accounting estimates

Definition

An **approximation** of the amount of an item in the absence of a precise means of measurement.

3.1 Introduction

This area is governed by ISA 540 *Auditing accounting estimates, including fair value accounting estimat*es, and related disclosures.

The auditors should ensure that where management have made estimates in the preparation of the financial statements – and this will, in effect, always be the case – they obtain sufficient, appropriate audit evidence.

Examples of typical circumstances where estimates are made are as follows:

(a) allowances to reduce inventory and receivables to their estimated realisable value

(b) provisions for depreciation

(c) accrued revenue

(d) provisions for deferred taxation

(e) provisions for losses on a legal dispute.

It is important to recognise that it is the directors and management who are responsible for making accounting estimates, not the auditors. The auditors will need to pay attention to this area, especially where the amounts are material, as there is a higher risk of misstatement. This is a complex area, and the auditor is more likely to need to exercise judgement in such situations as evidence available to support the estimate is not always conclusive.

3.2 Audit procedures on accounting estimates

The auditor should obtain sufficient, appropriate audit evidence as to whether an accounting estimate is reasonable in the circumstances and, when required, is appropriately disclosed.

It is important that the auditors gain an understanding of the procedures used by management when making estimates. If there is no objective data available to enable the auditors to assess the estimate, then they should consider the implications for their report.

Specific procedures that should be performed are as follows:

(a) **Review and test the process used by management to develop the estimate**

The auditor should:

(i) evaluate the data used, and consider the assumptions on which the estimates are based (are they realistic and reasonable?)

(ii) test the calculations used in the estimate

(iii) compare estimates made in prior periods with actual results of those periods (this will give comfort on how much reliance can be placed on management's procedures).This is a useful area for the application of analytical procedures

(iv) consider the review and approval procedures used by management.

(b) **Use of an independent estimate**

The auditors should either estimate the figure themselves or obtain a third party estimate. If they obtain a third party estimate then they should evaluate the data, consider the assumptions, and test the procedures used, in order to verify its accuracy. This independent estimate should then be compared with that of management and any differences investigated.

(c) **Review of subsequent events**

The auditors should review transactions after the period end which relate to the estimates made; these may remove the need to use estimates.

3.3 Evaluation of audit results

ISA 540 states that 'The auditor should make a final assessment of the reasonableness of the entity's accounting estimates based on the auditor's understanding of the entity and its environment and whether the estimates are consistent with other audit evidence obtained during the audit.'

The auditor should consider any differences identified between the accounting estimate and the results of their work. The materiality of the difference will affect their action:

(a) if the difference is reasonable then it is unlikely that adjustment will be required

(b) if the cumulative effect of all estimates or any one estimate is material then adjustment should be required

(c) if the directors refuse to make any required adjustment, then the auditors should consider the implications for their report.

Activity 1

Explain what is meant by an accounting estimate, and give three examples. For a suggested answer, see the 'Answers' section at the end of the chapter.

3.4 Conclusion

The use of accounting estimates is a subjective area; however, the auditor should still seek to obtain sufficient, appropriate audit evidence to verify their reasonableness and accuracy.

4 Summary

This chapter has introduced you to the application of standard audit testing procedures to substantive testing as used at the final stage of the audit. These procedures are used by the auditor to generate evidence that will enable the auditor to reach a conclusion on the financial statement assertions.

In carrying out these procedures the auditor should be aware of the theoretical framework within which financial statements are prepared (the IASB's Framework for the Preparation and Presentation of Financial Statements) and the particular audit problems resulting from accounting estimates.

We are now ready to move on to look at the application of these testing procedures to major areas of the financial statements.

Answers to chapter activities

Activity 1

An accounting estimate is an adjustment made to the financial statements about the nature and impact of uncertain future events. Examples include:

- Provisions and contingencies
- Useful economic lives of assets
- Net realisable value of inventory
- Going concern status of a business.

Audit verification work 2 – Inventory

7

Introduction

The following four chapters focus on audit field work across a number of areas. In this chapter we will look at the area of inventory within our audit. We will consider auditors work on inventory and risks associated and we will end with reviewing an audit programme for inventory.

SYLLABUS AREA

1.2 Describe the features of an accounting system.

2.10 Describe these verification techniques and their uses physical examination, vouching, reperformance, third party confirmation, documentary evidence and identification of unusual items.

3.3 Conduct tests, record test results and draw valid conclusions as specified in the audit plan.

3.4 Establish the existence, ownership, valuation and description of assets and liabilities and gather appropriate evidence to support these findings.

3.5 Identify all matters of an unusual nature and refer them promptly to the audit supervisor.

3.6 Identify and record material and significant errors, deficiencies or other variations from standard and report them to the audit supervisor.

CONTENTS

1 Inventory: Financial statement and audit implications

2 The auditor's work on the inventory count

3 The auditor's work on inventory valuation

4 Problem areas in the audit of inventory

5 An audit programme for inventory

1 Inventory: Financial statement and audit implications

Inventory, dealt with in this chapter, is perhaps the area on a typical statement of financial position, which has, historically given auditors more problems than any other. Many of the leading negligence cases involving auditors revolved around the approach taken to the audit of inventory. The implication is that inventory is often a high-risk area, requiring careful audit planning and often a high degree of judgement in carrying out audit procedures.

1.1 The importance of inventory and work-in-progress

The term inventory and work-in-progress includes raw materials, bought in parts, work-in-progress (manufactured goods in an incomplete state) and finished goods.

This asset is very important from the audit viewpoint for the following reasons:

(a) Misstatement of inventory balances has a direct effect on the reported profit of two accounting periods – closing inventory of one year is, of course, opening inventory of the next year. As a result of the subjective nature of many aspects of the inventory figure in the financial statements it is the easiest asset for management to manipulate.

(b) Inventory can be very difficult for an auditor to access.

- There may be thousands of different lines of inventory – the average UK supermarket carries approximately 40,000 different product lines and, of course, large quantities of each.
- There may be some inventory items of a very specialist nature – pharmaceutical or engineering companies may present this type of problem to the auditor.

(c) The quantities of inventory held at a given moment may be difficult to establish. It may not be possible to cease inventory movements during the inventory count with the effect that accurate inventory quantities may be hard to establish.

(d) Valuation may be difficult especially with specialist inventory and obsolete inventory. As a consequence net realisable values may be hard to establish. The amount of overheads that can be attributed to inventory may be subjective in nature.

(e) Inventory losses from pilferage, wastage, etc may be difficult to control.

1.2 Inventory valuation

For financial reporting purposes, accounting standards require that inventory should be valued at the lower of cost or net realisable value on an item by item basis.

You should be familiar with this from your financial accounting studies.

Definition

The **cost of inventory** shall comprise all costs of purchase, costs of conversion and other costs incurred in bringing the inventory to their present location and condition (IAS 2).

A major aspect of the auditor's work on inventory is, as we shall see later, verification of the valuation placed on inventory. In order to carry out this aspect of the audit verification work, the auditor must be fully aware of the IAS 2 inventory valuation principle shown above.

The key points to recall here are:

- Cost is based on activities conducted in the ordinary course of business. Abnormal costs, such as costs resulting from excessively high or low activity levels, should not therefore be included in the cost of inventory.
- Cost should only be included if it is incurred in bringing the item to its present location and condition, post production costs are therefore not to be included in the cost of inventory, but production overheads should be included if they fit into the definition given above.

Where individual items of inventory cannot be separately identified and valued they should be valued using either the FIFO (First In First Out) or the average cost basis.

Definition

Net realisable value is the estimated selling price in the ordinary course of business less the estimated costs of completion and the estimated costs necessary to make the sale (IAS 2).

1.3 Inventory quantities

In addition to valuing the inventory correctly, it is clearly important that the company can determine accurately the physical quantity of inventory on hand at any point in time.

Many companies will maintain accounting records of inventory, but from the audit point of view, the inventory records substantiated by physical inventory counts are important as inventory records by themselves are notoriously unreliable.

We are now going to examine in detail the audit work involved in reaching a conclusion on these two aspects of the final inventory figure in the valuation statements – the quantity of inventory in hand at the year-end date and the valuation to be placed on that inventory.

2 The auditor's work on the inventory count

2.1 Available inventory count methods

The two principal methods of systems of inventory count available to clients are continuous and periodic.

- Under a continuous system, some items of inventory are counted say every week or every month through the accounting period.
- Under a system of periodic inventory count, all inventory is counted at the same time, typically at the year-end date.

It is clearly important that the auditor should be aware of which system is in operation by the client in order that suitable audit arrangements can be made.

2.2 Continuous inventory counting

Where suitable accounting records of inventory are maintained, it is often backed up by a programme of continuous inventory counting as part of general inventory control procedures. In a continuous inventory counting system, inventory is counted on a regular on-going basis throughout the accounting period.

If such a programme of continuous inventory counting is in operation by a client, the auditor should ensure that:

(a) Each item of inventory is physically inspected and counted at least once a year, and more frequently in the case of items liable to loss, etc.

(b) Inventory records are kept up to date.

(c) The records are amended as a result of physical counting, and that there are appropriate reports and investigation procedures for discrepancies.

(d) Two people carry out each count, and there is a rotation of pairing of the checkers.

Providing the continuous inventory count procedures in place by a client are acceptable, auditors may use the information provided for audit purposes, even though this system means that all the inventory on hand at the year-end date was not counted at that date.

There are several advantages to be gained from a well organised system of continuous inventory checking.

(a) Disruption caused by the inventory count is minimised – each inventory count takes a shorter period of time to complete.

(b) More regular inventory counts will allow for earlier identification of errors and obsolete inventory.

(c) Increased discipline is imposed over storekeepers caused by the surprise elements of random checks. This should result in a higher level of control being exercised over inventory.

2.3 Periodic inventory counts

Under this system, inventory is counted only once in each accounting period.

The count will usually be undertaken on or near the financial year end. If undertaken shortly before or after the financial year end, the time gap between the physical count and financial year end should be kept to a minimum, so as to minimise the risk of inaccuracies arising in the final inventory figure.

Activity 1

A potential client has approached your firm as he is setting up a new company selling computer stationery. He has asked for advice on inventory count methods and informs you that he has heard of periodic and continuous inventory counting, but doesn't understand what these terms mean.

Explain the difference between these two methods.

2.4 Organisation of inventory counts

Regardless of the inventory count system in operation – continuous or periodic – it is vitally important both for financial reporting purposes and for audit purposes, that the count is carried out accurately.

It is the responsibility of management (not the auditor) to establish appropriate procedures to be followed by staff in organising and conducting the inventory count.

However, the auditor should carefully review the inventory count arrangements that a client has in place.

Clear procedures should be drawn up by the client well in advance of the inventory count taking place. These instructions should be made available to client staff who are going to be involved in the count so that they have a chance to review them, become familiar with their contents and clarify any areas of doubt or uncertainty.

In addition, the auditor should review a copy of the procedures before the inventory count is held by the client. In reviewing the procedures, the auditor is assessing their adequacy – will the client's procedures, if carried out effectively, ensure that a full and accurate count is taken, which can then be used as the basis for the quantity of inventory on hand at the year-end to be reflected in the financial statements.

Set out below are the main features that should appear in inventory count instructions.

1 The organisation of the inventory

(a) The inventory area is in a well organised, tidy condition in order to make the counting process as efficient as possible.

(b) Goods are clearly described and suitably labelled.

(c) Goods are protected against deterioration and misappropriation (restriction of access to stores).

(d) Goods held for third parties (i.e. goods not belonging to the company), and slow-moving, obsolete inventory, etc are identified and separated.

(e) There is an adequate plan of the area to be covered, which should be tidy.

2 Carrying out the inventory count

(a) The procedure to be followed by each relevant department, branch, division, etc, reflecting the circumstances of each part of the business.

(b) Competent supervisors should be appointed for each inventory area, with teams (pairs) of technically competent counters allocated to the supervisors. One person for each team should be responsible for counting, the other for recording and checking the count. The storekeepers should not be responsible for counting unless their work is independently checked (segregation of duties!)

(c) Inventory should be suitably marked to indicate that it has been counted e.g. chalk mark, docket/ticket, etc.

(d) A standardised pre-numbered form should be used for recording the inventory count, the issue and return of which should be controlled so that all inventory counted and areas are accounted for, and that proper accounting records are kept.

(e) Movement of inventory during the inventory count should be halted or closely controlled.

(f) Comparisons should be made as soon as practicable after the inventory count with the continuous inventory records so that any discrepancies may be investigated and adjusted.

2.5 The auditor's attendance at the inventory count

Standard audit practice requires the auditor to attend the client's inventory count if inventory is material to the financial statements and if the auditor is to rely on the inventory count as a source of evidence as to the physical quantities of inventory on hand. It follows from this that if:

- inventory is not material, or
- the accounting record rather than the inventory count is used as the source of inventory quantities,

then the auditor is not expected to attend the count. These exceptions are not encountered on a regular basis in practice.

The auditor's role

The auditor will usually attend the client's inventory count, the overall purpose of attendance being to assess the effectiveness of the client's inventory count procedures. Attendance at an inventory count is primarily a test of controls, not a substantive procedure. It is not the auditor's responsibility to count inventory, but the client's. The auditor will perform test counts but these tiny samples are not intended to be representative of the populations they are drawn from.

We can analyse the role of the auditor in connection with inventory counts under three headings:

- Before the inventory count
- During the inventory count
- After the inventory count.

Before the inventory count	**During the inventory count**	**After the inventory count**
The auditor should perform the following procedures: (a) Review prior year's working papers, familiarise himself with the nature, volume and location of inventory. The controlling and recording procedures over inventory should also be considered. (b) Identify problem areas in relation to the system of internal control and decide whether reliance can be placed on internal auditors. (c) If inventory held by third parties is material, or the third party is insufficiently independent or reliable, then arrange a inventory count attendance at the third party's premises, otherwise, arrange third party confirmation by way of letter to the auditor.	The main task here is to ensure that the client's staff are carrying out their duties effectively. Here, the auditor is using the audit testing procedure of observation. In addition to observing the inventory count process being carried out, the auditor should also: (a) Make two-way test counts from factory floor to inventory sheets, and from inventory sheets to factory floor. These are checked with the figures counted by the client and discrepancies investigated. The test counts are used for follow up audit work later. (b) Make notes of items counted, damaged inventory and instances where the procedures are not being followed. (c) Examine and test control over the inventory sheets. The client should keep a inventory sheet register.	The auditor should perform the following procedures after the inventory count. (a) Check the cut off details obtained at the inventory count are accounted for in the correct period. (b) Review the final inventory sheets and follow up test counts to the final statements of inventory. This test is designed to ensure that inventory quantities that actually existed at the date of the count are reflected in the final financial statements. (c) Ensure that continuous inventory records (if applicable) are adjusted or reconciled to the physical count.

Before the inventory count	During the inventory count	After the inventory count
(d) If the nature of the inventory is specialised then the auditor will need to arrange expert help or to review the client's own arrangements for identifying and valuing the inventory. (e) Examine the client's inventory –taking instructions, as explained above: If found to be inadequate, the matter should be discussed with the client with a view to improving them prior to the inventory count.	(d) Examine cut-off procedures. (e) Pay particular attention to goods held on behalf of third parties (for example, goods on consignment) and how these are segregated and recorded. (f) Reach and record a conclusion as to whether or not the inventory count was satisfactory, and hence provides reliable evidence supporting the final inventory figure. If the auditor in attendance at the inventory count does not feel that the procedures are being carried out adequately, he must bring this to management's attention immediately and seek to rectify the position as it may not be possible to obtain the relevant evidence at a later date.	

The cut-off concept

As financial statements are drawn up at a specific point in time, it is important that the right transactions are fully recorded in the right period. This is a simple but useful way of looking at cut off.

For example, if sales are recorded as a transaction of the current period by recognising a year end debtor, the corresponding cost of sales entry must also be made in the current period and the item must not be included in year-end inventory. This is an example of sales cut off.

Similarly, if goods are received during the current period and recorded in closing inventory, the year end creditor for the item must also be recorded. This is an example of purchase cut off.

Tests the auditor would carry out to ensure correct cut-off include the following.

(a) During inventory count attendance, note the serial numbers of the last sales invoice, despatch note and goods received note generated before the inventory count.

(b) After the inventory count, check the year-end despatch notes to sales invoices and the sales daybook and vice versa to ensure that despatches and the related invoice both fall before the year end.

(c) Similarly for purchases, ensure year-end goods receipts notes and related purchase invoices are correctly treated in the current period.

(d) Take a sample of goods received and goods despatched just after the year end and ensure that the related inventory was not included in the count in the case of goods received, and that it was included, in the case of goods despatched.

Activity 2

Explain the main reasons why the auditors attend the inventory count and state what action they would take if they identified that the client's laid down inventory count procedures were not being followed.

3 The auditor's work on inventory valuation

The main objective of the auditor attending the inventory count is to obtain evidence relating to the existence of inventory. Attendance will provide some evidence relating to the valuation of inventory – for example, the auditor should record details of any inventory showing signs of obsolescence – but much more work will be required before the auditor can reach an overall conclusion on inventory valuation. This section deals with that audit work.

The auditors need to perform additional valuation tests. The audit work which the auditor will need to perform in respect of the valuation of inventory will depend on the type of inventory items under review.

3.1 Raw materials and consumable supplies

As these items of inventory are in their raw state (no work has yet been done on them by the client), the principal element of cost to consider is their purchase price from the material supplier. In addition there may be incidental costs such as delivery charges to consider.

Typical audit procedures applied to the verification of these inventory items will be as follows:

(a) Ascertain what elements of cost are included e.g. carriage in, duties, etc.

(b) Ascertain the method of valuing inventory.

(c) If standard costs are used, enquire into standards: how and when the standards were set, how these compare with actual costs and how variances are treated.

(d) Check costs used with purchase invoices received, before the inventory count.

(e) Check quantities with inventory records with a particular aim of finding items which have been in inventory for an unduly long period. Discuss these items with a responsible official in order to find out when they might be used, if at all, in order to ascertain a reasonable net realisable value. Consider the need for any write down of the value of these items of inventory.

(f) Follow up valuation of all damaged or obsolete inventory noted during observance of physical inventory count with a view to establishing a net realisable value and again consider any write down which may be necessary.

3.2 Work-in-progress (i.e. part completed goods)

The range of costs to consider here will include labour costs and production overheads, in addition to materials, as some work has been done by the client on this type of inventory.

Typical audit procedures applied to the verification of these inventory items will be as follows:

(a) Ascertain what elements of cost are included. If overheads are included, ascertain the basis on which they are calculated and review this basis with the available costing and financial information. If labour is included, check the calculations to costing and payroll records.

(b) Ascertain how the state of completion of the work in progress is measured and if estimates are made, on what basis they are made.

(c) Ensure that any materials costs exclude any abnormal wastage factors – abnormal costs should not be included under IAS 2.

(d) Ensure that any addition for overheads includes only normal expenses based on normal production capacity and that any costs arising from under-utilisation of production facilities, excessive waste or exceptional circumstances (i.e. abnormal costs again) are not carried forward in the inventory valuation.

(e) Enquire into any old, obsolete or damaged items and ensure that these are valued at a reasonable estimated net realisable value. Check this with previous or subsequent sales of similar items.

3.3 Finished goods and goods for resale

Note that if these items have been manufactured or processed by the client, the cost will consist of the same elements as were identified in work in progress above. If the items were brought in by the client in their completed state, cost of the inventory will comprise the purchase price from the supplier.

Typical audit procedures applied to the verification of these inventory items will be as follows:

(a) Enquire into what costs are included, how these have been established and ensure that any overhead addition is based on normal costs and is reasonable in relation to the information disclosed by the draft accounts. If labour is included, check the calculations to costing and payroll records.

(b) Check the final cost with the client's official sales prices, bearing in mind any trade discounts which are normally granted off the list prices. This enables the auditor to ensure that inventory is valued at net realisable value if this is less than cost. For any such items, also check back and see if the relevant partly processed inventory and raw materials have also been written down.

(c) Follow up any items which inventory records show are more than, say, six months in inventory. Enquire into reasons for this and ascertain possible realisable value of such items.

(d) Follow up any inventory which at the time of observance of physical inventory taking were noted as being damaged or obsolete.

(e) Discuss with sales manager any possible policy of selling off certain lines at less than usual selling prices e.g. 'loss leaders' due to competition, substitute products on the market etc.

(f) Follow up valuation of all 'seconds' items and ensure that they are valued at a reasonable estimated net realisable value if less than cost.

4 Problem areas in the audit of inventory

4.1 Introduction

Certain practical matters which may cause difficulty in some audits are explained briefly below. Where relevant, the auditor should take them into consideration when verifying inventory.

4.2 Overheads

Definition

Overheads are expenses incurred in the manufacture of goods and include items like factory rates and lighting and heating.

Overheads should normally be included in the cost of goods being produced, based on the normal activity level of the company. An estimate of overheads to be incurred at this level of activity will need to be calculated, and allocated to the goods produced based on this activity level. If the company produces less goods than expected, then the unabsorbed overheads should be written off to the profit and loss account and not included in the inventory valuation.

In addition, most costing systems base overhead allocations on budgeted figures. These are obviously pre-determined figures, calculated before the actual overhead costs for the period are known and before the actual level of production is known. Activity levels in excess of that expected may require a reapportionment of overheads. If this is not done, it may result in an excessive amount of overhead being included in inventory valuation.

The overheads to be included in inventory should be only those relating to production; these are known as production overheads (the factory rates, etc).

4.3 Choice of overhead allocation method

There are many different ways of including overheads into the cost of inventory. Each company must make its own decision about which method to use. The method must give a close approximation to the actual cost of overheads incurred in making the inventory.

The auditor will need to apply judgement in order to evaluate the appropriateness of the method used by the client.

4.4 Net realisable value

Definition

Net realisable value is the estimated selling price in the ordinary course of business less the estimated costs of completion and the estimated costs necessary to make the sale.

As you are already aware, inventory should be valued at the lower of cost and net realisable value and it is not always easy to arrive at a figure for net realisable value. This is often another area where estimates will be used and where the auditor will need to assess the reasonableness of those estimates. A wide variety of sources of information may be available in order to assess net realisable value. These include:

- selling prices realised after the year end
- price lists.

Where net realisable value is found to be less than cost, the individual inventory lines affected should be revalued at the (lower) net realisable value. The only exception to this rule is for raw materials and components to be used in manufacture. These items may have their own net realisable value being less than cost. However, these items are not normally sold in their raw state. Because of this, no reduction in value is needed if it can be shown that the product made from these items can still be sold at above its cost.

There are several situations where net realisable value is more likely to be less than cost, including:

(a) increased costs of manufacture

(b) reduced selling prices of products

(c) deterioration of inventory (particularly food stuffs)

(d) obsolescence of products (perhaps due to technological changes)

(e) deliberate selling at loss (supermarket 'loss leaders')

(f) buying and production errors.

5 An audit programme for inventory

The following is an extract from a detailed audit programme for inventory.

Example

Audit programme

Sch Ref

HASTINGS & WARWICK

AUDIT PROGRAMME

CLIENT ____________ **PREPARED BY** ____________ **DATE** ____________

REVIEWED BY ____________ **DATE** ____________
(Audit senior in charge)

PERIOD ____________ **REVIEWED BY** ____________ **DATE** ____________
(Manager)

AUDIT AREA – inventory

The purpose of the auditing procedures set out in this section of the programme is to obtain reasonable assurance that inventory are not materially misstated.	*Work performed by*	*Ref to supporting working paper*
RELIANCE ON INTERNAL CONTROL PROCEDURES 1 Where we have placed reliance on the client's internal control procedures, test that the controls on which we are relying have been complied with, and record the details of such tests in the working papers.		

TESTS OF DETAIL

EXISTENCE AND OWNERSHIP

Planning our attendance at the inventory count

2 Where the date selected for the inventory count is an interim date we must be able to rely on the year-end book inventory records. Assess the past reliability of the book records by examining the materiality of differences disclosed by previous physical inventory-counts. If there are any doubts as to the reliability of the book records, discuss immediately with the manager whether we should request the client to conduct a year-end inventory count.

3 Review the adequacy of the client's inventory count instructions. Any serious shortcomings must be discussed immediately with responsible client officials so that they can be rectified before the inventory-count.

4 Select for test counting those inventory items expected to have the largest monetary value at the inventory count date.

5 Where the client maintains inventory of a technical nature which is not readily identifiable, or whose conditions we are not competent to ascertain, consider using independent experts.

6 Obtain a list of all inventory held by third party custodians. Ensure that the list is complete. In respect of these inventory:

(a) Establish the suitability of the custodian.

(b) Confirm the existence and title of such inventory directly with the custodians.

(c) Review the controls exercised by the client over this inventory (including cut-off) and consider whether there is any need for us to inspect them physically.

7 Arrange for the necessary audit staff to attend inventory count at the various locations. Brief the audit staff and ensure that they have a copy of the client's instructions for inventory count together with a list of the inventory items pre-selected in 4 above and the audit programme for procedures during inventory count which they will be required to complete.

Make arrangements for the audit staff to be present at the end of the inventory count.

8 On completion of the inventory count obtain and review the audit working papers prepared during our attendance at the various locations, and summarise the adequacy and effectiveness of the inventory count.

Procedures subsequent to inventory count

9 Obtain the client's count records and test that they are complete and accurate, as follows:

(a) Test for completeness, by comparing the numerical sequence of count records with the details recorded in our working papers at the time of the physical count.

(b) Scrutinise the count records to ensure that they have not been altered subsequent to our attendance at the inventory-count by comparing the records with details recorded in our working papers at the time of the physical count (e.g. photocopies).

Testing continuous inventory count procedures

10 Review the instructions issued to inventory counters and the procedures adopted by the client, in order to determine whether such instructions and procedures are adequate. Pay particular attention to controls revealed on the ICQ for the inventory system where inventory is not physically counted at the year-end date.

11 Arrange to attend at least one of the continuous inventory counts during the year. Review the inventory count reports or the inventory records to ascertain the extent to which inventory have been counted during the year, and also to determine (by reviewing any differences disclosed) the accuracy of the inventory records. In the light of this review, determine the extent of the counting to be performed under 12 (a) and (b) below. Test that the differences disclosed by inventory count have been adjusted in the inventory records.

12 Carry out audit tests as follows:

(a) Select from the inventory account at the year-end date a sample of inventory items, and check the quantities with the underlying inventory records and the valuation of the items with supporting documents.

(b Count a number of items that are in inventory, and check these by comparing them with the inventory account.

13 Summarise on a working paper our findings on the adequacy and effectiveness of the continuous inventory count procedures and on the reliability of the inventory records. Also indicate the approximate amount of the differences found during the year.

Checking quantities on inventory sheets

14 Test the casts of the inventory sheets by:

(a) Casting the pages to which counted items have been traced and follow the totals through to the inventory summary.

(b) Casting the final inventory summary, selecting individual page totals and casting these pages, at the same time selecting items for examination in procedure 15(a).

15 Test that the physical quantities shown on the final inventory sheets are neither overstated nor understated by performing the following procedures:

(a) Overstatement: Agree the details of those items selected in procedure 14 (b above with the client's count records, to ensure that the inventory sheets only incorporate count records from the inventory count.

(b) Understatement: Agree items which were counted by us, or in our presence, with the final inventory sheets.

Testing the cut-off of inventory

16 Test that there was a proper cut-off at the inventory count date, as follows:

(a) Select from the goods received reports for a few days either side of the inventory count date, and compare with the relevant inventory records (and vice versa) to ensure that goods received were recorded in the inventory records in the correct accounting period.

(b) Select from the despatch records for a few days either side of the inventory count date, and compare with the relevant inventory records (and vice versa) to ensure that goods despatched were recorded in the inventory records in the correct accounting period.

(c) Where necessary, test the cut-off on the internal movement of inventory.

VALUATION

Checking valuations and calculations on inventory sheets

17 Record in the working papers in detail the bases and methods of costing used, and obtain reasonable assurance that these bases and methods are being applied consistently, and are in accordance with generally accepted accounting practices and the stated accounting policies of the company.

18 Test the items selected in procedure 15 above as follows:

(a) Prove the unit costs on the inventory sheets by reference to appropriate supporting records (such as suppliers' invoices, labour cost analyses, overhead allocations and other appropriate records).

(b) Prove the extensions on the inventory sheets.

19 Where the costs have been obtained from standard cost records, review the variance reports or the entries in the variance accounts as appropriate in order to determine whether or not the standard costs are materially different from actual costs. If there are material differences, ascertain the reasons for these differences and consider the need to adjust the valuation of the inventory.

20 Examine the overheads included in the inventory valuation and ensure that:

(a) Their inclusion is in accordance with generally accepted accounting principles.

(b) They reflect the client's normal level of activity.

21 Ensure that inter-department or inter-branch profit included in inventory have been properly eliminated and that where inventory include goods purchased or transferred from group companies they have been identified as such and segregated on the inventory summary.

22 Check that the general ledger accounts have been adjusted to reflect the results of physical inventory count. Establish the reasons for any material differences disclosed.

TESTING THE NET REALISABLE VALUE OF INVENTORY

23 Apply the procedures set out in (a) to (e) below to ascertain whether or not inventory write-downs and provisions are adequate (but not excessive) so that inventory are stated at the lower of cost and net realisable value. In doing this, consider the following factors where applicable: the condition of the inventory, its saleability, the possibility of obsolescence, the levels of inventory in relation to current and expected sales or usage, the estimated costs of completing work in progress, and current and expected selling prices less reasonable costs of disposal.

(a) Test the amount at which inventory of finished products and of other items held for sale to customers is stated does not exceed the selling price less reasonable costs of disposal. Also test that the quantities held are not excessive. Compare inventory levels (where appropriate) with sales for the current year, with orders, and with sales forecasts.

(b) Test that work in progress is current and saleable. Also test that (where appropriate) it has been written down by the amount of any losses expected to arise on realisation – taking into account reasonable costs of completion and disposal.

(c) Test that the costs incurred to date on contract work in progress plus the estimated costs of completing the work do not exceed the net contract price. Inspect written contracts for significant projects undertaken during the year (whether complete or incomplete at the year-end date), noting prices, terms of delivery, possible penalties, and possible variations of the contract price. Where profit is taken on contracts in progress, review the bases and methods used in order to determine whether or not such bases are consistent with those used during the previous year and also reasonable and acceptable.

(d) Test that inventory of raw material and supplies which are defective, obsolete or surplus to production requirements have been adequately written down.

(e) Test that adequate provision has been made for any major purchase commitments which are surplus to requirements or which are at prices in excess of current replacement prices.

TESTING INVENTORY IN TRANSIT

24 In respect of inventory in transit:

(a) Examine the basis for recording any inventory that is in transit.

(b) Check that the inventory has been subsequently received and was validly in transit.

OVERALL REVIEW

25 Compare the inventory at the year-end date with those of the previous year, and obtain explanations for any significant differences. Compare inventory turnover rates with those of previous years. Generally consider whether inventory are stated on appropriate bases consistent with those stated in the preceding year.

6 Summary

Inventory is a material asset in the financial statements of many enterprises which is relatively easily manipulated. Auditors will often treat inventory as a relatively high risk area. This together with its materiality impact, means that auditors will devote a significant amount of audit time to inventory.

There are two main areas to consider:

- Audit evidence in relation to the existence of inventory is derived primarily from the auditor's attendance at inventory counts.
- Evidence is also required on the valuation of inventory, which should be in accordance with IAS 2 – the lower of cost (including relevant labour and overhead) and net realisable value.

Answers to chapter activities

Activity 1

Continuous inventory counting is where each line of inventory is counted throughout the year, and each inventory item is physically counted at least once a year. The frequency will be determined according to the risk level of the inventory item. This method requires that records are maintained up to date; these will be amended as a result of physical inspection where any errors are identified.

Periodic inventory counting is where all inventory are counted once a year, usually at the financial year end.

Activity 2

The auditor's attendance at the inventory count is a key step in the audit process. Inventory is often a material statement of financial position item and the auditors will want to assess the effectiveness of the client's inventory count procedures. By doing this they will obtain confirmation as to whether controls are working effectively and they can then decide the extent of their reliance on such controls.

If the client's inventory count procedures are not being followed, the auditor should raise the matter with management immediately so that action can be taken on the occasion of the count to ensure that adequate audit evidence is obtained.

7 Test your knowledge

Workbook Activity 3

Engco Ltd is a company which undertakes industrial maintenance services under short-term fixed-price contracts. All direct costs (labour and materials) relating to each contract are recorded in the company's job costing system which is integrated with the purchases and payroll applications. The job costing records are used by the finance director to estimate the value of work in progress for the monthly management accounts and the year-end financial statements. For the work in progress valuation, a percentage is added to the direct costs to cover overheads. The finance director determines the percentage by taking the production overheads figure in the management accounts as a percentage of direct costs in the management accounts.

Set out, in a manner suitable for inclusion in the audit plan, the audit procedures to be undertaken in order to ensure that work in progress is fairly stated in the financial statements.

Workbook Activity 4

For the following statements, select whether they are true or false in respect of inventory:

1 Inventory must be valued at the higher of cost and net realisable value.

2 The auditors attendance at the inventory count is a test of control.

3 Inventory is generally an immaterial balance on the financial statements.

Audit verification work 3 – Non-current assets

8

Introduction

This chapter focuses on non-current assets within the audit, both tangible and intangible. We will consider the various verification procedures used.

SYLLABUS AREA

1.2 Describe the features of an accounting system.

2.5 Identify account balances to be verified and the associated risks.

2.8 Select or devise tests in accordance with the auditing principles and agree them with the audit supervisor.

2.10 Describe these verification techniques and their uses physical examination, reperformance, third party confirmation, vouching, documentary evidence and identification of unusual items.

3.3 Conduct tests, record test results and draw valid conclusions as specified in the audit plan.

3.4 Establish the existence, completeness, ownership, valuation and description of assets and liabilities and gather appropriate evidence to support these findings.

3.5 Identify all matters of an unusual nature and refer them promptly to the audit supervisor.

3.6 Identify and record material and significant errors, deficiencies or other variations from standard and report them to the audit supervisor.

CONTENTS

1 Non-current assets: an introduction

2 Verification procedures: tangible non-current assets

3 Verification procedures: intangible non-current assets

4 Verification procedures: non-current assets investments

1 Non-current assets: an introduction

This chapter examines the audit verification procedures relating to all non-current assets. As you will probably be aware from your financial reporting studies, this includes three main categories of assets:

- tangible non-current assets
- intangible non-current assets
- non-current asset investments.

These assets will often be a material item in a client's statement of financial position, particularly in the case of a manufacturing company and represent another area where auditor judgement will be required – notably in the area of depreciation.

Definition

Non-current assets are those assets which are held for continuing use in the business and are not intended for resale.

Non-current assets can be analysed as follows:

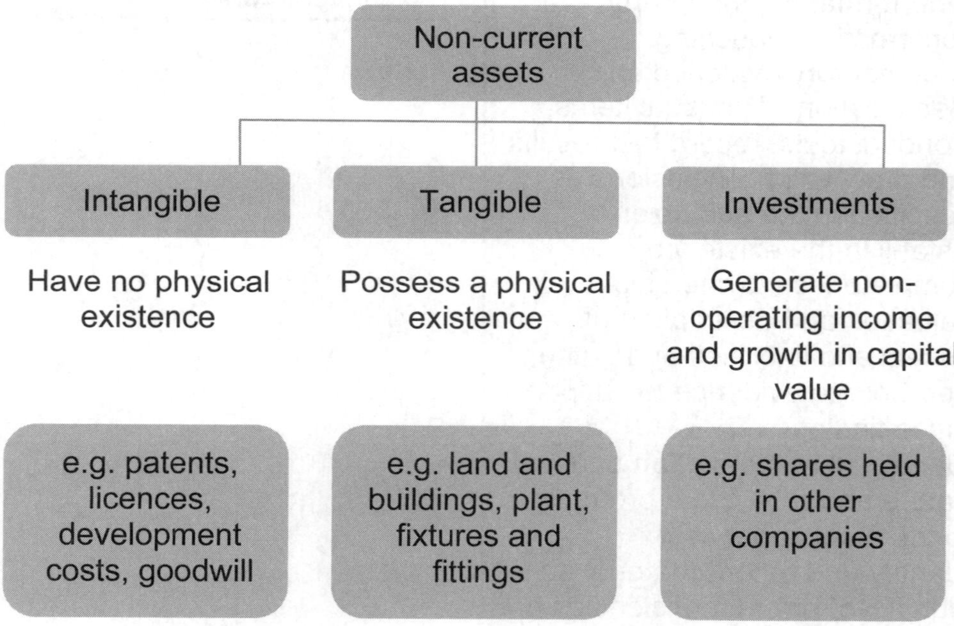

Any assets not intended for continuing use are treated as current assets regardless of when they will be realised.

1.1 Non current assets – major disclosure requirements

In order to satisfy UK legislation, a schedule of non-current assets is required in published financial statements. This provision applies to all three categories of non-current assets. An example is shown here relating to tangible non-current assets – similar schedules would also be published in respect of intangible non-current assets and non-current asset investments.

	Land and buildings	*Plant and machinery*	*Fixtures, fittings, tools and equipment*	*Payments on account and assets in course of construction*	*Total*
Cost or valuation	£	£	£	£	£
At beginning of year	X	X	X	X	X
Additions	X	X	X	X	X
Disposals	(X)	(X)	(X)	(X)	(X)
At end of year					
Accumulated depreciation					
At beginning of year	X	X	X	X	X
Disposals	(X)	(X)	(X)	(X)	(X)
Provisions for the year	X	X	X	X	X
At end of year	X	X	X	X	X
Net book amount: At end of year	X	X	X	X	X
At beginning of year	X	X	X	X	X

Statutory information requirements for tangible non-current assets.

The net book amount of land and buildings comprises:

	20X5	*20X4*
	£	£
Freehold	X	X
Long leaseholds	X	X
Short leaseholds	X	X
	X	X

Where tangible assets are included at a valuation the notes must disclose:

(a) the years in which the valuation took place, and for each year, the value of those assets

(b) for any valuation during the year the names of the valuers, or their qualifications, and the bases of valuation adopted.

It is also necessary to disclose:

(a) the accounting policies as regards the depreciation and to account for any permanent fall in the value of assets

(b) the net book value of plant and machinery and fixtures and fittings that are held under finance leases (see below). Leased assets should be split between short leases and long leases.

Short leases are leases that have less than 50 years to run at the year-end date. All other leases are long leases.

The above movement schedule, as it is often called, is useful as an introduction to the audit work on non-current assets. It highlights some of the key areas where the auditor will focus attention, for example, additions and disposals.

1.2 Cost or valuation

UK companies can choose to include tangible non-current assets in the statement of financial position at either cost or valuation. The most frequently encountered category of asset that is stated at valuation rather than cost is land and buildings.

The following points should be noted:

(a) The basis used i.e. cost or valuation, must be disclosed in the accounts.

(b) If the assets are revalued the surplus on revaluation should be credited direct to a revaluation reserve and disclosed in the Statement of changes in Equity.

(c) Revaluation of non-current assets in accounting practice is not compulsory unless there has been a permanent fall in value in which case the asset must be written down in the statement of financial position. Usually the debit is made in the statement of profit or loss account, but it can be taken to revaluation reserves in certain circumstances.

(d) Depreciation of revalued assets should be based on the revalued amount and current estimates of useful life.

(e) If the decision is made to revalue one asset or group of assets then all assets in that category must be revalued (e.g. all plant and machinery). These valuations must be kept reasonably up to date in subsequent periods.

The auditor should have special regard to ISA 620 Using the Work of an Auditor's Expert when considering the accuracy of asset values and the integrity/competence of the valuer.

1.3 Depreciation

Depreciation is a subjective area; it is important that the auditor considers the requirements of IAS 16 and CA 2006 in respect of the appropriate accounting principles and the disclosure requirements.

Important points which should be noted in respect of depreciation are as follows:

(a) Assessment of depreciation, and its allocation to accounting periods, involves the consideration of three factors:

  (i) cost (or valuation when an asset has been revalued in the financial statements)

  (ii) the nature of the asset and the length of its expected useful economic life to the business having due regard to the incidence of obsolescence

  (iii) estimated residual value of the asset at the end of its useful economic life in the business of the enterprise.

(b) If the asset's estimated useful life has been revised, the remaining NBV should be charged over the new estimated life.

(c) Profit/loss on disposal should be disclosed, if material.

(d) All assets with a finite economic life must be depreciated, even if market value exceeds NBV.

(e) Freehold land need not normally be depreciated – it has an infinite economic life.

(f) Buildings on freehold land should be depreciated – they have a finite life.

(g) The method by which depreciation is calculated for each category of assets should be disclosed in the accounts together with the effective useful lives assumed.

1.4 Leases and hire purchase contracts

Companies often choose to lease assets rather than purchase them. The type of the lease agreement affects its treatment in the accounts. The important principle is that financial statements should reflect the true 'substance' of the transaction rather than its legal form.

There are two types of lease i.e. finance lease or operating lease. An asset held under a finance lease is effectively considered to be 'owned' by the company leasing it as they usually hold the lease for the majority of its useful life and pay insurance and repair costs. Such assets are therefore required to be capitalised in the statement of financial position; whereas assets held under operating leases will not be capitalised and the lease cost is charged through the statement of profit or loss account.

1.5 Non-depreciation of non-current assets

You should note that some companies do not depreciate certain properties such as hotels and supermarkets on the grounds that the asset is constantly maintained to a high standard and that the residual value will always be higher than cost and that the property has an indefinite useful life (e.g. a well kept 500-year-old pub).

This argument, although not frequently encountered, can be acceptable providing that refurbishment costs are charged to the statement of profit or loss account in lieu of depreciation.

Also, under the provisions of IAS 40 Investment Property land and buildings which are held for rental and investment purposes, rather than held as operating assets of the enterprise, are not necessarily subject to depreciation. Companies have the option of showing investment properties at their revalued amount, with revaluation on an annual basis, or at cost less depreciation, calculated on the same basis as under IAS 16. All investment properties must be valued on the same basis, either revaluation or cost less depreciation.

1.6 Internal control over non-current assets

It is the responsibility of the directors to establish a system of internal control over non-current assets with the following objectives:

(i) non current assets are correctly recorded, adequately secured and properly maintained

(ii) acquisitions and disposals of non-current assets are properly authorised

(iii) acquisitions and disposals of non-current assets are for the most favourable price possible

(iv) non current assets are properly recorded, appropriately depreciated, and written down where necessary.

You should note that a key feature of control systems over non-current assets is the existence of a non-current asset register, containing full details of each individual asset under the control of the company.

2 Verification procedures: tangible non-current assets

2.1 Verification procedures

Remember that verification procedures are designed to support the financial statement assertions of:

(a) completeness

(b) ownership

(c) valuation

(d) existence

(e) classification.

There follows a summary of the principal verification techniques which will be used to generate evidence on these assertions. The techniques shown below are related to each major category of tangible non-current assets , but you should note that there are common themes, that apply to all of the categories. The assertions to which each procedure relates is also identified.

2.2 Freehold and leasehold land and buildings

(a) Examine a sample of title deeds, land registry certificates, conveyancing documentation from solicitors, and leases. Pay particular attention to any 'encumbrances' i.e. mortgages or other securities held over assets (ownership, rights and obligations and disclosure).

(b) Check a sample of entries in the non-current asset register and trace back to source documentation to ensure properly stated at cost (valuation).

(c) Review company policies for depreciation and ensure appropriate in the light of the useful life of the building (commonly over 50 years) and ensure that land is not depreciated (valuation and measurement).

(d) Check a sample of calculations of depreciation and ensure accurate and in line with company policy – note that freehold land should not normally be subject to depreciation (valuation and measurement).

(e) Review assets and establish the need for any write-down for permanent diminutions in value. Discuss with directors (valuation).

(f) If freehold or leasehold assets are let to third parties, inspect tenancy agreements, and perform analytical procedures on rental income. Note that this procedure is an example of a useful general auditing technique allowing the auditor to relate together statement of financial position and statement of profit or loss account items – if there is an asset on the statement of financial position, is there any related statement of profit or loss account impact of the assets? (completeness of income).

(g) Ensure freehold land and buildings are stated in accordance with Sch4 CA 2006 at cost or valuation less accumulated depreciation. If valuation performed in year of audit, give name or qualification of valuer and basis of valuation (disclosure).

(h) Ensure assets held under leases are appropriately disclosed as long-term or short-term (disclosure).

(i) Physically inspect a sample of assets (existence).

(j) Ensure non-current asset register reconciles to nominal ledger (valuation).

2.3 Plant, machinery, fixtures and fittings and motor vehicles

(a) Examine a sample of invoices, contracts, finance leases or other evidence of title to assets including vehicle registration documents (ownership).

(b) Review company policies for depreciation and ensure appropriate in the light of the useful life of the assets (valuation).

(c) Check a sample of calculations of depreciation and ensure accurate and in line with company policy (valuation and measurement).

(d) Review assets and establish the need for any write-down for permanent diminutions in value. Discuss with directors (valuation).

(e) Ensure that VAT is appropriately capitalised where it is not recoverable (valuation).

(f) Ensure assets are stated in accordance with legislation and that the NBV of assets held under finance leases is disclosed separately (disclosure).

(g) Physically inspect a sample of assets (existence).

2.4 Assets in the course of construction

Such assets are built by the company for itself and can include plant and machinery as well as buildings. The tests are as above except that there are no title deeds or documents of title to examine. Instead the auditor may perform the following tests on the company's own records.

(a) Ensure the company's system for allocating costs to the asset is appropriate. Some tests of control may be necessary here. Such costs include raw materials, goods taken from trading inventory, costs of labour and sometimes interest costs.

(b) Ensure that the costs that are included relate to the project by taking a sample of costs included and tracing back to costings and source documentation.

The danger is always that costs that should be expensed through the statement of profit or loss account and reducing profits, are in actual fact being capitalised in the statement of financial position, thus turning losses into assets!

The following is an example of a detailed audit programme for tangible non-current assets.

Example

Audit programme

HASTINGS & WARWICK | **Sch Ref**

AUDIT PROGRAMME

CLIENT ____________ **PREPARED BY** ____________ **DATE** ____________

____________ **REVIEWED BY** ____________ **DATE** ____________

AUDIT AREA – TANGIBLE NON-CURRENT ASSETS

The purpose of the auditing procedures set out in this section of the programme is to obtain reasonable assurance that tangible non-current assets are not materially misstated.	*Work performed by*	*Ref to supporting working paper*
RELIANCE ON INTERNAL CONTROL PROCEDURES		
1 Where we have placed reliance on the client's internal control procedures, test that the controls on which we are relying have been complied with, and record the details of such tests in the working papers.		

TESTS OF DETAIL

EXAMINING THE TRANSACTIONS DURING THE YEAR

2 Obtain or prepare working papers of non-current asset balances and a summary of the related general ledger transactions (including depreciation) and test that these have been properly prepared, as follows:

(a) Agree the totals with the general ledger accounts.

(b) Test the casts (additions) for overstatement.

(c) Agree the totals with the subsidiary records of non-current assets (e.g. non-current asset registers).

3 (a) Select the non-current assets to be examined, as follows:

(1) Select from the list of non-current assets at cost at the beginning of the financial year; and

(2) Select additions to non-current assets in the financial year by selecting from the debit entries in the non current asset control account in the general ledger. Test the casts of the debit entries in this account for overstatement.

(b) Test the additions selected in procedure (a) (2) above with the relevant supporting records and documents for:

(1) Approval by the board of directors or by other designated officials or committees.

(2) Other independent evidence of validity.

(3) Correctness of the allocations to the general ledger accounts.

(c) For the items selected in procedure (a) (2) above, examine the paid cheque for the correctness of the relevant details.

(d For each item selected under procedures (a) (1) and (2) above, perform the following procedures:

(1) Where the non current asset has not been disposed of, check that it is correctly included in the non current asset control account at the year-end date.

(2) Where the non current asset has been sold or otherwise disposed of during the financial year, check with the supporting evidence (such as correspondence, scrapping note, etc) and ensure that the profit or loss on disposal has been properly computed and has been correctly recorded in the general ledger accounts. Determine that the client has made a reasonable scrap recovery in the case of assets which have been scrapped.

CONFIRMING THE EXISTENCE AND OWNERSHIP OF NON CURRENT ASSETS

4 Confirm the existence and ownership of all non-current assets which have been examined under procedure

(a) In respect of freehold property, inspect the title deeds or obtain confirmation from independent third-party custodians.

(b) In respect of leasehold property, inspect the leases or obtain confirmation from independent third-party custodians.

(c) In respect of plant and equipment and other non-current assets, review the evidence of physical counts, or inspect the assets, or use other appropriate procedures. If the asset is permanently idle or obsolete, review the value of this asset in the accounts.

CONFIRMING THE BOOK VALUE OF NON CURRENT ASSETS

5 Test that depreciation has been correctly calculated by applying either procedure (a) or procedure (b) below:

(a) Prove the amount of depreciation in total.

(b) Test the amounts of depreciation on individual items selected in procedure 3 (a) above, by checking with the authorised depreciation rates and by checking the calculations in order to ensure that such items are not already fully depreciated. Also, test the casts of the depreciation records and the postings to the general ledger accounts.

6 Investigate and test the client's procedure which ensures that all amounts expended by the client on the acquisition of non-current assets are correctly recorded as non-current assets.

Note: *The purpose of this procedure is to ensure that the test for understatement of the accumulated provision for depreciation (in paragraph 5 above) is based on a population of non-current assets that is not materially understated.*

7 Ensure that depreciation:

(a) has been provided on a basis which is consistent with that of the previous year.

(b) is adequate but not excessive, by reviewing gains and losses on disposals or by other appropriate methods.

PROPERTY VALUATION

8 (a) Review the details of any valuation of assets made in the year, whether or not such valuations have been reflected in the accounts.

(b) Where there is reason to believe that the current market value of a property could be significantly different from the amount at which it is included in the accounts, and no valuation has been made in the current year, discuss with the manager the need to request the client to make such a valuation.

(c) Assess whether or not a true and fair view is shown by the statement of financial position if the current market value is materially below the book value and, if appropriate, consult the manager or partner.

REVIEWING AND TESTING CAPITAL COMMITMENTS

9 Obtain or prepare a working paper of capital commitments.

10 Test that they are correctly stated.

11 Consider possible additional commitments. Discuss these with responsible client officials and include in the working papers the date and outcome of the discussions and the names and status of the officials concerned.

3 Verification procedures: intangible non-current assets

3.1 Research and development expenditure

The accounting requirement on this area is the subject of IAS 38 Intangible Assets.

Research and development expenditure are distinguished by the following definitions:

(a) Research is original and planned investigation undertaken with the prospect of gaining new scientific or technical knowledge and understanding.

(b) Development is the application of research findings or other knowledge to a plan or design for the production of new or substantially improved materials, devices, products, processes, systems or services before the start of commercial production or use.

The cost of all research should be written off in the statement of profit or loss account as incurred.

In contrast development costs should be carried forward under certain circumstances:

(a) The project is technically feasible so that it will be available for use or sale.

(b) The company intends to complete the project and use or sell the results.

(c) The company is able to use or sell the results of the project.

(d) The company expects to generate probable future economic benefits (e.g. by demonstrating the existence of a market for the output of the project).

(e) The company has adequate technical, financial and other resources to complete the development and to use or sell the intangible asset.

(f) The company is able to measure reliably the expenditure attributable to the intangible asset during its development.

In theory, the company must capitalise expenditure on projects which meet these criteria, although it would be a simple matter to prepare pessimistic forecasts about the expected outcome of the project so that all costs had to be written off as incurred.

Once commercial production has commenced the development costs carried forward should be amortised over the period of production that has benefited from the development expenditure. This may be done on a time basis or using a 'unit of production' method.

Deferred development expenditure should be reviewed at the end of each accounting period and if the above six conditions can no longer be satisfied the expenditure should be written off immediately.

The main audit procedures that should be performed are to check that the conditions noted above have been complied with, but note that this is likely to be a high risk area of the audit because of the degree of technical knowledge required and the fact that the conditions from IAS 38 stated above require the use of forecasts and estimates.

3.2 Goodwill

In UK accounting practice, goodwill is defined as the excess of the value of a business as a whole over the value of its identifiable net assets.

IAS 38 does not deal with goodwill arising on acquisitions. Instead IFRS 3 *Business Combinations* requires that goodwill arising from the acquisition of a business or of another company should be carried as an asset in the statement of financial position, with no annual amortisation. The asset must, however, be reviewed for impairment every year. Essentially, this means that if the company decides that the goodwill is worth less to it than the book value then the book value has to be adjusted down to that reduced amount.

The auditors must satisfy themselves that the goodwill is calculated correctly and that the necessary impairment reviews have been conducted and adequate attention paid to any impairment.

3.3 Trademarks, patents and brand names

IAS 38 deals with most other intangible assets in a similar manner to research and development. Assets are deemed to have both a 'research' phase and a 'development' phase. Thus, a company that is paying consultants or using its own marketing staff to develop a new brand name might decide that the criteria listed above under development have been satisfied. This would permit the costs associated with that (which could be substantial) to be capitalised as intangible assets.

Cost is arrived at by accumulating the figures from the date that the project first satisfied the requirements listed under development. Thus, any costs incurred when the project was at a more tentative stage will have to be written off.

The subsequent treatment of those costs is very similar to that of development expenditure. Companies can opt for either a cost model or a valuation model. The first requires the cost to be amortised (written off) over the asset's expected useful life. The second requires the asset to be revalued regularly. This model is, however, only available if there is an active market in that asset. For example, the owner of a taxi licence might be able to observe similar licences being bought and sold in that city. That would permit the licence to be shown at fair value. A brand name such as Coca Cola will not have a similar open market value and so it would have to be valued at cost less amortisation.

4 Verification procedures: non-current assets investments

4.1 Classification of investments under the Companies Act 2006

An investment will be treated as a non-current asset in the financial statements if it is intended for use on a continuing basis in the company, otherwise it will be a current asset regardless of the date of its expected realisation. In practice, non-current assets tend to be those held for more than one year, current assets being those that are held for less.

Broadly a group undertaking is where a company owns more than 50% of the ordinary share capital of another company or can otherwise control the activities of the company.

A participating interest is where a company owns more than 20% of the ordinary share capital of another company.

Both of these categories require special accounting procedures for the preparation of additional financial statements – group accounts, otherwise known as consolidated accounts. You may well have come across these concepts in your financial accounting studies. These additional financial statements are outside the present syllabus but the individual company financial statements which show these investments are within the syllabus.

Non-current asset investments may be stated at historical cost, market value or other appropriate value as decided by the directors.

Current asset investments may be stated at historical cost or current cost.

Own shares refer to a situation where a company buys back some of its share capital and retains the shares either as non-current assets or current asset depending upon the expectation of reselling or cancelling them. The circumstances in which companies are permitted to do this are very limited and not likely to be encountered in this unit.

4.2 Statutory disclosure requirements

In general terms, the following items should be disclosed in relation to all investments:

(a) The accounting policy and valuation method relating to the investment.

(b) The difference between market value and book value of listed investments. If market value is lower there may be a need to consider adjusting for a permanent write-down in value.

(c) Details relating to investments consisting of shares in other companies including the proportion of shares held, the country of incorporation and the assets and results of those companies if they are not consolidated.

(d) Movements on investments during the year.

4.3 Internal control

Where a trading concern holds only a few investments, there is unlikely to be any systematic internal control system specifically for those investments. However, the auditor and the company should be aware that investments can result in the company suffering speculative losses – so authorisation procedures should be in place as a basic minimum control.

With a larger investment portfolio, there should be a system of internal control which will include:

(a) authorisation procedures for purchases and sales

(b) registers reconciled with control accounts

(c) control over dividend/interest receipts

(d) proper division of responsibility and supervision.

4.4 Verification procedures

Verification procedures should follow the general approach outlined for tangible non-current assets. However, the following specific points should be noted:

(a) **Existence and ownership**

Establishment of title and beneficial ownership of investments is not conclusively possible. However, evidence is available in the form of:

(i) share certificates, correspondence with nominees, etc

(ii) payments for securities, brokers 'bought notes' or 'contract notes'

(iii) dividends/interest from securities, dividend 'warrants'

(iv) internal control procedures.

(b) **Valuation**

Valuation of listed securities is easily confirmed with appropriate financial publications. Directors' valuation of unlisted securities is something on which the auditor's report, and the basis of the calculations must therefore be examined. The auditor must also consider whether any provisions for diminution in value are adequate, which may mean examining copies of accounts of companies in which investments are held.

An important point in respect of investment valuation is that they should be valued individually rather than on a portfolio basis – similar to the requirement in IAS 2 that inventory should be valued on an item by item basis. These requirements are essentially designed to avoid offsetting losses on some items with profits on other items.

(c) **Income**

Income from securities can be verified with known interest rates for fixed interest securities, and a share information service for listed shares. Unlisted share income must be verified with copies of the accounts. This is another example of the audit technique of relating together statement of financial position and statement of profit or loss account aspects of transactions.

5 Summary

This chapter has dealt with the principal audit verification techniques applicable to the three main categories of non-current assets – tangible, intangible and investments.

As with all verification work, the audit work can be structured around the financial statement assertions – existence, ownership, valuation, completeness and disclosure. You will have noted that there is lot of regulation of the accounting treatment of non-current assets by IFRSs and IASs – these requirements need to be fully reflected in the audit verification work.

6 Test your knowledge

Workbook Activity 1

During the audit of Ahoy! Ltd, a fishing supplies company, the auditor discovered that although the company maintained a non-current asset register, no checking procedures other than a reconciliation with the nominal ledger are undertaken.

Prepare extracts suitable for inclusion in a report to management of Ahoy! Ltd, which set out:

(i) the possible consequences; and

(ii) the recommendations that you would take in respect of this matter.

Workbook Activity 2

The objective of a substantive test will determine the population from which the sample for testing is selected.

For each of the following objectives, select the population from which the sample should be selected.

Obtain evidence of the existence of a non-current asset

(non current asset register/physical asset).

Obtain evidence of the valuation of a non-current asset

(non current asset register/purchase invoice).

Audit verification work 4 – Receivables, cash and bank

9

Introduction

In this chapter we will look at receivables and bank and cash. In particular, we will examine the use of receivables circularisations and bank letters as forms of evidence. We will end with looking at a relevant audit programme.

SYLLABUS AREA

1.2 Describe the features of an accounting system.

2.5 Identify account balances to be verified and the associated risks.

2.8 Select or devise tests in accordance with the auditing principles and agree them with the audit supervisor.

2.10 Describe these verification techniques and their uses physical examination, reperformance, third party confirmation, vouching, documentary evidence and identification of unusual items.

3.3 Conduct tests, record test results and draw valid conclusions as specified in the audit plan.

3.4 Establish the existence, completeness, ownership, valuation and description of assets and liabilities and gather appropriate evidence to support these findings.

3.5 Identify all matters of an unusual nature and refer them promptly to the audit supervisor.

3.6 Identify and record material and significant errors, deficiencies or other variations from standard and report them to the audit supervisor.

CONTENTS

1 The audit of receivable balances – general principles

2 Direct circularisation procedures

3 The audit of bank and cash balances

1 The audit of receivables balances – general principles

1.1 Introduction

This chapter deals with verification procedures for the remaining principal current assets of an enterprise – receivables and cash and bank balances.

The areas covered here represent useful examples of a number of standard audit verification principles, in particular the requirement for the auditor to collect reliable audit evidence. Written evidence is considered to carry a high degree of reliability – this type of evidence is central to verification work in these areas.

You should of course cover all aspects of the audit work on these important areas, but you might find it helpful in focusing your attention to bear in mind where the major audit problems might arise. In the case of receivables this is the subjective area of provisions for potential irrecoverable balances. In the case of cash and bank, the audit problem results from the fact that this is the asset most likely to be subject to misappropriation – strong control procedures should be in place backed up by rigorous audit testing. In the case of receivables, we are largely concerned that clients may want to overstate the figures and therefore the audit emphasis is usually on existence.

1.2 Internal control over receivables

The objectives of internal controls in this area are to ensure that:

(a) all goods despatched are invoiced

(b) invoicing is at correct price and discount

(c) goods are only despatched on credit to approved customers

(d) invoices are recorded and related to subsequent cash receipts

(e) receivables are controlled and outstanding receivables pursued

(f) credit notes are approved.

Note that there are very close links to the sales accounting system here.

In addition internal controls over receivables should ensure that the possibility of any falsification of the receivables' accounts is eliminated. Segregation of duties is an important part of the controls. So, for example, the cashier should not have access to the sales ledger, and the sales ledger clerk should not have access to cash received. Thus, the possibility of teeming and lading (i.e. stealing a receivables' payment and then concealing the fact by juggling subsequent receipts so that a sum received a few days later from another receivable is credited to the first account, then a later receipt goes to the second account and so on indefinitely) could only be brought about by collusion. Collusion is an inherent limitation of any system of internal control.

1.3 The audit of receivables – general approach

In order to verify the figure in the financial statements for receivables the auditor would perform a number of substantive procedures as outlined below.

Control account

The auditor should obtain a list of the receivables ' balances in the sales ledger from the client and agree the total with the control account. This acts as a check on the completeness and accuracy of the listing of receivables balances which will be extensively used in the following detailed audit verification work.

Year end receivables account balances

(i) Obtain an aged receivables listing and discuss any significantly overdue balances with management to identify action to be taken, and whether or not the receivables are likely to be paid (this will assist the auditor in verifying the reasonableness of the provision for irrecoverable receivables).

(ii) Check the authorisation for receivables written off as irrecoverable and review external correspondence relating to these receivables.

(iii) Carry out direct confirmation of receivables balances. This is known as circularisation and will be considered further in the next section.

(iv) Check that the balances are made up of specific invoices relating to recent transactions and enquiring into any balances which appear to be in dispute, or old.

(v) Check the purchase ledger balances for customers who are also suppliers and to whom the client owes money. Contra entries should be made to net off the two amounts to avoid overstating both assets and liabilities.

(vi) Review the individual accounts of major customers and those that appear unusual either by nature, composition or size of the balances or the transactions therein.

(vii) Review and test the year end cut-off procedures for sales, as dealt with in a previous chapter.

Analytical procedures

The auditor would typically perform the following analytical procedures in respect of receivables:

(i) A comparison of receivables days ratio $\frac{\text{receivables}}{\text{sales}} \times 365$ with budget and/or prior years. Separate computations may be appropriate to take into account different classes of business, varying credit terms and other factors.

(ii) A comparison of the proportion of the receivables in different age bands to prior years. This information should be available directly from the client.

A high or increasing incidence of old receivable balances may indicate either poor or deteriorating economic conditions or credit control. In such instances the work on irrecoverable receivables will become critical.

Irrecoverable receivables

This is one of the more subjective areas involved in the audit of receivables balances.

Audit procedures to establish appropriate provisions for potentially irrecoverable balances include consideration of:

(i) the company's previous experiences

(ii) evidence from the receivables ' circularisation

(iii) aged analysis of receivables

(iv) post year-end events (see below and later chapters).

In the light of this information the auditor will have to consider whether the provision made by management in the accounts is adequate.

Both specific and general provisions may be made. Specific provisions are made for those balances which are known to be doubtful. General provisions (usually a percentage of total receivables) are based on past experience.

Returns inwards and credit notes

There should be strict internal controls over returns inwards and credit notes issued, to prevent the fraudulent cancellation of a company receivable.

From an audit point of view the major problem is likely to be the issue of a substantial volume of credit notes after the year end to cancel false sales made before the year end. This is known as 'window dressing' – recording a sale and the resulting receivable in the current period and then issuing a credit note to reverse the transaction in the following period (it could be seen as another example of a cut-off problem). For this reason, both the system, and post-year-end events, should be carefully examined to detect any possible misstatement of annual profits resulting from this procedure.

Prepayments

These are often disclosed in the financial statements under the general heading of receivables and similar audit considerations apply. However, prepayments are typically immaterial in amount and in this connection may attract relatively little audit attention. On the other hand, this is an area where subjective accounting estimates will often be required. Analytical procedures – comparing one period with another and seeking an explanation for major differences – are often extensively used in this area.

Prepayments are commonly made for rent, gas, electricity and telephone standing charges and other items where the expenditure has been paid for in the current period, but relates to the next period.

Audit evidence may include:

(i) considering the client's own system (if any) for accounting for prepayments

(ii) obtaining a schedule of prepayments, ensuring that it is cast correctly and comparing it with prior year prepayments and performing other analytical procedures

(iii) test checking a sample of prepayments for correct calculation, referring to supporting documentation.

2 Direct circularisation procedures

2.1 Introduction

Circularisation is one of the most effective methods for confirming receivables balances. The auditor communicates directly with the customers of the client to seek direct confirmation of the amounts outstanding.

Replies to the circularisation will generally be considered to constitute reliable evidence – they arise outside the client under audit and they are in a written form.

The auditor must ask the client's permission before writing to the receivables , but, if the quality of the evidence is to be preserved, it is important that the process is under the auditor's control. So for example the replies should be sent direct to the auditors, not to the client to preserve their integrity as an item of audit evidence.

The circularisation of receivables satisfies a number of objectives:

(a) Reliable evidence is provided as to whether receivables are overstated – customers can usually be relied on to complain if the balance they are supposed to owe is too large. This in turn will help us gain some comfort over the existence of the balance.

(b) Evidence, albeit weaker, is provided as to whether receivables are understated – customers are less likely to complain if the balance is too small.

(c) Indirect evidence is generated of the accuracy of the sales figures.

(d) Evidence of the functioning of internal controls is generated – accurate receivables balances result from effective control procedures.

(e) Evidence is provided of the efficiency of the cut-off procedures if carried out at the year end.

(f) Evidence of the collectability of receivables is generated. If a customer maintains that the client's balance on their account is overstated, this may represent a receivable recorded by the client which requires to be written off or provided for.

It does not however give evidence as to recoverability. Our receivable may agree that he owes us a lot of money; this does not guarantee that he will pay us!

2.2 Timing and form of circularisation

Ideally the circularisation should be carried out at the year end, as this provides direct evidence of the statement of financial position figures. In practice, pressures to complete the audit by a deadline may mean that the circularisation is often carried out one or two months before the year end, and balances are then 'rolled forward' to the year end.

In the latter case movements on the control accounts should be reviewed in the period between the circularisation and the year end for reasonableness.

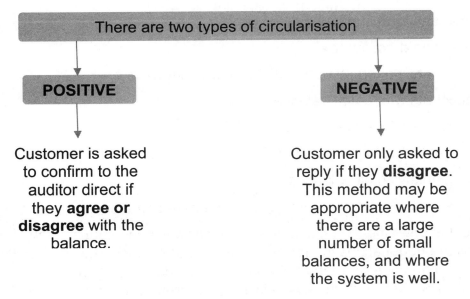

There are two types of circularisation

POSITIVE

Customer is asked to confirm to the auditor direct if they **agree or disagree** with the balance.

NEGATIVE

Customer only asked to reply if they **disagree**. This method may be appropriate where there are a large number of small balances, and where the system is well.

Positive circularisations are now generally used as these provide better quality evidence. A non- reply to a negative circularisation request will be taken by the auditor indicating agreement – but in fact the letter may never have been received by the customer or the customer may have taken a decision simply not to reply.

It is useful if the circularisation letter or form is accompanied by a copy of the customers' ledger account in the client's books; this makes it easier for the customer to reconcile differences between their records and the client's records.

Examples of letters used in the two types of methods are shown later in this chapter.

2.3 Control of circularisation

As stated earlier it is important that in all cases the circularisation must be controlled by the auditor if the reliability of the audit evidence generated is to be preserved and maximised. This control by the auditor should be reflected at all the key stages in the circularisation process, as indicated below:

Selection

Customers to be circularised should be selected by the auditor from a sales ledger listing which agrees to the nominal ledger control accounts. The auditor is primarily concerned with the possible overstatement of receivables . When we come to look at payables, where we are primarily concerned with understatement, we will see that we will not necessarily select our sample from the year-end list of payables.

Particular attention should be given to:

(i) old unpaid accounts

(ii) accounts written off during the period under review

(iii) accounts with credit balances

(iv) accounts with large balances.

The following should not be overlooked:

(i) accounts with nil balances

(ii) accounts which have been paid by the date of the examination.

If a client is unwilling to circularise a particular balance because, say, there are delicate negotiations in progress, the auditor should establish that the reason is a genuine one (and not an attempt to 'cover up' a problem balance), and then perform alternative procedures such as those noted below.

Despatch of letters

The letters should be checked for accuracy by the auditor once they have been prepared and should be kept under the control of the auditor until they are posted. In checking the letter, particular attention should be paid to the client's address and to the account balance circularised. The letter is sent from the client on their letter headed paper.

The auditor's working papers should contain a control schedule recording all relevant details of the circularisation.

Response

Responses should be sent directly to the auditor. The auditor should check the replies against his schedule. A reminder should be sent if no replies are received.

2.4 Replies and non-replies

The audit work on the response to the circularisation will typically involve the following:

<table>
<tr><th>REPLIES</th><th>NON REPLIES</th></tr>
<tr><td>

Agreed replies

- If the reply agrees with the balance circularised, the auditor should check that the letter has been signed and dated by a responsible official of the company and that the reply gives no cause for suspicion on the part of the auditor.
- If the auditor is happy the reply is filed.

Disagreed but reconciled

- If the reply indicates that the customer disagrees with the balance circularised, the auditor (or the client on behalf of the auditor) should attempt to reconcile the two balances.
- Reconciling items may be timing differences e.g. as goods or cash in transit or credit notes not yet recorded. These must be checked carefully. For example, the timing of the despatch of goods in transit must be agreed to delivery records to prove that the customer owed that amount at the confirmation date.

Once the auditor is happy with the reconciling items, these can be filed and treated as agreed replies.

</td><td>

- Send a second letter
- Fax/email customer
- Telephone customer
- Check after circularisation date
- Cash received
- Check receivable is genuine, look for evidence of:
  – Signed order
  – Signed GRN.

Consider overall existence of receivable if insufficient evidence – discuss with client possible provision/ adjustment.

Could also perform alternative procedures such as after-date cash testing.

</td></tr>
</table>

Disagreed – not reconciled • Disagreement of balances may result from more serious problems, indicating errors in the client's receivables balances or possibly weaknesses in the accounting and control systems e.g. sales invoices posted twice, cash received not recorded or disputes relating to prices charged or the availability of settlement discounts. These replies should be reviewed carefully by the auditor and discussed with client management.	

2.5 Evaluation of the results of the circularisation

After the completion of the circularisation it will form a key part of the evidence in relation to the receivables figure.

The auditor will summarise the results of the circularisation in the current audit file and will need to evaluate the results in terms of:

(a) percentage response

(b) number of disagreements

(c) outcome of follow-up of disagreements

(d) the materiality of the amounts involved.

2.6 Examples of receivables circularisation letters

(a) **Positive method**

Example

Swallow Limited
Bird Estate
Highcity
Beds

30 April 20XX

Hugh Allen Limited
Brow Estate
Lowtown
Beds

Dear Sirs

CONFIRMATION OF INDEBTEDNESS

1 In accordance with the request of our auditors, ABC & Co, we shall be obliged if you will confirm directly to them your indebtedness to us at 31 March 20XX which, according to our records, amounted to £1,457.67, as shown by the enclosed statement.

2 If you are in agreement with the balance shown, please sign this letter in the space provided below and return it intact DIRECTLY TO OUR AUDITORS in the enclosed reply paid envelope.

3 If you disagree with the balance, please notify our auditors, giving full details of the difference.

PLEASE NOTE THAT THIS IS NOT A REQUEST FOR PAYMENT.

We thank you for your co-operation in the above matter.

Yours faithfully

Swallow Limited

Reply to: ABC & Co
Certified Accountants
2 Low Close
Downtown
Beds

The balance shown above is correct/incorrect*

Signature Position:

Date:

Details of difference: (If relevant)

*Please delete as appropriate.

(b) **Negative method**

Example

Dear Sirs

CONFIRMATION OF INDEBTEDNESS

(Paragraph 1 per positive method)

(Paragraph 2 omitted)

If you disagree with the balance, please inform our AUDITORS DIRECTLY, giving full details of the difference by completing the form below . . . .

Yours faithfully etc

The balance shown above is incorrect.

Signature: Position:

Date:

Details of difference:

2.7 Example of a circularisation summary

The results of a receivables circularisation exercise are summarised as follows to facilitate evaluation.

Example

HASTINGS & WARWICK

Receivables circularisation summary

CLIENT	**PREPARED BY**	**DATE**
	REVIEWED BY (Audit senior in charge)	**DATE**
PERIOD	**REVIEWED BY** (Manager)	**DATE**

	No of accounts	% of total accounts	Value £	% of total value	Ref to supporting schedules
Population total		100.0	£	100.0	
Sample for confirmation					
Statistical selections					
Additional selections					
Total sample					
Results of confirmation			£		
Confirmed by:					
(a) Letter					
(b) Fax/email					
(c) Telephone					
Replies reconciled					
Non-replies agreed by alternative procedures					

Total balances agreed						
Balances in dispute						
Total sample		£				

Date initial circularisation letter despatched ____________

Percentage reply on initial circularisation ____________

Date of follow-up letter ____________

2.8 Audit programme: receivables and prepayments

The following is a detailed example of a typical audit programme for receivables and prepayments.

Example

Audit programme

HASTINGS & WARWICK

AUDIT PROGRAMME

Sch Ref

CLIENT ____________ **PREPARED BY** ____________ **DATE** ____________

REVIEWED BY ____________ **DATE** ____________
(Audit senior in charge)

PERIOD ____________ **REVIEWED BY** ____________ **DATE** ____________
(Manager)

AUDIT AREA – TANGIBLE NON CURRENT ASSETS

The purpose of the auditing procedures set out in this section of the programme is to obtain reasonable assurance that inventory is not materially misstated.	*Work performed by*	*Ref to supporting working paper*
RELIANCE ON INTERNAL CONTROL PROCEDURES		
1 Where we have placed reliance on the client's internal control procedures, test that the controls on which we are relying have been complied with, and record the details of such tests in the working papers.		

TESTS OF DETAIL

CONFIRMING THE EXISTENCE OF TRADE RECEIVABLES

Note: *Receivables may be confirmed at the year-end date or at an interim date. If an interim date is chosen the follow-up procedures set out in paragraph 9 of this AP must also be applied.*

2 Obtain a list of trade receivables at the confirmation date and test these receivables for overstatement by carrying out the audit procedures set out in paragraphs 3, 4 and 5 below. Wherever possible, use the list the client's analysis of receivables accounts.

3 Test the list as follows:

(a) Agree or reconcile the total of the list with the receivables control account in the general ledger.

(b) Test the casts of the list for overstatement.

(c) Test the individual items on the list for overstatement, by applying the procedures set out below:

(1) Select either debit balances from the list of receivables or invoices outstanding by use of sub-sampling techniques.

(2) In respect of the selected balances, send out positive confirmation requests.

(3) Where the receivable will not confirm the balance in writing, try (with the client's permission) to obtain confirmation by fax or telephone.

(4) Review each reply that we receive. In cases where the receivable disputes the balance, request the client to investigate the reasons for all differences. Establish the validity of the differences and prepare a schedule of the differences and their subsequent disposal.

Note: *It is important to investigate thoroughly any instances where the receivable disputes the amount paid by him or the date on which the client's records indicate payment was received. Factors such as these may indicate 'teeming and lading'*

4 Where we are unable to obtain confirmation of a receivable's balance, obtain evidence (by applying appropriate procedures) that the balance was a bona fide receivable of the client at the confirmation date. The appropriate alternative procedures consist of:

(a) Checking the opening balance of the account with the list of balances at the previous year end, testing the casts of the account during the year and agreeing the balance.

(b) Testing the outstanding items with independent evidence of validity – including customers' orders, despatch records and subsequent payments (where these can be substantiated by remittance advices or other independent means).

(c) Testing for the understatement of payments etc by discussing the outstanding items with a responsible official who is independent of the cash receiving function.

The purpose of the auditing procedures set out in this section of the programme is to obtain reasonable assurance that receivables *are not materially misstated.*

5 Where confirmation procedures are not applied, select individual balances from the list of receivables and carry out the procedures listed in paragraph 4 above.

6 Prepare a summary of the confirmation procedures applied under paragraphs 2 to 5 previously and of our conclusions.

TESTING THE VALUATION OF TRADE RECEIVABLES

7 Test trade receivables for collectability and for understatement of the provision as follows:

(a) Obtain reasonable assurance that the client's listing of overdue accounts has been correctly prepared by checking it with the sample selected in procedure 3 (c) (1). Check the casts of each column and agree the total with the receivable's control account.

(b) Select overdue items from the client's listing of overdue accounts and check and investigate the extent to which they are collectable by reviewing credit reports, correspondence and other independent evidence.

(c) Establish the reasonableness of formulae used to calculate general provisions. Review generally the client's irrecoverable receivable experience for the current and recent financial years and establish the reasons for significant differences. Check the calculations on which the provision is based.

8 Test the receivable balances written off against the provision during the year for overstatement by selecting balances written off and checking them with such independent evidence of validity as correspondence with solicitors, debt collection agencies, etc.

FOLLOWING UP AN INTERIM CONFIRMATION OF TRADE RECEIVABLES

9 Where the procedures in paragraphs 2 to 8 previously were applied to a date other than the year-end date, apply the following additional procedures:

(a) Test for overstatement of trade receivables at the year-end date by examining the transactions in the intervening period from the confirmation date to the year-end date, as set out below:

(1) Test the credit sales in the intervening period for overstatement as follows. Select debit entries from the receivables control account and compare these with the final sales records. Select individual transactions by sub-sampling these final records and the related intermediate and initial sales records. Check these transactions with independent evidence of validity, such as customer orders, delivery notes signed by the receivables, despatch records, etc.

(2) Test the sales returns and allowances in the intervening period for understatement, as follows. Examine the evidence of sales returns and allowances (such as goods returned records, correspondence with customers, and the relevant sales invoices). Trace major items in these records to the credit notes and (via the accounting records) to the credit of the receivables control account. In doing this ensure that these sales returns were recorded in the correct financial year.

(3) Test the receipts from receivables in the intervening period for understatement, as follows. Examine customers' remittance advices, and any other available independent evidence. Trace major items in these records (via the accounting records) to the credit of the receivables control account. In doing this, ensure that these receipts were recorded in the correct financial year.

(b) Review and summarise the movements on the receivables control account from the confirmation date to the year-end date and establish the reasons for all unusual fluctuations. Compare the individual balances which were selected for confirmation at the interim date with the corresponding balances at the year-end date, and investigate major differences.

TESTING THE CUT-OFF OF RECEIVABLES

10 Test for any overstatement of receivables as at the year-end date that has arisen from recording transactions in the wrong financial year. Do this by testing for overstatement of sales and for understatement of sales returns and receipts, in the following manner:

(a) Test for overstatement of credit sales in the period immediately preceding the year end, as follows. Compare major billings as recorded in the receivables control account (or other appropriate accounting record of billings) in the last few days of the year, with evidence of the date on which goods were despatched or services were rendered. In doing this, ensure that the billings are for sales made during the financial year under review. (The evidence of despatch should preferably comprise the customer's acknowledgement of delivery or service (such as signed delivery notes) or, failing that, the client's despatch records).

(b) Test for understatement of sales returns and allowances in the period immediately preceding the year end, as follows:

(1) Examine the evidence of sales returns and allowances (such as goods returned records, correspondence with customers, and the relevant sales invoices) for the last few days of the year and the first few weeks after the year end. Trace major items in these records to the relevant credit notes and (via the accounting records) to the credit of the receivables control account. In doing this, ensure that the sales returns and allowances have been recorded in the correct financial year or, alternatively, that adequate provision for sales returns and allowances has been made as at the year end.

(2) Compare major sales credit notes in the first few weeks after the year end with the relevant supporting evidence (such as goods returned records, correspondence with customers, and the relevant sales invoices). In doing this, ensure that these credit notes have been recorded in the correct financial year or, alternatively, that adequate provision for sales returns and allowances has been made as at the year end.

(c) Test for understatement of receipts from receivables in the last few weeks of the year, as follows. Examine customers' remittance advices, listings of remittances, and any other independent evidence. Trace major items in these records (via the accounting records) to the credit of the receivables control account. In doing this, ensure that these receipts were recorded in the correct financial year.

REVIEWING THE TRADE RECEIVABLES

11 Review generally the list of balances as at the year-end date. Compute trade receivables as a percentage of sales and as the number of days' sales outstanding. Compare these ratios with those of preceding years and obtain satisfactory explanations for any significant differences.

Determine that the balances have been correctly classified for statement of financial position purposes and in particular that:

(a) Material credit balances have not been deducted from receivables (except where there is a right to set-off).

(b) Inter-group balances have been classified correctly.

(c) Balances due from any person or company which is in any way 'connected' with the client arise from bona fide transactions on an 'arm's length' basis.

TESTING OF OTHER RECEIVABLES AND PREPAYMENTS 12 Obtain a list of other receivables as at the year-end date or, where appropriate, as at an interim date. Test this for overstatement, as follows: (a) Agree the list with the balances on the relevant accounts in the general ledger. (b) Test the casts of the list for overstatement. (c) Determine the nature and bona fides of all significant receivables , paying particular attention to amounts due from any person or company which is in any way connected with the client. 13 Obtain a list of prepayments as at the year-end date or, where appropriate, as at an interim date. Test this for overstatement, as follows: (a) Agree the list with the balances on the relevant accounts in the general ledger. (b) Test the casts of the list for overstatement. (c) Select prepayments from the list and test them for overstatement by comparing them with supporting independent documentation and with the corresponding amounts in prior years. **LOANS TO DIRECTORS OR EMPLOYEES** 14 Identify loans made to, or balances due by either directors, or employees, and consider the disclosure of such loans in the accounts.		

3 The audit of bank and cash balances

3.1 Introduction

Because of their liquidity, these assets represent the most vulnerable of all the company's assets. On the other hand, they are amongst the most easily verified, because they are objective in nature and they lend themselves to being confirmed directly by third parties or by physical counts.

3.2 Internal controls over bank and cash

Due to the vulnerability of liquid assets, internal controls are usually very tight in order to eliminate (or minimise) the possibility of fraud. The objectives of cash internal controls are as follows.

(a) All sums are received and subsequently accounted for.

(b) No payments are made which should not be made.

(c) All receipts and payments are promptly and accurately recorded.

3.3 Verification – bank accounts

There are two aspects to the verification work on a client's bank balances:

- Direct confirmation from the bank or other financial institution, of the account balance. This gives the auditor written external evidence from a very reliable source.
- Examination of the bank reconciliation.

Each of these is now dealt with in more detail.

3.4 Direct bank confirmation – bank confirmation letter

This is achieved via a **bank confirmation letter** (also known as a bank certificate).

Definition

A **bank certificate** is a standard request letter sent by the auditor to the bank requesting details of the client's financial arrangements managed by the bank.

The auditor should obtain a bank certificate as part of every audit. A standard request letter has been agreed with the clearing banks; this is shown below, together with the standard procedure followed by auditors.

Standard procedure

(a) The standard letter should be sent in duplicate on each occasion by the auditors on their own note paper to the manager of each bank branch with which it is known that the client holds an account or has dealt with since the end of the previous accounting period.

(b) Auditors should ensure that the bank receives the client's authority to permit disclosure. The clearing banks state that this authority must be evidenced by either:

  (i) the client's countersignature to the standard letter

  (ii) a specific authority contained in an accompanying letter, or

  (iii) a reference in the standard letter to a standing written authority given on a specified earlier date, which remains in force.

(c) Wherever possible, the letter should reach the branch manager at least two weeks in advance of the date of the client's financial year end. Special arrangements should be made with the bank if, because of time constraints, a reply is needed within a few days.

(d) In reviewing the bank's reply it is important for auditors to check that the bank has answered all questions in full.

3.5 Example of a Standard Letter

Example

STANDARD LETTER OF REQUEST FOR BANK REPORT FOR AUDIT PURPOSES

(i) The form of the letter should not be amended by the auditor.

(ii) Sufficient space should be left for the bank's replies.

The Manager,

.... (Bank)

.... (Branch)

Dear Sir,

.... (Name of customer)

STANDARD REQUEST FOR BANK REPORT FOR AUDIT PURPOSES FOR THE YEAR ENDED ....

In accordance with your above-named customer's instructions given

(1) hereon)
(2) in the attached authority) Delete as
(3) in the authority dated ....already held by you) appropriate

Please send to us, as auditors of your customer for the purposes of our business, without entering into any contractual relationship with us, the following information relating to their affairs at your branch as at the close of business on..........and in the case of items 2, 4 and 10 during the period since .... For each item, please state any factors which may limit the completeness of your reply; if there is nothing to report, state 'none'.

We enclose an additional copy of this letter, and it would be particularly helpful if your reply could be given on the copy letter in the space provided (supported by an additional schedule stamped and signed by the bank where space is insufficient). If you find it necessary to provide the information in another form, please return the copy letter with your reply.

It is understood that any replies are in strict confidence.

Information requested	Reply
Bank accounts	
(1) Please give full titles of all accounts whether in sterling or in any other currency together with the account numbers and balances thereon, including NIL balances:	
(a) where your customer's name is the sole name in the title	
(b) where your customer's name is joined with that of other parties	
(c) where the account is in a trade name.	
(2) Full titles and dates of closure of all accounts closed during the period.	
(3) The separate amounts accrued but not charged or credited at the above date, of:	
(a) provisional charges (including commitment fees), and	
(b) interest.	
(4) The amount of interest charged during the period if not specified separately in the bank statement.	
(5) Particulars (e.g. date, type of document and accounts covered) of any written acknowledgement of set-off, either by specific letter of set-off, or incorporated in some other document or security.	
(6) Details of:	
(a) overdrafts and loans repayable on demand, specifying dates of review and agreed facilities	
(b) other loans specifying dates of review and repayment.	

Customer's assets held as security

(7) Please give details of any such assets whether or not formally charged to the bank.

Customer's other assets held

(8) Please give full details of the customer's other assets held, including share certificates, documents of title, deed boxes and any other items listed in your Registers maintained for the purpose of recording assets held.

Contingent liabilities

(9) All contingent liabilities.

Other information

(10) A list of other banks, or branches of your bank, or associated companies where you are aware that a relationship has been established during the period.

Yours faithfully

Disclosure authorised

For and on behalf of

____
(Official stamp of bank)

(Name of customer)

____
(Authorised signatory)

____

____

____
(Signed in accordance with the mandate for the conduct of the customer's bank account)

____
(Position)

____
(Date)

The authority to release such information must be obtained from the enterprise, and this is generally done by asking the enterprise to communicate with the bank directly.

Important factors

The following matters are important:

- The standard form of the letter (reproduced above) should not be amended by the auditor.
- Where the style of letter is used for non-statutory engagements (e.g. the presentation of accounts of a sole trader) any reference to 'audit' should be deleted.
- The standard letter should be sent in duplicate by the auditor, on the note paper of his firm, to each bank branch where the client is known to have an account.
- The letter should reach the relevant branch at least two weeks in advance of the date of the client's year end.
- If it is necessary to request supplementary information from the bank, this request should be sent at the same time as the standard request.
- The authority to disclose may be granted by the client counter-signature on the letter or by a written request. Joint account holders must all give their consent when authorising a bank to disclose information to the auditor.
- In reviewing the bank's reply, the auditor must check that the letter has been answered in full.

Syllabus note

For the purposes of the External Audit Assessment you do not need to know the precise wording of the letter – be familiar with the information that the auditor is requesting!

3.6 Examination of the bank reconciliation

You should be very familiar with the bank reconciliation process from your basic accountancy studies. From the point of view of audit verification work, the auditor needs to check the reconciliation between the cash book figure, which will appear in the financial statements and the bank statement figure which has been the subject of direct confirmation by the bank.

This stage is of great importance to the auditor.

The reconciliation should establish that:

(i) differences between the bank and the client's records can be specifically identified

(ii) the differences are differences of timing which should clear in the post year-end period

(iii) no very old differences are outstanding

(iv) any differences other than timing differences (e.g. errors or omissions by the bank or the client) are advised to the bank or adjusted in the client's accounting records.

Audit procedures on the reconciliation

Reconciliations usually start with the balance per the cash book and reconcile this to the balance per the bank statement, although the reverse is also acceptable. A simple example might show:

Example

Bank reconciliation as at 31 July 20X4

	£
Balance per cash book	12,345.22
Add Unpresented cheques	223.46
Less Outstanding lodgements	(16.34)
Difference	1.34
Balance per bank statement	12,553.68

- **Reconciling items** are usually due to timing delays. Cheques will have been sent to suppliers on the last day of the period but the suppliers will not have had a chance to bank the cheques. These cheques are 'unpresented'.
- **'Outstanding lodgements'** are cheques received by the company and paid into the bank, but not yet credited by the bank i.e. there is usually a delay of two to three days for the cheques to be cleared.
- **All unpresented cheques** and outstanding lodgements should be checked to ensure that they do 'clear' shortly after the period end by reviewing bank statements just after the period end. Any old items should be considered carefully. If a cheque has not been presented to the bank after six months, it may be that the supplier has lost it or has gone out of business. In any case the cheque will be 'out of date' and the bank will not honour it even if it is presented. The auditor should consider the need for the creditor to be reinstated and a new cheque issued, or the need for the cheque to be written back as income.

Differences, even small differences must be investigated as they may represent large errors in both directions that net each other off. If there are known errors or omissions affecting the cash book, the normal procedure is to adjust the cash book for these items and then reconcile the adjusted cash book figure with the bank statement figure. For example:

Example

	£
Draft balance per cash book as at 31 July 20X4	12,153.32
Add sundry receipts per bank statement not in cash book	123.45
Less direct debits per bank statement not in cash book	(21.55)
Add error in addition of cash book	90.00
Adjusted balance per cash book as at 31 July 20X4	12,345.22

Again, all of the adjusting items need to be checked to their source. As these are cash book errors and the cash book forms part of the double entry system, there is likely to be a double entry effect of these adjustments which the auditor should establish has been correctly dealt with.

Reconciliations are normally performed on a monthly basis and should show evidence of review i.e. who reviewed it and on what date. The auditor should check that they are cast correctly.

3.7 Verification – cash balances

The amount of audit verification work that the auditor will carry out on cash balances will be very much dependent on their materiality. If, for example, the only cash balance held in a large company is a small petty cash float where controls are strong, the auditor may carry out no substantive work at all. However, in situations where cash balances are more material, standard audit procedures would include:

- attendance at a cash count at the year-end date
- if cash is held at more than one location, all cash at all locations should be counted simultaneously
- if the auditor counts the cash himself he should do so in the presence of two or more officers of the company and obtain a signed receipt when the cash is handed back to the client
- the auditor should agree the balance on hand with the figure in the accounting records and check the validity of any reconciling items.

3.8 Audit programme: cash and bank balances

The following is an example of a detailed cash and bank audit programme.

Example

Audit programme for cash and bank balances

HASTINGS & WARWICK

AUDIT PROGRAMME

Sch Ref	

CLIENT ____________ **PREPARED BY** ____________ **DATE** ____________

REVIEWED BY ____________ **DATE** ____________

(Audit senior in charge)

PERIOD ____________ **REVIEWED BY** ____________ **DATE** ____________

(Manager)

AUDIT AREA – BANK AND CASH BALANCES

The purpose of the auditing procedures set out in this section of the programme is to obtain reasonable assurance that inventory is not materially misstated.	*Work performed by*	*Ref to supporting working paper*
RELIANCE ON INTERNAL CONTROL PROCEDURES		
1 Where we have placed reliance on the client's internal control procedures, test that the controls on which we are relying have been complied with, and record the details of such tests in the working papers.		
TESTS OF DETAIL		
CONFIRMING BANK BALANCES		
2 Obtain or prepare a list of all bank accounts that were open at any time during the year. Send out requests for confirmation to the banks concerned at least two weeks before the confirmation date, usually the year end.		
3 Obtain, and retain, a copy of the client's bank reconciliations as at the confirmation date. Test the reconciliations as follows:		
(a) Check the casts of the reconciliations and agree the balances with the general ledger (or where appropriate with the cash books) and with bank statements.		

(b) Obtain bank statements for a sufficient period (usually ten working days) immediately subsequent to the confirmation date. (If there are any suspicious circumstances, obtain these statements direct from the bank). Carry out the following procedures:

(1) Test for understatement of outstanding cheques and other items which decrease the cash book balance as follows. Select from payments recorded by the bank in the subsequent period and comparing these with the payment records to ensure that they were recorded in the correct accounting period. Compare the cheques recorded prior to the confirmation date with the reconciliation.

(2) Check for overstatement of any unbanked receipts and other items which increase the balance at the bank. Do this by selecting from the list of unbanked receipts and comparing with paying-in slips and with bank statements. Investigate the reasons for any delay in banking receipts.

(3) Test for worthless cheques deposited to cover shortages by scrutinising the bank statements for dishonoured cheques in the first ten working days after the year end.

4 Agree bank certificates with the balances shown on the reconciliations as being due to or from the banks. Also check that all other information given on the certificates agrees with the client's records and is properly reflected in the accounts.

FOLLOWING UP AN INTERIM CONFIRMATION OF BANK BALANCES

5 Where the confirmation date differs from the year-end date:

(a) Review the client's reconciliations as at the year-end date. Obtain certificates from banks, agree the reconciliations with the ledger balances and the bank certificates, check any unusual reconciling items, and test the casts of the reconciliations. Check that all other information given on the certificates agrees with the client's records and is properly reflected in the accounts.

(b) Review the changes in the bank balances from the confirmation date to the year-end date and establish the reasons for all unusual fluctuations.

WINDOW DRESSING

6 Test for window dressing by reviewing material payments and receipts in the last month of the year and for a sufficient period immediately after the year-end date.

SETTING-OFF OF BALANCES

7 Ensure that:

(a) A legal right of set-off exists where bank balances have been set-off.

(b) The client has made all known material set-offs in the accounts.

CONFIRMING CASH BALANCES

8 Obtain or prepare a list of all petty cash funds, undeposited receipts, unclaimed wages and other items. Include, where appropriate, negotiable instruments, title deeds, share certificates, etc. Agree this list with the general ledger accounts or other appropriate records.

9 Where cash balances are material, count them (on the date chosen for the confirmation of bank balances) as follows:

(a) Count and list notes, coins and cheques, vouchers and any negotiable instruments. Control all funds and other items to ensure that there can be no substitution. Carry out the count in the presence of the custodian of the funds and do not, at any time, assume sole custody of these funds. Where there is a significant difference between the book records and the count, consult the client's officials immediately.

(b) In respect of cheques:

(1) Ensure that these have been entered correctly in the receipt records. If they have not yet been entered, obtain a copy of the client's paying-in slip which records them and, subsequently, check that they have been properly recorded.

(2) Check that these items are lodged in the bank promptly. Also check that there are no undeposited receipts on hand at the date of our count.

(3) Where cashed cheques are part of petty cash funds, ensure that these are controlled, that they are not post-dated and that they are banked promptly. Review with an appropriate official of the client any cheques which are for a relatively large amount or are signed by the custodian or are in any way suspicious.

(c) In respect of vouchers:

(1) Inspect these for approval, for authenticity and for date.

(2) Check that the vouchers have been recorded in the cash fund records. If they have not been recorded, prepare a list of the items in sufficient detail to enable this check to be carried out at a subsequent date.

(3) Examine the cash fund records to ensure that those vouchers that have been used to support a cash fund balance do not also support previous payments.

FOLLOWING UP AN INTERIM CONFIRMATION OF CASH BALANCES

10 Where the confirmation date differs from the year-end date:

(a) Review all movements from the confirmation date to the year-end date and establish the reasons for all unusual fluctuations.

(b) Prepare a working paper which reconciles the balances at the confirmation date with those at the year-end date and which shows the totals of payments and receipts. Agree the receipts with the main cash book and the payments with the monthly ledger posting.

4 Summary

Receivables may be a major asset of the company and therefore may require significant audit attention.

The principal audit verification procedure involves the circularisation of a sample of receivables which generates high quality, written, external evidence for the auditor. The auditor must control the circularisation and carefully analyse the replies received.

Bank balances are readily verifiable with a third party through the use of bank confirmation letters. These should be in a standard format and used by the auditor in accordance with a standard procedure agreed with the banking industry. The bank letter can also be used to ask other questions such as about bank guarantees. The other major aspect of the auditor's work on bank balances is a careful examination of the bank reconciliation statement.

The amount of audit work on cash balances will depend on the materiality of the amounts involved – it will revolve primarily around the auditor attendance at cash counts.

5 Test your knowledge

Workbook Activity 1

During the external audit of Perch Plc, the audit junior was requested to add up 10 pages of the cash book from throughout the year. 9 pages added up correctly but one page had a transposition error leading it to be undercast by £69.

The turnover of Perch was £3.5m for the year and the profit was £469,000.

In respect of this matter, select whether the audit junior should take no further action or refer to the supervisor.

Workbook Activity 2

During the external audit of Peppa Ltd, the audit junior sent out receivables confirmations. Several of the balances do not agree due to cash in transit and goods in transit. The audit junior is unsure how to deal with these items.

For each of the following, select whether they should be added on or deducted from the balance on Peppa Ltd's receivables ledger:

(a) Cash in transit should be ....?

(b) Goods in transit should be ....?

Audit verification work 5 – Liabilities, shareholders' funds and statutory books

10

Introduction

This chapter introduces liabilities and how we may go about verifying these. We will look at an audit programme for payables, accruals and provisions and then we will consider auditing share capital.

SYLLABUS AREA

1.2 Describe the features of an accounting system.

2.5 Identify account balances to be verified and the associated risks.

2.8 Select or devise tests in accordance with the auditing principles and agree them with the audit supervisor.

2.10 Describe these verification techniques and their uses physical examination, reperformance, third party confirmation, vouching, documentary evidence and identification of unusual items.

3.1 Identify account balances to be verified and the associated risks.

3.3 Conduct tests, record test results and draw valid conclusions as specified in the audit plan.

3.4 Establish the existence, completeness, ownership, valuation and description of assets and liabilities and gather appropriate evidence to support these findings.

3.5 Identify all matters of an unusual nature and refer them promptly to the audit supervisor.

3.6 Identify and record material and significant errors, deficiencies or other variations from standard and report them to the audit supervisor.

CONTENTS

1 An introduction to liabilities: the audit approach

2 Provisions and contingencies

3 The audit approach to share capital

4 Auditing reserves

1 An introduction to liabilities: the audit approach

1.1 Introduction

The usual testing procedures can be used to cover the financial statement assertions. However, there is likely to be a change in the emphasis of the audit work when dealing with liabilities as compared with assets. In the case of assets, the view is that clients are more likely to overstate the figures than to understate – hence audit emphasis is usually on existence. The auditor will want to ensure that all the assets which the company assert that they have, do actually exist. By contrast any deliberate misstatement of liabilities is likely to understate the figures (this will present a better picture of financial performance). So, much of the audit evidence relating to liabilities focuses on completeness – the auditor will want to ensure that all liabilities, which exist, are recorded in the financial statements.

For this reason many auditors find reaching a conclusion on liabilities more difficult than reaching a conclusion on assets balances. In the case of assets, you are starting from a figure given by the client and setting out to verify that the assets representing that figure exist. In the case of liabilities the auditor is looking for items that are not listed – the auditor is searching for unrecorded liabilities.

In addition to dealing with all significant categories of liabilities, this chapter also covers (more briefly) shareholders' funds and a company's statutory books and records.

1.2 Classification

Liabilities can be classified as follows:

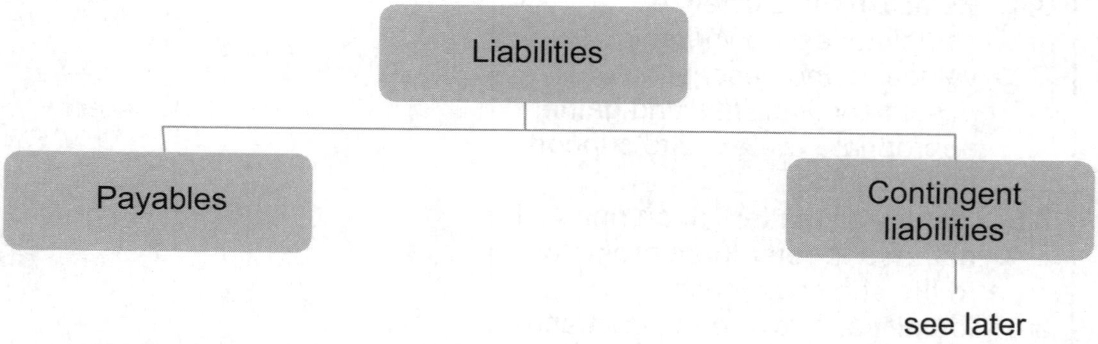

- Trade payables.
- Accruals and deferred income.
- Debenture loans.

- Bank loans and overdrafts.
- Payments received on account.
- Amounts owed to group undertakings.
- Other payables including taxation and social security.

Amounts falling due within one year **(current)** must be shown separately in the financial statements from amounts falling due after more than one year **(long-term)** for each item.

1.3 Current liabilities

Of the types of payable in the above listing, the item requiring most work under the general heading of current liabilities will be trade payables. Many companies will have a large number of trade payable accounts – the audit approach to this will therefore usually involve sampling.

The other items are likely to be checked in detail, where material. Some of the items are not included in your assessment as they require accounting knowledge which has not been covered. The items that are relevant are covered below.

1.4 Internal controls over trade payables

Internal controls over trade payables are designed to ensure that:

(a) purchased goods/services are ordered under proper authorities and procedures

(b) purchased goods/services are only ordered as necessary for the proper conduct of the business operations and are ordered from suitable suppliers

(c) goods/services received are effectively inspected for quality, quantity and conditions

(d) invoices and related documentation are properly checked and approved as being valid before being entered as trade payables

(e) all valid transactions relating to trade payables (suppliers' invoices, credit notes and adjustments), and only those transactions, should be accurately recorded in the accounting records.

1.5 Trade payables – substantive procedures

Always bear in mind that the audit emphasis here will be on completeness – have all liabilities that exist been fully recorded in the financial statements? The main verification procedures are as follows.

(a) Obtain a schedule of the trade payables with appropriate age analysis and check this with the control account and the payables' ledger.

(b) Debit and credit balances should be separated, debit balances being included in receivables.

(c) Review the individual accounts with the largest throughput of transactions during the period (not necessarily the largest balances at the year-end).

(d) Review the year-end cut-off procedures for purchases.

The following should be considered during the tests of individual balances:

(i) Is the balance made up of specific items outstanding for a reasonable period?

(ii) Does the amount agree or can it be reconciled with payables' statements? This is an important step – the auditor is using written, external evidence as a source for verification. It is also a means whereby the auditor may detect possible unrecorded amounts.

(iii) Consider the need to perform a payables circularisation. Because external evidence exists in the case of payables – in the form of supplier statements – auditors do not always undertake a payable circularisation. However, if controls are weak or suppliers statements are unavailable or considered to be unreliable, a circularisation of a sample of payable balances may be appropriate.

(iv) Review payments to payables just after the year end.

(e) Review the internal control over the purchases system which ensures that all goods received are properly recognised as liabilities of the company.

(f) Perform analytical procedures on payables, comparing age analysis with previous periods and payable days $\frac{\text{payables}}{\text{cost of sales}} \times 365$. This again may help the auditor to detect possible unrecorded liabilities – any major changes in the ratio over time should be investigated in the light of this possibility.

(g) A general review for unrecorded liabilities should be carried out. In addition to analytical procedures, the auditor's knowledge of the business can be very helpful here. For example, if the auditor knows that X plc is a major supplier of inventory items to the client, but the amount shown as owing to X plc is zero at the year-end date, this would warrant some investigation by the auditor.

Activity 1

Trade payables usually form the major component of a company's liabilities, and as such will therefore require a substantial amount of audit work.

Tasks

(a) Explain why a company should ensure that there is a satisfactory system of internal control over payables.

(b) State what the auditor should consider when testing individual balances.

For a suggested answer, see the 'Answers' section at the end of the chapter.

1.6 Bank overdrafts

Bank overdrafts are shown under liabilities even though there may be balances on other accounts which are shown as assets the only exception being if there is a legal right of set-off.

Verification of bank overdrafts is in other respects identical to the verification of bank balances as dealt with in the previous chapter.

1.7 Accruals

Accruals, like prepayments are commonly made for rent, gas, electricity, telephone and other items where the expenditure has been incurred in the current period but where no invoice has yet been paid. Accruals are often immaterial and reliance is often placed on analytical procedures. Nevertheless, as year-end adjustments, there are rarely any controls over accruals and any errors are likely to be those of understatement.

Audit procedures, similar to those applied to prepayments, will include:

(i) Considering the client's own system (if any) for identifying and recording accruals.

(ii) Obtaining a schedule of accruals, ensuring that it is cast correctly. It should be compared with prior year accruals subject to other analytical procedures. Again, the auditor should use his knowledge of the business to identify possible unrecorded accrued liabilities. Areas that companies often miss in establishing year end accruals include employee and directors bonuses, sales staff commission and employee holiday pay.

(iii) Checking a sample of accruals for correct calculation, referring to supporting invoices received in the next period.

(iv) Include confirmation of the completeness of accruals in the management representation letter.

(v) Reviewing invoices received post year-end and ensuring costs are accrued if they relate to the previous period.

1.8 Long-term bank loans

The audit procedures are the same as for a similar item under current liabilities. It should also be appreciated that if all or part of the loan has a due date of payment within one year of the year-end date, then that loan (or the part payable within one year) must be disclosed under current liabilities.

Particular points to note in respect of these items include:

- Circularisation might be advisable if amounts are particularly material or controls are considered to be weak.
- Evidence relating to bank loans can be obtained from the standard bank confirmation letter already dealt with.
- In addition to verifying the amount outstanding on the loan itself, the auditor should consider the adequacy of any accrual for unpaid interest.
- The auditor can recalculate the interest paid on the loan based on the loan agreements and check this to the actual amounts.

Definition

A debenture loan is a written acknowledgement by a company, usually under seal, of a loan made to it, containing provisions as to payment of interest and repayment of capital.

1.9 Debenture loans

(a) **Issue**

The auditor should refer to the client's memorandum and articles to ascertain the borrowing powers of the company, since, although a trading company has implied power to borrow up to any amount, it is possible that such power may be restricted by the memorandum or articles. Legal difficulties may arise if the company exceeds its borrowing powers.

When a new issue of debentures takes place in the year it is necessary to disclose the class of debentures issued, the amount issued for each class and the consideration received. The auditor should ensure that the cash proceeds are received and properly recorded by the company. Any discounts or costs of the issue should be properly recorded – but this can now be a complex issue under financial reporting practice and is beyond the scope of this unit.

(b) **Redemption**

Debentures may be redeemable according to the terms of the issue, at specified dates, by annual or other drawings (a process for selecting which debentures are to be redeemed that year), or at the option of the company, after due notice has been given of intention to repay. The auditor should examine the provisions of the debenture deed or the debenture bonds relating to the redemption, and ascertain that they are duly complied with.

The auditor's principal duties with regard to the redemption are to:

(i) examine the debenture deed as to the terms of the redemption, and note that these have been complied with

(ii) check the payment of cash to the debenture holders

(iii) inspect the cancelled bonds.

Definition

There may be uncertainty as to the amounts or timing of a future payment. **IAS 37 *Provisions, Contingent Liabilities and Contingent Assets*** lays down the treatment for such balances.

2 Provisions and contingencies

A provision is a liability of uncertain timing or amount. In other words, it is a liability which can be estimated with reasonable accuracy as to the amount and timing of the payment. For example, the company might have sold goods and given customers a warranty against break downs. The company knows that it is very likely to have to make some payments under the terms of the warranty and can use prior experience to arrive at a reasonable estimate of the amounts that must be paid, but the precise amounts cannot be predicted with any certainty.

Provisions must be recognised in the statement of financial position, but described as provisions rather than as other liabilities to alert readers to the fact that the sum stated is an estimate.

A contingency may be defined as a condition which exists at the year-end date where the ultimate outcome (gain or loss) will only be confirmed by the occurrence or non-occurrence of one or more uncertain future events. For example, a pending court case against the company might result in it paying damages, but the case has yet to be heard.

Contingencies cannot be recognised in the statement of financial position because the uncertainty is too great to make it sensible to do so. Instead, they should be disclosed in the notes to the financial statements, unless the likelihood of payment is so remote that it would be misleading to make disclosure.

The distinction between a provision and a contingent liability is a matter of judgement. It really depends on the extent of the uncertainty. It is, therefore, very important to consider whether a contingent liability should actually be recorded into the accounts as a liability or merely disclosed as a note to the accounts. This is another example of an area where judgement is required. It is also likely to be the case than management will prefer the note disclosure approach, whereas the auditor may feel that recording is required if a true and fair view is to be presented.

Typical contingent liabilities include:

(a) Guarantees given by the client in respect of loans to third parties e.g. to guarantee a subsidiary company's overdraft. If the subsidiary fails to repay the overdraft the bank may enforce the guarantee against the client.

(b) Damages and costs in legal actions still undecided.

(c) Claims under guarantees, warranties arising out of past transactions.

The auditor's judgement in this area may often be helped by advice from experts, typically lawyers.

Contingent assets should not be provided for. If there is a reasonably high probability that the sum will be received then it should be disclosed by note.

2.1 Disclosure

The Companies Act 2006 requires that for any contingent liability not provided for in the financial statements disclosure should be made of:

(a) the amount or estimated amount of that liability

(b) its legal nature

(c) whether any valuable security has been provided by the company in connection with that liability and if so, what.

2.2 Sources of audit evidence

We have already stressed the point that the auditor needs to search for the possibility of unrecorded liabilities. This aspect of the audit work is particularly relevant to the area of contingencies, as the client may have failed to recognise the existence of these items in the draft financial statements.

There are a wide range of sources of information available to the auditor which can be used in a search for possible contingencies. The major sources are set out below:

(a) **Standard letter of request to the bank**

This is likely to provide the necessary evidence in respect of any guarantees. This letter is considered in an earlier chapter as the primary method of verifying bank balances.

(b) **Pending legal matters**

Pending lawsuits and other actions against the company often present problems to the auditors. They should take the following steps:

(i) Review the client's system of recording claims including the procedure for bringing them to the attention of management.

(ii) Discuss with the client's legal department or company secretary the procedures for instructing solicitors.

(iii) Examine board or management minutes for indications of possible claims.

(iv) Examine correspondence with solicitors, including bills rendered.

(v) Obtain a list of matters referred to solicitors with the company's estimates of possible liabilities.

(vi) Obtain a letter of representation from the relevant director that he is not aware of any other matters referred to solicitors.

The auditor may consider it useful to obtain the client's consent to send a letter requesting confirmation of specific matters to the client's solicitor. An example of such a letter is shown below:

Example

In connection with the presentation and audit of our accounts for the year ended ……. the directors have made estimates of the ultimate liabilities (including costs) which might be incurred, and which are regarded as material, in relation to the following matters on which you have been consulted. We should be obliged if you would confirm that in your opinion these estimates are reasonable.

Matter	Estimated liability including cost
Libel action against the company in connection with statements appearing in newspaper.	£25,000

Signed ……………………………………

Dated ……………………………………

Etc

(c) **Letter of representation**

The knowledge of contingent liabilities may very well be confined to management and is therefore a suitable matter for inclusion in such a letter. In addition it will remind the directors of their responsibility to disclose such matters to the auditor.

2.3 The audit of accounting estimates

ISA 540 *Auditing accounting estimates, including fair value accounting estimates, and related disclosures* requires that auditors obtain sufficient appropriate evidence of accounting estimates. Estimates include estimates of provisions for depreciation, deferred tax, write-downs to net realisable value, losses on long-term contracts, legal claims against the company, other contingent liabilities, and other areas in which a significant element of judgement is required.

Areas such as those described above are inherently more risky than non-judgmental items and control risk is usually higher as these are non-routine transactions. The auditor should pay special attention to such items and would perform the following steps:

(a) review and test the process used by management to develop the estimate

(b) use an independent estimate (generated by the auditor) to compare with management's estimate

(c) review subsequent events.

Where in the case of contingent liabilities, subsequent events 'crystallise' the liability, there will be no need to review management's processes or use independent estimates.

The auditor will normally test the calculations of the estimate, assess the assumptions made (e.g. the court is 90% likely to find in our favour), compare estimates with those made in previous periods and ensure that the estimate is in accordance with the auditor's knowledge of the business and the other audit evidence obtained.

2.4 Audit programme: payables, accruals and provisions

The following is a detailed example of an audit programme for trade payables, accruals and provisions.

Example

Audit programme

HASTINGS & WARWICK

AUDIT PROGRAMME

Sch Ref

CLIENT ____________ **PREPARED BY** ____________ **DATE** ____________

REVIEWED BY ____________ **DATE** ____________
(Audit senior in charge)

PERIOD ____________ **REVIEWED BY** ____________ **DATE** ____________
(Manager)

AUDIT AREA – PAYABLES AND ACCRUALS *The purpose of the auditing procedures set out in this section of the programme is to obtain reasonable assurance that inventory is not materially misstated.*	*Work performed by*	*Ref to supporting working paper*
RELIANCE ON INTERNAL CONTROL AND INTERNAL AUDIT PROCEDURES 1 Where we have placed reliance on the client's internal control or internal audit procedures: (a) List the internal control or internal audit procedures that we consider are essential to the system of internal control or internal audit. (b) State whether each procedure is, or is not, documented in writing. (c) Test that the controls have been complied with, and record the details of our tests in the working papers.		

TESTS OF DETAIL

TESTING TRADE PAYABLES FOR UNDERSTATEMENT

Confirmation date

2 Obtain a list of payables at the confirmation date and apply the following procedures:

(a) Agree or reconcile the total of the list with the general ledger account(s).

(b) Cast the list.

(c) Establish whether or not the list appears reasonable by reviewing it for payables which are obviously misstated, or which, clearly, have been omitted (e.g. by comparing the list with the balances at the beginning of the period and with the general ledger debit sample).

3 Test the subsidiary records of trade payables (normally the payables ledger or a listing of unpaid invoices) for understatement or omission of amounts due to suppliers at the confirmation date. Do this by selecting suppliers for confirmation as follows:

(a) Determine the length of the average trade payables cycle by dividing the larger of the trade payables balances at the most recent month end or at the preceding year end (or the estimated current year-end balance if it is expected to be significantly larger) by the average monthly payments to trade payables.

(b) Select suppliers' accounts for confirmation by selecting a sample for a period of two trade payables cycles (or three months if longer) prior to the examination date from either:

(1) the cash payment records, or

(2) the general ledger debits (i.e. in purchase and expense accounts).

4 For the period we used in 3 (b) above, do one of the following:

(a) If we have sampled from the cash payment records, determine the total payments made in the period to each supplier we have selected.

(b) If we have sampled from the ledger debits, determine the total purchases made in the period from each supplier we have selected.

Note: *The purpose of this step is to enable us to evaluate the results of the confirmation procedures.*

5 Request each supplier selected in 3 (b) above to confirm his balance in writing. If we receive no reply send second requests or apply other procedures (e.g. telex or telephone calls made under our control) that might be expected to produce a direct reply from the supplier.

6 (a) Reconcile each reply that we receive with the subsidiary records of trade payables and investigate any differences by examining supporting documents, direct contact with the supplier or other appropriate means.

(b) Where we are unable to obtain a direct reply from the supplier, either:

(1) Obtain a payables statement from the client, scrutinise it for evidence of alteration, and reconcile the balance at the examination date as in (a) above, or

(2) If a statement is not available, examine purchase invoices and documents supporting cash payments to that supplier for a period of one trade payables cycle following the confirmation date to determine the adequacy of the liability recorded at that date. Sample also the debit entries to the payables' account and establish their validity by examining paid cheques, credit notes or other relevant evidence. Agree the opening payables balance on the account with the list of payables at the previous year end and test the casts of the account.

Note: *For the purpose of 6 previously, our reconciliation with supporting documentation will include selecting purchase items on a judgement basis and tracing them to the goods received records and the inventory records.*

7 Consider whether the extent of the errors we discover necessitates our extending the confirmation procedures.

Following up an interim confirmation of payables

Note: *If trade* payables *have been confirmed at the year-end date omit procedures 8 to 10.*

8 Test debit entries to the trade payables recorded between the confirmation date and the year-end date as follows:

(a) Select items from the cash payments records and examine supporting documents (including each related cancelled cheque) to determine whether a liability recorded at the confirmation date has been satisfied.

(b) Trace the selected items to the credits in the subsidiary records of trade payables.

(c) Review the level of purchase returns and allowances. If they are material, select a sample of purchase returns and allowances from the debit entries to the payables control account and ensure that they are both valid and recorded in the correct accounting period by comparing them with supporting evidence (such as goods returned records, inspection records, correspondence with suppliers and the relevant credit note).

9 Review and summarise the movements on the payables control account from the confirmation date to the year-end date, and establish the reasons for any unusual movements.

10 Compare the individual balances which we selected for confirmation at the confirmation date with the corresponding balances at the year-end date, and investigate any major differences.

Year-end date

11 Select a sample of items from the cash payments records for one trade payables cycle, or (if shorter) the period between the year-end date and the approximate date of completion of fieldwork.

12 Where the completion of fieldwork occurs later than one trade payables cycle from the year-end date, select all further top stratum payments until the date of completion of fieldwork.

13 Test the items selected in 11 and 12 above with supporting documents and determine whether those payments that satisfied a liability at the year-end date satisfied a recorded liability at that same date.

14 Test for understatement of credit purchases in the period immediately preceding the year end by selecting items on a judgement basis from the purchase and expense records for the first few weeks after the year end, and ensuring that those purchases and expenses which relate to the period before the year-end were accrued as liabilities at the year end.

15 Enquire whether any old, disputed or questionable liabilities (either recorded or unrecorded) exist, and investigate as we deem appropriate.

16 Review the level of trade payables and its relationship to purchases. Compare with the previous year and investigate any significant changes in the composition of the trade payables between the opening balance and the balance at the year-end date. Record the results of the investigation in a working paper.

17 Evaluate the errors we discover during our work. If the revised monetary precision is unacceptable, apply any or all of the following procedures: (a) Extend the confirmation at the year-end date. (b) Extend the tests conducted in 8 to 14 above. (c) Request the client to re-check the recorded liabilities at the year-end date. (d) Request the client to record an acceptable adjustment based on the estimated population error in the evaluation for trade payables.		
18 Review unpaid suppliers' invoices and unmatched receiving reports shortly before the completion of fieldwork. Identify any items that represent unrecorded liabilities at the year-end date.		
TESTING ACCRUALS AND PROVISIONS		
19 Test for omission and other understatement of accrued liabilities and provisions. Do this by examining documentation and by checking calculations to ensure that adequate (but not excessive) provision has been made for the items listed in (a) to (j) below. Where there is no independent evidence available concerning the amount of an accrual, test the debits to the accrual accounts by comparing with internal evidence of validity and with paid cheques, etc. (a) Periodic payments (e.g. rent, utilities, insurance, etc). (b) Accrued salaries, wages and employer's social security contributions. (c) Accumulated holiday pay. (d) Accrued commissions and bonuses. (e) Payroll deductions (e.g. PAYE, NI, and pension scheme contributions). (f) Professional charges. (g) Directors' remuneration. (h) Royalties and similar charges. (i) Further expenditure for 'completed work' and for after-sales service (e.g. warranties). (j) VAT.		
20 In addition, test for omission of other accruals and provisions, by comparing with accruals and provisions in previous years, by comparing with expenses incurred during the year, by making enquiry, and by other appropriate methods. Ensure that the basis for recognising provisions conforms with IAS 37.		

3 The audit approach to share capital

3.1 Statutory requirements relating to share capital

Shares issued by a company must have a nominal or par value which is determined by the company itself. The share capital account of the company must be maintained at the nominal value of the shares. It is unlawful for a company to issue shares for a price below their nominal value (i.e. at a discount). If shares are issued at a premium (i.e. above their nominal value), the excess must be recorded in a share premium account. This is then treated as part of the capital of the company (so, for example, a dividend cannot be paid out of the share premium account).

The statement of financial position of a company shows share capital as the nominal value of the **called up** share capital. Any called up share capital not paid at the year-end date is shown as part of receivables.

> **Definition**
>
> The **called up** share capital is the amount of nominal value of the shares which the company has asked the shareholders to pay as at the year-end date.

In the notes to the accounts, the authorised and issued share capital must be disclosed by class of share e.g. preference or ordinary shares.

> **Definition**
>
> The **authorised** share capital is the total amount of shares which the company is allowed to issue under its Memorandum of Association.
>
> The **issued** share capital is the total amount of the authorised share capital which has actually been issued.

In addition, full details must be given of any changes in the share capital during the year (e.g. new share issues).

3.2 Audit of share capital

As any change in share capital is likely to be a material transaction (by reference to its nature, even if not material by reference to its size) which is subject to special legal requirements, all changes should be subject to examination by the auditor. Sampling would not be appropriate except for an issue of shares for cash involving a substantial number of shareholders.

Appropriate procedures would be as follows:

(a) check authorised capital limit to Memorandum and Articles

(b) check changes to issued capital in year and agree to board minutes

(c) trace all transactions involving cash to the cash book and bank statement

(d) ensure that appropriate returns have been made to the Registrar of companies

(e) ensure that all transactions are legal and that premiums in particular have been accounted for in accordance with legislation.

It is also important that the auditor performs tests in respect of any dividends paid/proposed; these tests should include checks that the dividends do not contravene the distribution provisions of the Companies Act 2006.

4 Auditing reserves

4.1 Introduction

Definition

A company's **reserves** represent the total net assets of a company in excess of its issued share capital (remember that total shareholder funds = share capital + reserves).

Possible categories of reserves include the following:

(a) Share Premium account, as referred to above

(b) Revaluation Reserve arising on a revaluation of non-current assets

(c) capital redemption reserve, a technical reserve which may arise if a company buys back from its shareholders or redeems part of its issued share capital

(d) reserves provided for by the articles of association e.g. a capital reserve.

(e) other reserves e.g. plant replacement reserve, designed to build up a pool of funds to finance the replacement of non-current assets at the end of their economic lives

(f) statement of profit or loss.

Syllabus note

Some of these are highly specialised and beyond the scope of the External Audit paper. Those reserves which you need to be aware of are dealt with in more detail below.

4.2 Disclosure

Under the Companies Act disclosure rules, reserves must be presented under the headings shown in the previous section. In addition, the Act requires that the movement for the period on each reserve should be disclosed in the financial statements. This movement will involve a detailed reconciliation of the differences between the opening and closing balances on each reserve.

4.3 Share premium

Definition

If a company issues shares for a consideration in excess of the nominal value of the shares, the excess is known as **share premium.**

Example

A company issues 10,000 shares at a price of £1.20 each; the nominal value of the shares is £1.00. The company would record the following amounts to the share capital and share premium accounts:

	£
Share capital (10,000 × £1.00)	10,000
Share premium (10,000 × £0.20)	2,000

The Companies Act imposes restrictions on the uses to which the balance on the share premium account should be put.

The auditor should confirm that share premium entries shown above are made correctly and that the provisions restricting the uses of the share premium account are complied with.

The principal permitted uses of the share premium account are as follows:

- providing for a fully paid issue of bonus shares
- writing off preliminary expenses (formation costs) of a new company
- writing off cost of share or debenture issues including discounts on issues
- writing off premiums on redemption of debentures and, in limited circumstances, premiums on redemption of shares.

4.4 Revaluation reserve

If a company makes use of the alternative accounting rules allowed by legislation (rather than using historical cost) then any profit or loss arising from the revaluation must be transferred to the revaluation reserve. This reserve must be shown separately on the statement of financial position.

The most common example of the use of the alternative accounting rules is showing tangible non-current assets in the statement of financial position at market value.

If a revalued asset suffers a permanent fall in value, the amount of this reduction can be charged to the revaluation reserve **up to a maximum of the extent of the revaluation of that asset.**

The audit of the revaluation reserve will involve:

(a) assessment of the reason for the revaluation, the basis of valuation and its reasonableness in the light of the auditor's judgement.

(b) evaluation of the qualifications and experience of the valuer, which must be disclosed in the year in which the valuation takes place (the year of the valuation is given in subsequent years)

(c) ensuring that adequate disclosures are made and that any difference between market value and the recorded value is disclosed.

4.5 Capital reserve

The term capital reserve is not a reserve required by statute or any accounting standards. Nevertheless, on occasions, a company's articles may require that certain profits of a capital nature (for example, profits on sale of property) be transferred to a capital reserve account.

The auditor must ensure, therefore, that the company has complied with the relevant rules contained in the articles.

4.6 Statement of profit or loss

This represents accumulated retained profits of the business. The balance at the year-end consists of the balance brought forward from the previous year plus the retained profit for the current year.

Activity 2

You are the audit senior for a client, Hasels Ltd and are about to commence the audit for the year end 31/1/X5. Hasels Ltd revalue their non-current assets annually. The land originally cost £10,000 on 31/1/X1 and has been subsequently revalued as follows:

31/1/X2	£20,000
31/1/X3	£30,000
31/1/X4	£35,000

The revaluation reserve was £50,000 as at 31/1/X4. This includes £25,000 relating to the land and £25,000 relating to other revalued non-current assets. You are aware that there has been a recent slump in the property market which is not expected to recover and are concerned that the asset is overstated.

Following discussions with management they inform you that the land has fallen in value to £8,000 and they will be transferring £27,000 from the revaluation reserve.

Tasks

(a) Explain whether this treatment is permissible.

(b) Outline the audit procedures that you would perform to verify the value of the reserve.

5 Summary

This chapter completes your work on substantive audit procedures. The main area to focus on is the audit of liabilities. Bear in mind that the auditor's main area of interest here is completeness – have all liabilities that exist been recorded. This can make the audit of liabilities a more challenging area than the audit of assets.

The audit of share capital and reserves is an important area in practice but typically not a major area in External Audit assessments. The work here mainly consists of checking that the various legal requirements and disclosures have been complied with.

Answers to chapter activities

Activity 1

(a) A company should ensure it has a proper system of internal control over its payables for the following reasons:

- to ensure all goods/services purchased are authorised
- to ensure goods/services purchased are only ordered for business purposes and from appropriate suppliers
- to ensure all goods/services received are inspected as to quality and quantity
- to ensure all invoices and supporting documentation are checked and approved to ensure their validity
- to ensure only valid transactions are accurately processed.

(b) When verifying individual payable balances, the auditor should consider the following factors:

- whether or not the balance comprises items outstanding within a reasonable timescale
- whether the outstanding items have been authorised for payment
- whether the amount can be reconciled to the payable's statements
- whether a payable's circularisation is required
- whether payments made to payables just after year end relate to specific outstanding items.

Activity 2

(a) Following a permanent fall in value of a revalued asset it is permissible to transfer an amount from the Revaluation Reserve but only to the extent of the revaluation. In respect of Hasels Ltd, the maximum amount that can be transferred is £25,000 (i.e. £35,000 – £10,000) even though the reserve is £50,000 as the remaining £25,000 relates to other assets. £2,000 of the total £27,000 will have to be recorded in the statement of profit or loss.

(b) The audit procedures that should be performed are as follows:

- identify the reason(s) for the revaluation(s), the basis of revaluation and whether or not these appear to be reasonable
- assess whether the valuer was suitably qualified and experienced and confirm that these details are disclosed in the year of valuation
- ensure that all appropriate disclosures have been made including any differences between the market value and the recorded value.

6 Test your knowledge

Workbook Activity 3

During the year ended 31 December 20X2, Nerja Ltd acquired a fleet of 10 new lorries for distribution, at a cost of £7m payable in 3 annual instalments on a finance agreement at 8%.

Set out in a manner suitable for inclusion in the audit plan:

(i) the audit risks relating to the loan

(ii) the procedures to be undertaken in order to ensure that the loan is properly classified and disclosed in the financial statements.

Completion stages of an audit

11

Introduction

In this chapter we are assuming that we are coming to the end of the audit assignment and we will consider the various steps we must take before we are ready to submit our audit opinion, including satisfying ourselves that the company can continue in business for the foreseeable future.

SYLLABUS AREA

1.4 Explain the concept of assurance and why an organisation needs to be audited.

4.1 Prepare and submit clear and concise draft reports with recommendations.

4.2 Use management feedback when reporting.

4.3 Agree preliminary conclusions and recommendations with the audit supervisor.

4.4 Follow confidentiality and security procedures at all times.

5.1 Explain the legal and ethical duties of auditors, including the content of reports and the definition of proper records.

5.2 Explain the liability of auditors under contract and negligence including liability to third parties.

5.3 Explain the relevant legislation and auditing standards.

CONTENTS

1 The completion stages

2 Review of audit working papers

3 Compliance with accounting standards and statute

4 Management representations to auditors

5 The going concern basis in financial statements

1 The completion stages

1.1 Introduction

The completion stages of any audit will primarily be concerned with a detailed review of both the audit working papers and the financial statements. Such procedures are aimed at providing the auditor with final assurance on the following matters.

- That the evidence which has been gathered and recorded is sufficient to support the opinion which is to be given in the auditors' report.
- That the financial statements comply with accounting standards, statute and any other regulations.
- That the accounting policies selected and disclosure given in the financial statements are such that they render the statements as a whole true and fair.
- That the financial statements are materially correct.

2 Review of audit working papers

The work performed by each member of the audit team must be reviewed by a more senior member to:

- ensure that the work has been adequately performed
- confirm that the results support the audit conclusions reached.

2.1 Audit functions at final review

The audit functions fulfilled by the final review are as follows:

- The figures in the draft accounts are consistent with the audit evidence.
- The impact of any unadjusted errors is assessed and the decision to press for further adjustments taken.
- All appropriate disclosure and other requirements are complied with in the accounts.

- There is sufficient, relevant and reliable audit evidence to support the audit opinion.
- Recommendations to be made to the client in the management letter are considered.
- To assist next year's audit, a schedule of relevant points forward is prepared and the permanent audit file is left up to date.

2.2 Audit senior

The audit senior's principal responsibilities may be to:

- review in detail the work of all juniors
- check that all current and permanent file working papers are complete
- prepare 'interim notes' linking interim and final visits (see below)
- update the results of the overall analytical procedures
- prepare a summary of unadjusted errors
- prepare or review the tax computations
- draft the representation letter (see later in this chapter)
- complete a disclosure checklist (see later in this chapter)
- review post year-end events
- prepare a list of points for partner (see below) draft the audit opinion (see Chapter 12)
- prepare the management letter (see Chapter 12)
- complete staff evaluations for audit juniors
- prepare a schedule of points forward to the next audit (see overleaf) and update permanent file.

2.3 Interim notes

If a separate interim audit visit is made, it is usual to complete all work on internal controls at this time. Any unfinished work must be documented by the senior with brief details of what needs to be done at the final visit. The interim notes should also summarise results to date and any implications for materiality and risk. For example, if controls are stronger than expected (i.e. control risk is lower) less detailed testing may be proposed.

2.4 Points for partner

This schedule should be restricted to material points and include brief explanations of the following:

- the results and financial position as shown by the draft accounts, and any changes from prior years, budget and expectations
- any audit problems including areas where major judgements have been exercised
- outstanding work which has proved impossible to complete
- variances from budget on the costs to date (and estimated costs to completion).

2.5 Points forward

The purpose of this schedule is to provide a link between this year's final visit and next year's planning. Points may include the following:

- recommendations to reduce audit work in specific areas
- recommendations to use alternative procedures to overcome difficulties encountered
- client's future plans for changes in the accounting systems and internal controls
- major changes in the business (e.g. new products, factory closures)
- changes in legislation and accounting standards
- proposals for improvements in timetabling and staffing arrangements.

2.6 Audit manager

The audit manager's principal responsibilities may be to:

- review the working papers in the context of the audit plan and later facts emerging
- ensure there is sufficient appropriate evidence to support the audit opinion
- at the end of the interim visit, review interim notes and take appropriate action
- consider results of analytical procedures and the sense of the accounts review unadjusted errors and make recommendations for further adjustment/audit opinion
- review tax computations
- review the management representation letter
- review draft accounts for compliance with requirements

- review and edit the points for partner and recommend action thereon review the management letter to ensure it is commercially realistic and professionally sound
- review time costs summary, variances from budget and staff evaluations
- review points forward and ensure permanent file updated, and
- before the audit opinion is to be signed, ensure all evidence documented and post year-end event review updated.

2.7 Audit partner

At the completion stage of the audit, the audit partner will usually:

- review audit files in sufficient detail to be assured that the audit has been done satisfactorily
- take decisions on the points for partner
- clear all material outstanding points (meet with client/consult with another partner)
- approve the final management letter for submission to the client
- approve the form and content of the accounts
- review and approve the representation letter
- agree wording of the auditors' report.

The partner should also:

- approve the final typed accounts
- sign and date the auditors' report.

3 Compliance with accounting standards and statute

3.1 Introduction

For the majority of audit assignments, the auditor will need to consider whether the financial statements comply with:

- International Financial Reporting Standards (IFRSs) and International Accounting Standards (IASs), and
- the Companies Act 2006.

These are both concerned with accounting policies and disclosure.

The Companies Act 2006 also prescribes formats for both statement of financial position and statement of profit or loss.

You should be familiar with the detailed requirements of the IFRSs, IASs, and CA 2006 in respect of the matters outlined above.

3.2 Accounting policies

For each audit area:

- establish the accounting policy
- consider whether the stated policy has been complied with
- consider whether the stated policy is appropriate and complies with any relevant IFRS or IAS or statutory provision.

3.3 Disclosure

The auditor will need to be satisfied that:

- all matters that should be disclosed have been disclosed, and
- the information which has been disclosed is correct.

The first objective is best achieved by the use of a detailed disclosure checklist.

The second objective can be achieved in most cases by referring back to audit work already performed. (For instance, the figure disclosed as 'depreciation charge' should have been audited as part of the non current asset work.)

However, certain items may need further validation, as follows.

3.4 Directors' loans and transactions

Directors have several areas of potential conflict of interest with the company. It is important that the members are made aware of any such conflict in order for the accounts to give a true and fair view and, in some cases, in order for the members to vote on the directors' proposed actions.

The areas of potential conflict include:

- remuneration, and
- loans, quasi-loans and credit transactions from the company to the directors or their connected persons (e.g. spouse).

Consequently there are a number of statutory regulations concerning the legality and the disclosure in the financial statements of such transactions.

3.5 Directors' remuneration

The Companies Act 2006 requires that the remuneration received by the directors and chairman must be accurately disclosed in the financial statements. This is a particularly sensitive area and the auditor will need to ensure that disclosure is correct – the concept of materiality is thus applied in a different manner to this area of the financial statements.

The figure which is included in the financial statements may be verified by referring to:

- Articles of Association
- Board minutes
- P11Ds
- Letters of confirmation of emoluments.

3.6 Directors' loans

S330(1) of the Companies Act 2006 states that no company may make, guarantee, or provide security for a loan to any of its directors or to any of the directors of its holding company.

Nor may a company assume or have assigned to it any transaction which would have contravened the above provision if it had actually been entered into by the company. (Otherwise, for example, A Ltd might avoid the provision by making a loan to the directors of B Ltd in return for B Ltd's lending money to A Ltd's directors).

If any company enters such a transaction with one of its directors, then:

- the details have to be disclosed in the financial statements (irrespective of the amount)
- it would be considered to be an illegal transaction if the amount of the loan exceeded £5,000.

3.7 Quasi-loans

Definition

Quasi-loans: Where a company pays or promises to pay a third party on behalf of a director (or connected person), and the director (or connected person) undertakes to repay the company in due course.

A quasi-loan is thus an indirect loan. Examples of quasi-loans are where a company settles a liability owed by a director or buys goods on his behalf.

If such transactions exceed £5,000 or are not repaid within two months, they will be illegal, but only if the company concerned is a relevant company (i.e. a plc, or part of a group containing a plc). (This applies to quasi-loans given to directors of a relevant company, or their connected persons.) Quasi-loans will never be illegal if given by a private company.

However, the details of such transactions must always be disclosed, irrespective of amount and also irrespective of the type of company concerned.

3.8 Credit transactions

Definition

Credit transactions: Where goods or services are supplied and payment is deferred or paid by instalments (e.g. leases, hire-purchase transactions or normal trade credit).

Credit transactions are illegal if:

- the company concerned is a relevant company,
- the transaction is with a director or a connected person, and
- they exceed £10,000*

The details of all credit transactions in excess of £5,000* must be disclosed in the financial statements, irrespective of the type of company concerned. (*Note the different monetary limits for legality and disclosure.)

3.9 Disclosure

When auditing a relevant company it can be seen from the above regulations that there are potentially far more transactions which the auditor must ensure are disclosed in the financial statements. The details to be disclosed for loans, quasi-loans and credit transactions are:

- the name of the director (or connected person)
- the amount of the 'loan' outstanding at the beginning and end of the year
- the maximum amount outstanding at any point in the year
- any provisions made by the company against non-payment of interest or capital.

3.10 Audit work

- Establish clients' procedures for ensuring all disclosable transactions are identified and recorded.
- Inspect board minutes and records of transactions with directors.
- Inspect agreements and contracts involving directors and check details to source documentation.
- Check whether transactions are on commercial terms. · Consider:
  - whether amounts due are recoverable – the legality of these transactions
  - the effect of post year-end events (e.g. receipt of after-date cash).
- Obtain a statement from the directors confirming the details of disclosable transactions.

4 Management representations to auditors

4.1 Introduction

During an audit many representations are made to the auditors, either unsolicited or in response to specific enquiries. They may consider certain of these representations to be critical to obtaining sufficient appropriate audit evidence on which to base their audit opinion. The auditors may also require representations on general matters, for example that the directors have made all accounting records available to the auditors.

The possibility of misunderstandings between auditors and management is reduced when oral representations are confirmed in writing. Written confirmation of representations may take the form of:

- a representation letter from management, or
- a letter from the auditors outlining their understanding of management's representations, duly acknowledged and confirmed in writing by management, or
- minutes of meetings of the board of directors, or similar body, at which such representations are approved.

Auditors must obtain written confirmation of appropriate representations from management before their report is issued.

4.2 Procedures

It is advisable for auditors to discuss such matters with those responsible for giving the written confirmation before they sign it to ensure that they understand what it is that they are being asked to confirm.

When representations to the auditors relate to matters which are material to the financial statements, they must:

- seek corroborative audit evidence
- evaluate whether the representations made by management appear reasonable and are consistent with other audit evidence obtained, including other representations, and
- consider whether the individuals making the representations can be expected to be well-informed on the particular matters.

Representations by management cannot be a substitute for other audit evidence that auditors expect to be available.

If auditors are unable to obtain sufficient appropriate audit evidence regarding a matter which has, or may have, a material effect on the financial statements and such audit evidence is expected to be available, this constitutes a limitation on the scope of the audit, even if a representation from management has been received on the matter. In these circumstances it may be necessary for them to consider the implications for their report (see Chapter 12).

4.3 When obtained

In certain instances, such as where knowledge of the facts is confined to management (e.g. when the facts are a matter of management intentions), or when the matter is principally one of judgment or opinion (e.g. on the trading position of a particular customer), management representations may be the only audit evidence available. In some exceptional cases, the matter may be of such significance that the auditors refer to the representations in their report as being relevant to a proper understanding of the basis of their opinion.

4.4 If contradicted

If a representation appears to be contradicted by other audit evidence, the auditors should investigate the circumstances to resolve the matter and consider whether it casts doubt on the reliability of other representations.

The investigation of apparently contradictory audit evidence regarding a representation received usually begins with further enquiries of management, to ascertain whether the representation has been misunderstood or whether the other audit evidence has been misinterpreted, followed by corroboration of management's responses. If management is unable to provide an explanation or if the explanation is not considered adequate, further audit procedures may be required to resolve the matter.

4.5 Basic elements of a management representation letter

Addressee

When requesting a management representation letter, auditors request that it be addressed to them, that it contain specified information and that it be appropriately dated and approved by those with specific knowledge of the relevant matters.

Board approval

Auditors usually request that the management representation letter be discussed and agreed by the board of directors or similar body, and signed on their behalf by the chairman and secretary, before they approve the financial statements, to ensure that the board as a whole is aware of the representations on which the auditors intend to rely in expressing their opinion on those financial statements. The auditors may also wish to consider whether to take the opportunity to remind the directors that, under section 389A of the Companies Act 2006, it is an offence to mislead the auditors.

Dating

A management representation letter is normally dated on the day the financial statements are approved. If there is any significant delay between the date of the management representation letter and the date of the auditors' report, the auditors may consider it necessary to obtain further representations regarding the intervening period.

4.6 Action if management refuses to provide written confirmation of representations

If management refuses to provide written confirmation of a representation that the auditors consider necessary, the auditors should consider the implications of this scope limitation for their report. In such circumstances, it may no longer be appropriate for the auditors to place reliance on other representations made by management during the course of the audit.

4.7 Illustration

Set out below is an example of a letter of representation based on the Appendix to the ISA 580 *Written representation*. It is not intended to be a standard letter because representations by management can be expected to vary not only from one enterprise to another, but also from one year to another in the case of the same audit client.

Example

(To Auditor) (Date)

This representation letter is provided in connection with your audit of the financial statements of ABC Company for the year ended December 31, 20X1 for the purpose of expressing an opinion as to whether the financial statements give a true and fair view of the financial position of ABC Company as of December 31, 20X1 and of the results of its operations and its cash flows for the year then ended in accordance with the Companies Act 2006.

We acknowledge our responsibility for the fair presentation of the financial statements in accordance with (indicate applicable financial reporting framework).

We confirm, to the best of our knowledge and belief, the following representations:

- There have been no irregularities involving management or employees who have a significant role in internal control or that could have a material effect on the financial statements.
- We have made available to you all books of account and supporting documentation and all minutes of meetings of shareholders and the Board of Directors.
- We confirm the completeness of the information provided regarding the identification of related parties.
- The financial statements are free of material misstatements, including omissions.
- The Company has complied with all aspects of contractual agreements that could have a material effect on the financial statements in the event of noncompliance. There has been no noncompliance with requirements of regulatory authorities that could have a material effect on the financial statements in the event of noncompliance.
- The following have been properly recorded and, when appropriate, adequately disclosed in the financial statements:
  - (a) the identity of, and balances and transactions with, related parties
  - (b) losses arising from sale and purchase commitments
  - (c) agreements and options to buy back assets previously sold
  - (d) assets pledged as collateral.

- We have no plans or intentions that may materially alter the carrying value or classification of assets and liabilities reflected in the financial statements.
- We have no plans to abandon lines of product or other plans or intentions that will result in any excess or obsolete inventory, and no inventory is stated at an amount in excess of net realisable value.
- The company has satisfactory title to all assets and there are no liens or encumbrances on the company's assets.
- We have recorded or disclosed, as appropriate, all liabilities, both actual and contingent, and have disclosed in Note X to the financial statements all guarantees that we have given to third parties.
- Other than . . . described in Note X to the financial statements, there have been no events subsequent to period end which require adjustment of or disclosure in the financial statements or Notes thereto.
- The ...claim by XYZ Company has been settled for the total sum of XXX which has been properly accrued in the financial statements. No other claims in connection with litigation have been or are expected to be received.
- There are no formal or informal compensating balance arrangements with any of our cash and investment accounts. Except as disclosed in Note X to the financial statements, we have no other line of credit arrangements

....

Senior Executive Officer Senior Financial Officer

5 The going concern basis in financial statements

5.1 Accounting requirements

IAS 1 *Presentation of Financial Statements* requires that an entity should prepare its financial statements on a going concern basis unless:

- it intends to liquidate, or
- the directors have no realistic alternative but to liquidate the entity or to cease trading.

In such circumstances the financial statements can be prepared on another basis, other than the going concern basis.

When preparing the financial statements the directors should assess whether there are any significant doubts about an entity's ability to continue as a going concern.

5.2 Impact on financial statements

If the going concern basis is inappropriate, this affects the manner in which assets and liabilities are shown in the financial statements:

- amounts recorded in respect of assets may not be recovered (through use/realisation)
- amounts and dates of maturities of liabilities may change
- further liabilities may need to be recognised, e.g. redundancy costs/contract severance charges.

If there are any material uncertainties that may cast significant doubt upon the ability to continue as a going concern, the financial statements should include note disclosures about the matters giving rise to the concern.

5.3 Impact on audit

When forming an opinion as to whether financial statements give a true and fair view, auditors should consider a company's ability to continue as a going concern and any relevant disclosures.

5.4 Audit evidence

Auditors should assess the adequacy of the means by which the directors have satisfied themselves that the going concern basis is appropriate (with any necessary disclosures). For this purpose the auditor should:

- make enquiries of directors and examine appropriate available information
- plan and perform procedures to identify material matters which could indicate concern about the entity's ability to continue as a going concern.

5.5 Sources of information

When the auditor is assessing the adequacy of the going concern basis, there are a number of sources of information they would look to:

- Client's system for timely identification of warnings of risks and uncertainties.
- Budgets, forecast information, etc.
- Obligations, undertakings, guarantees with lenders, suppliers, group companies for giving or receiving support. The auditor might want to check that these guarantees are still relevant.
- Bank borrowing facilities and suppliers' credit, e.g. the company might be losing their borrowing facility.

5.6 Matters to consider

There are a number of issues an auditor would be on the lookout for when assessing the going concern assumption and these are as follows:

- Liabilities exceed assets/net current liabilities.
- Necessary borrowing facilities not agreed.
- Breach of loan agreement/covenants.
- Normal trade credit terms refused by suppliers.
- Fundamental market/technological changes.
- Loss of key management/suppliers/customers/product.
- Major litigation.

5.7 Procedures

The extent of audit procedures is influenced primarily by how far there is an excess of financial resources available over the financial resources required in the foreseeable future. For a stable business with uncomplicated circumstances discussions with the directors may suffice. Cash budgets, management accounts, etc. are not required as a matter of course.

The auditor would usually review forecasts in order to see if management's assumptions are in line with their going concern assumption.

5.8 Examination of borrowing facilities

It may be necessary for the auditor to:

- obtain confirmation of existence and terms of bank facilities, and
- make his own assessment of the bankers' intentions.

5.9 Written confirmation of management representations

Written management representations may be needed regarding:

- the directors' assessment of the entity as a going concern
- any relevant disclosures in the financial statements.

If the auditor is unable to these representations, he must consider whether there is a limitation on the scope of the audit, requiring modification to the auditors' report (see next chapter).

5.10 Assessing disclosures

When forming an opinion on whether the financial statements show a true and fair view, the auditor should consider:

- the entity's ability to continue as a going concern, and
- any relevant disclosures made in the financial statements.

If the going concern basis is inappropriate or significantly uncertain, and the financial statements do not give disclosure, the audit opinion may need to be modified on the grounds of disagreement with disclosure.

5.11 Reporting on financial statements

Where there is a significant level of concern, but the auditors do not disagree with the preparation of the financial statements on the going concern basis, they should include an emphasis of matter paragraph in their report.

It is important to note that they do not affect the audit opinion. These paragraphs simply draw the readers' attention to a matter that is fundamental to the readers' understanding of the financial statements.

Please see below for an example paragraph:

Emphasis of matter

In forming our opinion, we have considered the adequacy of the disclosures made in note 1 of the financial statements concerning the uncertainty as to the continuation and renewal of the company's bank overdraft facility. In view of the significance of this uncertainty we consider that it should be drawn to your attention but our opinion is not modified in this respect.

Opinion should not be modified on these grounds alone, provided disclosures are adequate. The disclosures required are as follows:

- statement that the financial statements are prepared on the going concern basis
- statement of pertinent facts
- nature of concern
- statement of directors' assumptions (must be clearly distinguishable from facts)
- details of any relevant actions by directors.

If disclosure is inadequate in any material respect, the audit opinion will be modified (see Chapter 12).

5.12 Adverse opinion

An adverse audit opinion should be issued if the auditors disagree with preparation of the financial statements on the going concern basis.

Disclosure alone cannot be sufficient to give a true and fair view.

5.13 Financial statements not prepared on going concern basis

In rare circumstances, in order to give a true and fair view, directors may prepare the financial statements on a basis other than going concern.

If the financial statements contain the necessary disclosures, the audit opinion should not be modified in this respect. (The basis on which the financial statements are prepared may be referred to in the introductory paragraph.)

5.14 Disclaimer

If the auditor concludes that the directors have not taken adequate steps to satisfy themselves that the going concern basis is appropriate then the auditor will not be satisfied that they have obtained sufficient appropriate evidence and a disclaimer of opinion may be appropriate.

6 Summary

You should now appreciate that the completion stages of an audit are particularly important and have an understanding of some of the issues which must be considered at this stage, including:

- whether the financial statements comply with IFRSs, IASs and relevant legislation
- whether there is proper disclosure of all relevant directors' loans and transactions in the financial statements
- the need for written management representations
- whether the business is a going concern.

As well as appreciating the issues, you should also understand how they are likely to be addressed in practice.

7 Test your knowledge

Workbook Activity 1

List 3 issues an auditor would be on the lookout for when assessing the going concern assumption of the client.

The reporting function

12

Introduction

Having satisfied ourselves that we have gathered sufficient and appropriate evidence, we must now draft reports to management. This chapter examines the management letter and the statutory audit opinion that we submit at the end of our audit assignment. We will consider both unmodified and modified opinions and in addition audit opinions where there is some kind of significant uncertainty.

SYLLABUS AREA

2.4 Record significant weaknesses in control.

2.12 Explain how management feedback can be used when planning an audit.

4.1 Prepare and submit clear and concise draft reports with recommendations.

4.2 Use management feedback when reporting.

4.3 Agree preliminary conclusions and recommendations with the audit supervisor.

4.4 Follow confidentiality and security procedures at all times.

5.1 Explain the legal and ethical duties of auditors, including the content of reports and the definition of proper records.

CONTENTS

1 Reports to directors or management

2 Evaluation of misstatements

3 Statutory auditors' reports

4 Modified opinion

5 Additional paragraphs

1 Reports to directors or management

1.1 Introduction

It is common practice for all auditors to report to management. However, for external auditors, reports to management are a by-product of the statutory audit rather than a main objective.

The auditor's report to the shareholders on the financial statements is the principal objective at which the whole external audit procedure is aimed.

The principal purposes of reports to directors or management are for auditors to communicate points that have come to their attention during the audit:

- on the design and operation of the accounting and internal control systems and to make suggestions for their improvement
- of other constructive advice, for example comments on potential economies or improvements in efficiency, and
- on other matters, for example comments on adjusted and unadjusted errors in the financial statements or on particular accounting policies and practices.

1.2 Material deficiencies in the accounting and internal control systems

When material deficiencies in the accounting and internal control systems are identified during the audit, auditors should report them in writing to the directors, the audit committee or an appropriate level of management on a timely basis.

Definition

A material deficiency in the accounting and internal control systems is a condition which may result in a material misstatement in the financial statements.

If the directors or management have detected a material deficiency and, in the view of the auditors, have taken appropriate corrective action, the auditors do not need to report to directors or management on the matter. In these circumstances they normally document the considerations which resulted in their conclusion that no report to directors or management in respect of this matter is needed.

1.3 Form of report

Usually, material deficiencies in the accounting and internal control system are communicated to directors or management in a written report issued by the auditors. In some circumstances it may be appropriate for the relevant matters to be raised orally with directors or management, followed by a file note circulated to those attending the meeting to provide a record of the auditors' observations and any responses of the directors or management.

When no material deficiencies in the accounting and internal control systems are identified during the audit, the auditors may choose not to issue a report to directors or management. When auditors do not intend to issue a report to directors or management they may consider it appropriate to inform them that no report is to be issued.

1.4 Other matters

In the course of the audit, the auditors may identify deficiencies in the accounting and internal control systems other than material deficiencies, or other matters which they consider appropriate to bring to the attention of directors or management. Usually these matters are included in a report to directors or management, together with details of any material deficiencies, although they may be issued in a separate report. The auditors may consider it appropriate to raise these matters orally with directors or management and in these circumstances they normally prepare a file note to provide a record of their observations.

1.5 Disclaimer

In any report to directors or management, auditors explain that the report is not a comprehensive statement of all deficiencies which exist or of all improvements which may be made, but that it documents only those matters which have come to their attention as a result of the audit procedures performed.

1.6 Timing

To be effective, a report to directors or management is best made as soon as possible after completion of the audit procedures giving rise to comment. Where the audit work is performed on more than one visit, it is often appropriate to report to directors or management after the interim visit as well as after the final audit visit, but making clear that the overall audit work is only partially complete and further matters may still arise. Where an interim report details serious deficiencies, the auditor will review corrective action taken by management during the final audit.

1.7 Management's response

Normally, auditors ask for a reply to the points raised in a report to directors or management, indicating the actions that the directors or management intend to take as a result of the comments made in the report.

1.8 Disclosure to third parties

Auditors normally state in their report to directors or management that:

- the report has been prepared for the sole use of the entity
- it must not be disclosed to a third party, or quoted or referred to, without the written consent of the auditors, and
- no responsibility is assumed by the auditors to any other person.

An express disclaimer of liability normally provides protection against an unforeseen liability to a third party.

1.9 Structure of the report

The letter should be as clear, concise and constructive as possible. To achieve this, the comments are presented to management using the following standard structure.

Explanation

The nature of each deficiency is described. The description is concise but specific, and the extent of the error quantified if possible.

Consequence

This points out to management the possible consequences of the deficiency in terms of the financial statements (e.g. they could contain errors), and/or the business's assets (e.g. financial loss may result).

Recommendation

For every deficiency a recommendation is made as to how the problem could be overcome. Such recommendations are as practical and cost-effective as possible in order to encourage management to adopt them.

If a recommendation is not adopted, and the same deficiency still exists in the following year, reference to this would be made in the following year's management letter. However, the consequence or recommendation may need to be revised to get the deficiency resolved.

The management letter usually deals with the most serious deficiencies first in order to lend weight to the report as a whole.

2 Evaluation of misstatements

In accordance with ISA 450 *Evaluation of misstatements identified during the audit* all misstatements should be communicated to management on a timely basis, unless they are clearly trivial. Management should be asked to correct **all** misstatements identified during the audit.

If management refuses to adjust the identified misstatements the auditor should:

- try and obtain an understanding of management's reasons for refusing to adjust
- determine whether uncorrected misstatements are material in aggregate or individually, and
- consider the potential impact on their audit report of material misstatements.

Prior to evaluating the significance of uncorrected misstatements the auditor should reassess materiality to confirm whether it remains appropriate to the financial statements.

Finally, the auditor should obtain a written representation from management and those charged with governance that they believe the effect of the uncorrected misstatements is immaterial, individually and in aggregate.

Once these procedures have been completed the auditor should consider the impact of uncorrected misstatements on their reporting. This is considered in more detail.

3 Statutory auditors' reports

3.1 Legal background

The external auditor's principal purpose in performing the work described in the preceding Chapters is to produce a report to the members of the company. He is obliged to produce such a report by S235 of the Companies Act 2006.

The auditors' report will be included, together with the financial statements, in the annual report which is laid before the members at the Annual General Meeting.

3.2 Unmodified opinions

The following is the text of a specimen audit report provided in accordance with ISA 700 *Forming an opinion and reporting on financial statements:*

Example

INDEPENDENT AUDITOR'S REPORT TO THE SHAREHOLDERS OF XYZ LIMITED

We have audited the financial statements of XYZ Limited for the year ended 31 December 20X1 which comprise the Statement of Profit or Loss, the Statement of Financial Position, the Cash Flow Statement, the Statement of Changes in Equity and the related notes. These financial statements have been prepared under the accounting policies set out therein.

Respective responsibilities of directors and auditors

The company's directors are responsible for the preparation of the financial statements in accordance with applicable law and United Kingdom Accounting Standards (United Kingdom Generally Accepted Accounting Practice).

Our responsibility is to audit the financial statements in accordance with relevant legal and regulatory requirements and International Standards on Auditing (UK and Ireland).

We report to you our opinion as to whether the financial statements give a true and fair view and are properly prepared in accordance with the Companies Act 2006. We also report to you if, in our opinion, the Directors' Report is not consistent with the financial statements, if the company has not kept proper accounting records, if we have not received all the information and explanations we require for our audit, or if the information specified by law regarding directors' remuneration and other transactions is not disclosed.

We read the Directors' Report and consider the implications for our report if we become aware of any apparent misstatements within it.

Basis of audit opinion

We conducted our audit in accordance with International Standards of Auditing (UK and Ireland) issued by the Auditing Practices Board. An audit includes examination, on a test basis, of evidence relevant to the amounts and disclosures in the financial statements. It also includes an assessment of the significant estimates and judgements made by the directors in the preparation of the financial statements, and of whether the accounting policies are appropriate to the company's circumstances, consistently applied and adequately disclosed.

We planned and performed our audit so as to obtain all the information and explanations which we considered necessary in order to provide us with sufficient evidence to give reasonable assurance that the financial statements are free from material misstatement, whether caused by fraud or other irregularity or error. In forming our opinion we also evaluated the overall adequacy of the presentation of information in the financial statements.

Opinion

In our opinion the financial statements:

- give a true and fair view, in accordance with United Kingdom Generally Accepted Accounting Practice, of the state of the company's affairs as at 31 December 20X1 and of its profit for the year then ended, and
- have been property prepared in accordance with the Companies Act 2006.

Registered auditors

Date *Address*

3.3 Opinions

The report is addressed to the shareholders of the company, and gives an indication of the scope of the auditor's work (i.e. that work has been done in accordance with ISAs). The auditor must give his opinion on two matters:

- whether the financial statements give a true and fair view of the profit or loss of the company for the period and its state of affairs at the year end, and
- whether the financial statements have been properly prepared in accordance with the Companies Act 2006.

These are known as the auditor's express opinions.

There are, however, further matters upon which Companies Act 2006 requires to be reported on by exception. These are known as the implied opinions:

- proper records of account have been kept by the company
- the accounts agree with the underlying records

- returns from branches not visited by the auditor are adequate for audit purposes
- all information and explanations necessary for audit purposes have been obtained
- the information given in the director's report is not inconsistent with the accounts.

APB Bulletin 2010/2 requires these points to be included in UK audit reports (even if there are no problems) to aid the users' understanding of what the audit entails.

In addition, if matters relating to directors' emoluments and other transactions are not properly disclosed in the accounts, they will be included in the auditors' report and disclosed there. The audit opinion will be modified on the grounds that the financial statements have not been properly prepared in accordance with the Companies Act.

3.4 The meaning of the term 'true and fair'

Although it is difficult to define the term exactly, as you saw in Chapter 1, in practice, if the auditor states that in his opinion the 'financial statements show a true and fair view', this generally implies that:

- IFRSs and IASs have been complied with as necessary, or
- if an IFRS or IAS has not been complied with, the non-compliance was necessary in order to give a true and fair view
- the financial statements have been otherwise drawn up using acceptable bases and conventions.

3.5 The meaning of the term 'financial statements'

In the context of the auditors' report, the 'financial statements' that are within the scope of the auditor's examination are:

- the statement of profit or loss
- the statement of financial position
- statements of cash flows and changes in equity
- notes required by the 4th Schedule of the Companies Act 2006.

The directors' report is not part of the financial statements and therefore the auditor is not required to consider whether it shows a true and fair view. The auditor's only responsibility in relation to the directors' report is to state that it is inconsistent with the financial statements, if this is the case.

3.6 Date and signature of the auditors' report

The date of the auditors' report is the date on which the auditors sign (in manuscript) their report expressing an opinion on the financial statements for distribution with those statements. This will be following:

- receipt of the financial statements and accompanying documents in the form approved by the directors for release
- review of all documents which they are required to consider in addition to the financial statements (for example the directors' report, chairman's statement or other review of an entity's affairs which will accompany the financial statements), and
- completion of all procedures necessary to form an opinion on the financial statements (and any other opinions required by law or regulation) including a review of post year-end events.

The report may be signed in the name of the auditors' firm, the personal name of the auditor, or both, as appropriate. The signature is normally that of the firm because the firm as a whole assumes responsibility for the audit. To assist identification, the report normally includes the location of the auditors' office. Where appropriate, their status as registered auditors is also stated.

4 Modified opinion

4.1 Introduction

A modified opinion is issued when either of the following circumstances exist:

- the financial statements as a whole are not free from material misstatements, or
- the auditor has been unable to obtain sufficient appropriate evidence to conclude that the financial statements as a whole are free from material misstatement.

If the auditor comes to either of the above conclusions they must consider how significant the matter is. If the matter is considered immaterial then it should not affect the wording of the opinion.

However, if the auditor believes that the matter is material they will modify the wording of the opinion. If the auditor considers the matter to be pervasive to the financial statements, then this must also be incorporated in to the audit opinion.

Pervasive means that the matter is:

- not confined to specific elements of the financial statements;
- if confined, represents a substantial proportion of the financial statements; or
- is fundamental to users understanding of the financial statements
- the affects on the audit opinion can be summarised in the table below:

	Auditor's judgement	
Nature of matter	**Material but not pervasive**	**Material and pervasive**
Financial statements are materially misstated.	Qualified opinion	Adverse opinion
Inability to obtain sufficient appropriate evidence.	Qualified opinion	Disclaimer of opinion

When the auditor modified the opinion they include a 'Basis for Modification Paragraph' in the audit report that describes the matter. This paragraph is included before the opinion paragraph.

4.2 Qualified opinion

With a qualified opinion the auditor is stating that whilst there are material misstatements, they are confined to a specific element of the financial statements but the remainder may be relied upon. Therefore, the opinion usually states that "except for the matters described in the basis for modification paragraph, the financial statements present fairly….."

The text which follows is based on ISA 705 *Modifications to the opinion in the independent auditors' report.*

We have audited ... (remaining words are the same as illustrated in the specimen unmodified report above).

We conducted our audit in accordance with ... (remaining words are the same as illustrated in the specimen unmodified report above).

As discussed in Note X to the financial statements, no depreciation has been provided in the financial statements which practice, in our opinion, is not in accordance with International Accounting Standards. The provision for the year ended 31 December 20X1, should be xxx based on the straight-line method of depreciation using annual rates of 5% for the building and 20% for the equipment. Accordingly, the non-current assets should be reduced by accumulated depreciation of xxx and the loss for the year and accumulated deficit should be increased by xxx and xxx, respectively.

In our opinion, except for the effects of the matter described in the Basis for Modification Opinion paragraph, the financial statements present fairly, in all material respects, (or give a true and fair view of) the financial position of XYZ Ltd as at.... (remaining words are the same as illustrated in the specimen unmodified report above).

4.3 Adverse opinion

If the auditor concludes that the matter is pervasive they are claiming that the financial statements cannot be relied upon in any part. The opinion will be reworded to state that the financial statements "do not present fairly...."

The text which follows is based on ISA 705.

We have audited ... (remaining words are the same as illustrated in the specimen unmodified report above).

We conducted our audit in accordance with ... (remaining words are the same as illustrated in the specimen unmodified report above).

In our opinion, because of the significance of the matter discussed in the Basis for Adverse Opinion paragraph, the financial statements do not present fairly (or do not give a true and fair view of) the financial position of XYZ Ltd as at 31 December, 20X1, and of their financial performance and their cash flows for the year then ended in accordance with

United Kingdom Generally Accepted Accounting Practice and do not comply with the Companies Act 2006.

Note that the adverse opinion is an extreme form of modification. It effectively recommends that the shareholders should not make any use of the financial statements.

4.4 Disclaimer of opinion

If the auditor gives a disclaimer of opinion they will state that they "do not express an opinion on the financial statements."

The text which follows is based on ISA 705.

We were engaged to audit the accompanying statement of financial position of the XYZ Company as of 31 December 20X1, and the related statements of income and cash flows for the year then ended. These financial statements are the responsibility of the Company's management. (Omit the sentence stating the responsibility of the auditor).

(The paragraph discussing the scope of the audit would either be omitted or amended according to the circumstances).

We were not able to observe all physical inventories and confirm accounts receivable due to limitations placed on the scope of our work by the Company.

Because of the significance of the matters discussed in the Basis for Disclaimer of Opinion paragraph, we have not been able to obtain sufficient appropriate audit evidence to provide a basis for an audit opinion. Accordingly, we do not express an opinion on the financial statements.

As with the adverse opinion, this is such an extreme form of modification that it should be avoided unless the situation is so extreme that only a disclaimer would suffice.

Activity 1

For each of the following situations which have arisen in two unrelated audit clients, select whether or not the audit opinion on the financial statements would be modified.

(i) Alpha Ltd capitalised costs of £150,000 in respect of repairs and maintenance and included these costs in non-current assets. The amount capitalised represents 30% of Alpha Ltd's profit before tax. The directors refuse to make any adjustments in respect of this matter.

(ii) There is a significant uncertainty about Beta Ltd's ability to continue as a going concern. The directors of Beta Ltd have prepared the financial statements on a going concern basis and have fully disclosed the uncertainty in the notes to the financial statements.

5 Additional paragraphs

Having formed their opinion there are circumstances where the auditor must draw the reader's attention to additional matters. These are categorised as follows:

- matters already disclosed in the financial statements that are fundamental to understanding the financial statements. These are presented in 'Emphasis of Matter' paragraphs; and
- other matters relevant to either understanding the audit, the auditor's responsibilities or the audit report. These are presented in 'Other Matter' paragraphs.

5.1 Emphasis of matter paragraphs

These paragraphs draw the reader's attention to a note already disclosed in the financial statements. The matters referred to have to be fundamental to the readers' understanding of the financial statements. They are included immediately after the opinion paragraph. It is important to note that they do not affect the audit opinion.

Examples of where it may be necessary to include an Emphasis of Matter paragraph are as follows:

- an uncertainty relating to the future outcome of exceptional litigation
- early application of new accounting standards that has a pervasive effect on the financial statements
- a major catastrophe that has had a significant effect on the entity's financial position
- uncertainty surrounding the going concern of the entity.

The text which follows is based on ISA 706 *Emphasis of matter paragraphs and other matter paragraphs in the independent auditor's report*.

In our opinion ... (remaining words are the same as illustrated in the specimen unmodified report above).

Without qualifying our opinion we draw attention to Note X to the financial statements. The Company is the defendant in a lawsuit alleging infringement of certain patent rights and claiming royalties and punitive damages. The Company has filed a counter action, and preliminary hearings and discovery proceedings on both actions are in progress. The ultimate outcome of the matter cannot presently be determined, and no provision for any liability that may result has been made in the financial statements.

5.2 Other matter paragraphs

Circumstances where these may be included are as follows:

- When national regulations require the auditor to elaborate on their responsibilities.
- If there is a material inconsistency between the audited financial statements and the 'other information' contained in the annual report.
- When there is an inability to obtain sufficient appropriate evidence imposed by management but the auditor cannot withdraw from the engagement due to legal restrictions.

6 Summary

It is important that you understand the following matters:

- the matters to be included in reports to management
- the matters to be included in the auditors' report:
  - in all cases, and
  - by exception only
- the meaning of the term 'financial statements' in the context of the auditors' report
- the factual matters required by statute to be included in the auditors' report if they are not included in the financial statements
- the contents of the ISA on auditors' opinions and in particular:
  - the distinction between disagreement, scope limitation and inherent uncertainty
  - the circumstances giving rise to uncertainties and disagreement
  - the format and wording of an unmodified opinion
  - the auditors' report wording associated with the various forms of qualification.

Answers to chapter activities

Activity 1

(i) Modified.

(ii) Unmodified.

7 Test your knowledge

Workbook Activity 2

During the external audit of Beech Ltd, the audit junior identified an invoice for the cost of school fees for the managing director's children. The purchase ledger clerk informed the audit junior that the managing director had told her to hide the costs in sundries. The amount of the school fees are insignificant in terms of key figures in the financial statements.

In respect of this matter, select whether the audit junior should take no further action or refer to the supervisor.

Workbook Activity 3

During the audit of Media Ltd, a film production company, it was discovered that although the company maintained a non-current asset register to record the details of its cameras and other equipment, no checking procedures other than reconciliation with the nominal ledger are undertaken.

Prepare extracts suitable for inclusion in a report to management of Media Ltd, which set out:

(i) The possible consequences; and

(ii) The recommendations you would make in respect of this matter.

Workbook Activity 4

Described below are situations which have arisen in separate audits. For each situation describe the effect on the audit report.

1 Ash Ltd uses leased motor vehicles which have been accounted for as operating leases. However, you believe that these leases are finance leases and should have been capitalized at £51,000. The current treatment does not comply with accounting standards which require finance leases, where the user takes on the risks and rewards of ownership, to be included within non-current assets and capitalized. Profit for the year would then have been reduced by £4,000. The pre-tax profits for the year were £600,000 and total assets were £5.4 million.

2 A fire in the warehouse of Oak Ltd destroyed the inventory sheets which were the only record of the company's inventory at the year-end. The company has included an estimated inventory figure of £780,000. The pre-tax profits for the year were £1.1 million and total assets were £6.5 million.

3 Elm Ltd has included a note in the financial statements explaining that 90% of its revenue is derived from a national retailer with whom it has a three year renewable contract. This contract is due for renewal in September. However, the directors require the audit report to be signed on 31 May.

4 Ben and Holly Ltd has included a provision for doubtful debts of £100,000 in the year end accounts. Obviously the provision cannot be estimated with complete accuracy but the reporting partner believes it should be materially higher.

13 The legal and professional framework

Introduction

In this chapter, we will discuss the legal requirements of auditors according to the Companies Act 2006 and how an auditor is appointed and removed from their position. We will consider the rights and duties of both auditors and directors and will reintroduce the concept of independence.

SYLLABUS AREA

5.1 Explain the legal and ethical duties of auditors, including the content of reports and the definition of proper records.

5.2 Explain the liability of auditors under contract and negligence including liability to third parties.

CONTENTS

1 Legal requirements
2 Eligibility and ineligibility
3 Appointment of auditors
4 Vacation of office
5 Duties and rights of auditors
6 Duties of directors in accounting and reporting matters
7 Independence of auditors

1 Legal requirements

1.1 The legal and professional framework

The Companies Act 2006 provides the legal framework within which the auditor operates. Although the law relating to auditors is quite detailed, the subject matter is not essentially difficult.

The auditor carries out his role in accordance with the profession's ethical guidance and regulations.

Regulations are designed to ensure that members of professional bodies:

- are independent
- are competent, and
- conduct their affairs in a professional manner.

The regulations of the **Institute of Chartered Accountants in England and Wales (ICAEW)** take the form of guidelines on professional ethics, backed up by a disciplinary system which investigates allegations of professional misconduct. The **Association of Chartered Certified Accountants (ACCA)** issues Rules of Professional Conduct.

1.2 Legal rules

Most external audit work is concerned with companies registered under the Companies Act 2006. This Act also regulates the auditors of such companies.

The legislation relating to the auditor is designed to:

- ensure the competence of auditors by requiring a professional qualification
- secure the auditor's independence by disqualifying certain people from eligibility for appointment and by controlling his removal or resignation
- ensure the auditor's integrity by requiring him to be a member of a body which enforces high ethical standards
- define the auditor's duties and the matters covered by his report, and
- give the auditor the rights needed to carry out his defined duties.

1.3 Statutory requirement for an audit

A company registered under the Companies Act can be limited by shares (public or private), limited by guarantee or unlimited (private).

S384 requires registered companies to appoint an auditor.

There are two exceptions (subject to specified criteria being met):

- dormant companies (S250)
- companies with a turnover of less than £6.5 million (S249A) (effective January 2004).

1.4 The auditor's function

S235 CA 2006 requires the auditor to report on the annual accounts laid before the members at the AGM which is within his term of office.

The auditor holds office from the conclusion of the general meeting at which he is appointed until the end of the next general meeting when accounts are presented to the members.

S237 requires the auditor to carry out such investigations as will enable him to form his opinion.

Note that the Companies Act does not say (in as many words) that a company's accounts or financial statements must be audited. But taken together, the following requirements mean that this is the case:

- S240 CA 2006 – Auditors' report to be annexed to accounts.
- S235 and 237 CA 2006 – Duty of auditors to report to members and to carry out any investigations necessary.
- S384 CA 2006 – Requirement for companies to appoint auditors.

1.5 Unincorporated businesses

There is no overall statutory requirement for unincorporated businesses to have an audit; any regulations in this respect would depend on legislation peculiar to a specific type of business (e.g. the Building Societies Act 1986), or on the terms of the engagement as agreed between auditor and client.

2 Eligibility and ineligibility

2.1 Who can be an auditor?

To be an auditor a person or firm (a body corporate or partnership) must fulfil certain criteria (S25 CA 2006). They must be a member of a recognised supervisory body and have an approved qualification.

2.2 Members of a Recognised Supervisory Body (RSB)

RSBs are currently:

- Institute of Chartered Accountants in England and Wales (ICAEW)
- Institute of Chartered Accountants of Scotland (ICAS)
- Institute of Chartered Accountants in Ireland (ICAI)
- Association of Chartered Certified Accountants (ACCA).

2.3 Appropriate qualification

The auditor must be a person appropriately qualified or a firm controlled by persons who are appropriately qualified (S31 CA 2006) i.e. either:

- a member of one of the bodies listed above
- a holder of a qualification from a Recognised Qualifying Body (RQB), or
- a holder of a similar non-UK qualification.

All four chartered bodies mentioned above have RSB and RQB status.

2.4 Who may not be an auditor?

The following persons are ineligible for appointment as auditor (S27 CA 2006):

- an officer or employee of the company (or any associated undertaking), or
- a partner or employee of an officer or employee of the company.

The officers of a company are generally agreed to be the directors and the company secretary.

2.5 Effect of ineligibility

If an existing auditor becomes disqualified he should:

- resign immediately, and
- give notice to the company.

The penalty for failing to do so is a fine (S28 CA 2006).

If the company auditor was ineligible for any part of the period during which the audit was conducted, the Secretary of State can direct the company to retain a person who is eligible to:

- carry out a second audit
- review the first audit and report, giving reasons why a second audit is needed (S29 CA 2006).

3 Appointment of auditors

3.1 Introduction

The main statutory provisions for the appointment of auditors are contained in S384 CA 2006 and are summarised below.

3.2 Appointment by members

When	How
• At AGM (or any other meeting Ordinary resolution. where annual accounts are presented):	• Ordinary resolution.
– to reappoint retiring auditor	
– to appoint an auditor other than the retiring auditor – to reappoint an auditor appointed by the directors.	• Ordinary resolution with special notice (28 days).
• Private companies only. No AGM necessary to reappoint retiring auditor (automatic annual reappointment for as long as election remains in force).	Elective (– 100%) resolution with ordinary notice. Revoked by ordinary resolution
• To fill a casual vacancy (e.g. if the auditor dies) if the directors do not.	• Ordinary resolution with special notice.

3.3 Appointment by directors

When	How
• To fill a casual vacancy. • To appoint first auditors, between the date of incorporation and the first AGM.	• Reappointment must be by members at next AGM, by ordinary resolution with special notice.

3.4 Appointment by Secretary of State

When	How
• If at the conclusion of the AGM no auditor is appointed.	• Company must inform the Secretary of State within one week.

The members do not 'ratify' an audit appointment made by the directors. Where the directors are empowered to make an appointment they may do so without the approval or consent of the members. When the term of office of an auditor appointed by the directors expires, the members may choose to:

- re-appoint the retiring auditor, or
- make a new appointment.

The auditor's remuneration is fixed by those who appoint him. In practice, this task is usually delegated to the directors.

4 Vacation of office

4.1 Introduction

The main statutory provisions for the vacation of the office of auditor are contained in Ss391–394 CA 2006 and are summarised on the next page:

4.2 Removal (before expiry of term of office)

Method

- Ordinary resolution with special notice (28 days).
- Notice of resolution to state if auditor has made representations.

Auditor's rights

- To have written representations of a reasonable length circulated to all members.
- To receive notice of, attend and be heard at the meetings at which:
  - his term of office would have expired, and
  - It is proposed to appoint a new auditor.

4.3 Resignation Method

Method

- Auditor must submit written notice to the company.
- Company must notify:
  - the registrar of companies, and
  - all parties entitled to receive copies of accounts.

Auditor's rights

- To requisition an EGM to consider reasons for resignation.
- To require the company to circulate a statement in advance of the meeting:
  - at which his term of office would have expired
  - to appoint a new auditor, or
  - he has requisitioned.

4.4 Statement by person ceasing to hold office as auditor

Whenever an auditor ceases to hold office (for whatever reason) he must deposit at the registered office of the company either:

- a statement that there are no circumstances connected with his ceasing to hold office which he considers should be brought to the attention of the members or payables, or
- a statement of any such circumstances.

A notice of resignation is not effective unless accompanied by either statement. In the case of failure to seek reappointment, the statement is required at least 14 days before the next auditors are appointed. In any other case, this statement must be deposited within 14 days of ceasing to hold office.

Reason for vacation	**When deposited**
• Resignation	• Failure to seek reappointment
• With notice of resignation	• At least 14 days before next auditor appointed (usually AGM)
• Other.	• Within 14 days of ceasing to hold office.

If there are circumstances to be brought to the attention of members or payables the company must send a copy to every person entitled to receive a copy of the accounts.

The purpose of these provisions is to ensure that the members are made aware of any important circumstances surrounding the removal or resignation, such as disagreement over an accounting policy which is making the directors remove the auditor.

Note that the auditor may not use his rights to secure publicity for defamatory material about the client's directors or anyone else. The Court has the power, on application by the company or any other aggrieved person, to order the representations not to be circulated or read out, on the grounds that it is defamatory.

5 Duties and rights of auditors

5.1 Primary duty

The primary duty of an auditor is set out in S235 of the Companies Act 2006, which requires him to report to the company's members on every set of accounts (i.e. statement of financial position, statement of profit or loss, etc and accompanying notes) of which a copy is laid before the members in respect of an accounting reference period.

The auditor's report must be read to the members at the general meeting (normally the AGM) and must be available for their inspection.

The report must state whether in the auditor's opinion:

- the accounts have been properly prepared in accordance with the Companies Act 2006, and
- a true and fair view is given of the state of affairs of the company at the end of its financial year, and of the profit or loss for that year.

5.2 Other duties

In preparing his report an auditor is required by S237 to carry out such investigations as will enable him to form an opinion as to whether:

- proper accounting records have been kept by the company;
- proper returns, adequate for audit purposes, have been received from any branches not visited by the auditor, and
- the accounts are in agreement with the records and returns.

If the auditor forms the opinion that any of these are not the case he must say so in his report.

Also, if either of the following situations arises he should state the fact in his report:

- if he has been unable to obtain all the information and explanations necessary for his audit (S237), and
- if there is any inconsistency between the accounts and the directors' report (S235).

The following mnemonic may help you to remember these requirements:

R eturns from branches

A greement with records and returns

P roper accounting records

I nformation and explanations

D irectors' report consistent.

S237 also requires that if the accounts do not contain the necessary information on the director's emoluments, loans and transactions, then the particulars must be included in the auditors' report.

5.3 Rights of auditors

The following rights are given to the auditors of a company by the Companies Act 2006 to enable him to carry out his duties effectively and to make his report to the members:

- to have access at all times to the books, accounts and vouchers of the company (S389A)
- to require from the officers of the company any information and explanations which he thinks necessary for the purposes of his audit
- to receive notice of and attend any general meeting of members (S390), and to be heard at any general meeting on business which concerns him as auditor.

S389A(3) CA 2006 extends the right to require information and explanations from the company's officers. It is the duty of subsidiary companies and their auditors to make any information available to the holding company's auditors to enable them to carry out their duties.

In addition, the auditor has important rights under the other sections already dealt with – in particular the rights associated with his removal or resignation.

6 Duties of directors in accounting and reporting matters

6.1 Introduction

A director can be described as an agent having a fiduciary relationship with a principal, i.e. the company that employs him. (A fiduciary relationship is one of trust.)

6.2 Duties in respect of company accounts

- To keep books of accounts and proper accounting records (S221 CA 2006).
- To produce an statement of profit or loss and statement of financial position in such a fashion as to show a true and fair view (S226–227 CA 2006).
- To produce a directors' report (S235 CA 2006) which is consistent with the financial statements and contains certain specified information.

6.3 Special matters affecting directors' transactions with the company

The directors are obliged to:

- disclose any loans or credit arrangements permitted under CA 2006
- disclose all emoluments received by them in respect of their office and any payments received as compensation for loss of office (these sums must be approved by the company in general meeting)
- ensure that the financial statements give, to the best of their knowledge and belief, all the statutory information required by the Act
- not to give misleading or reckless information to the company auditors (a criminal offence for directors or officers under S389(A) CA 2006).

7 Independence of auditors

7.1 Introduction

Without doubt, the most important professional attribute of an auditor (whether external or internal) is his independence; unless he is totally independent so that his ability to express his opinion is never subordinated to the will of a client's management, the objectivity, and thus the value of his report to the client's members or proprietors, is lost. The IFAC Code of Ethics require auditors to consider whether their independence might be questioned by external parties because of:

- business relationships
- personal relationships
- long association with the client
- fee dependence; and
- non audit services provided.

Where there is a lack of independence in the external auditor, shareholders' interests can be at risk from:

- auditors and directors colluding to produce financial statements containing wrong information or suppressing information, and
- auditors yielding to directors on matters of principle in order to preserve their appointment.

7.2 Opportunities for directors to overrule auditors

1 Where the directors are in a position to exert influence over the members

In many cases where shareholders are not involved with the day-to-day running of a company, and especially where no one member or group of members holds a sizeable proportion of the share capital, it is not easy for them to oppose moves made by directors without making common cause at an annual general meeting. Thus if a director or directors (acting as members) propose a change of auditors, they stand a good chance of carrying the proposals despite any representations made by the existing auditors.

There are, of course, very many companies, whose directors themselves hold all or a majority of the shares, and where the auditor's position is potentially even weaker.

2 Where the auditor is in any way dependent on the client

For example, where:

- a substantial part of his fee income derives from that client
- he is in some way personally involved with the client, and
- he receives preferential treatment from his client (e.g. substantial discounts on the client's products).

In such cases, an auditor is more likely to capitulate when a disagreement arises between himself and a client's directors. The ultimate sanction (of qualification of the auditors' report) may not be invoked if the resulting loss of the audit would have a material effect on the auditor himself and/or his firm.

In practice, the majority of firms have their own rules preventing involvement with their clients, and the guidelines for professional ethics published by each of the professional bodies advises against most of the above mentioned situations, but the efficiency of this safeguard obviously depends greatly on the integrity of the auditor.

7.3 Objectivity

Objectivity is a state of mind, but in certain roles the preservation of objectivity needs to be protected and demonstrated by the maintenance of an auditor's independence from influences which could affect his or her objectivity.

An auditor's objectivity must be beyond question if he or she is to report as an auditor. That objectivity can only be assured if the auditor is, and is seen to be, independent.

7.4 Areas of risk regarding an auditor's objectivity

- Objectivity may be threatened or appear to be threatened by undue dependence on any audit client or group of connected clients regarding fees.
- An auditor's objectivity may be threatened or appear to be threatened as a consequence of a family or other close personal or business relationship.
- A member's objectivity may be threatened or appear to be threatened where he or she holds a beneficial interest in the shares or other forms of investment in a company upon which the practice reports.
- Where a partner or member of staff holds shares in any capacity in a company which is an audit client of the practice they should not be voted on at any general meeting of the company in relation to the appointment, removal or remuneration of auditors.
- Objectivity may be threatened or appear to be threatened by a loan to or from an audit client.
- The existence of significant overdue fees from an audit client or group of connected clients can be a threat or appear to be a threat to objectivity akin to that of a loan.
- Objectivity may be threatened or appear to be threatened by acceptance of goods, services or hospitality from an audit client.
- There are occasions where objectivity may be threatened or appear to be threatened by the provision to an audit client of services other than the audit.

7.5 Review procedures

To guard against loss of independence, every audit firm should establish review procedures, including an annual review, to:

- satisfy itself that each engagement may be accepted/continued, and
- identify situations where independence may be at risk so that appropriate safeguards can be applied.

Wherever the review procedures indicate that an audit assignment should be accepted or continued only with additional safeguards against loss of independence, the engagement partner's decision and the range of safeguards appropriate to the assignment should be subject to an independence review by a partner unconnected with the engagement.

Safeguards against loss of independence should include the following, according to the size and circumstances of the practice and the size and circumstances of the clients:

- the inclusion of a manager or other qualified employee in the audit team
- rotation of the engagement partner, and
- rotation of senior members of staff.

It may be prudent to adopt a procedure under which staff engaged on an audit assignment are able in the last resort to report any area of concern to a partner other than the engagement partner.

7.6 Confidentiality – Improper disclosure

Information confidential to a client or employer acquired in the course of professional work should not be disclosed except where consent has been obtained from the client, employer or other proper source, or where there is a legal right or duty to disclose.

Where a member is in doubt as to whether he or she has a right or duty to disclose he should, if appropriate, initially discuss the matter fully within his firm or organisation. If that is not appropriate, or if it fails to resolve the problem, he should consider taking legal advice and/or consult his RSB.

7.7 Improper use of information

A member acquiring or receiving confidential information in the course of his or her professional work should neither use nor appear to use that information for his personal advantage or for the advantage of a third party.

When a member changes his or her firm or employment he is entitled to use experience gained in the previous firm or employment but not confidential information acquired there.

7.8 IFAC code of ethics

In addition to independence, auditors must comply with the IFAC code of ethics which has 5 fundamental principles as follows:

- **Integrity**

  Integrity refers to the honesty of an auditor's actions.

- **Objectivity**

  Objectivity has been discussed previously.

- **Professional competence and due care**

  Auditors have a duty to maintain their professional knowledge and ensure all their work is planned and completed to a high standard.

- **Confidentiality**

  This has been discussed above.

- **Professional behaviour**

  Auditors must not act in such a way that could bring the accountancy profession in to disrepute.

8 Summary

The legal provisions are an essential part of the framework within which the external auditor operates. You should ensure that you are familiar with the:

- requirement for an audit and the position of dormant and small companies
- rules governing eligibility and ineligibility
- rules governing the appointment, removal and resignation of auditors
- duties and rights of the auditor
- duties of directors in accounting and reporting matters, including the need to maintain proper accounting records.

Professional ethics is quite a detailed topic. It is important that you appreciate the spirit of the guidance. The most important statements cover the following key areas:

Integrity, objectivity and independence

Areas of risk are:

- undue dependence on an audit client
- family and other personal relationships
- beneficial interests in shares and other investments · voting on audit appointments
- loans
- overdue fees
- goods and services: hospitality
- provision of other services to audit clients.

Review procedures are an important safeguard.

Confidentiality

- Improper disclosure.
- Improper use of information.

9 Test your knowledge

Workbook Activity 1

In relation to the appointment of auditors, when will appointment by the Secretary of State take place?

(a) To fill a casual vacancy.

(b) If at the conclusion of the AGM, no auditor is appointed.

(c) To appoint the first auditors on incorporation.

Responsibilities and liabilities of the auditor

14

Introduction

This final chapter examines auditor's liability to third parties and focuses on the importance of quality control procedures within an audit firm. We will finish with discussing the role of auditors with relation to fraud.

KNOWLEDGE

5.2 Explain the liability of auditors under contract and negligence including liability to third parties.

CONTENTS

1 The auditor's liability in contract and tort

2 Quality control

3 Review procedures

4 Fraud and the role of the auditor

1 The auditor's liability in contract and tort

1.1 Introduction

The responsibilities and resulting liabilities of an auditor arise in both statute and common law. The auditor's statutory responsibilities are set out principally in the Companies Act 2006 and are not considered further in this chapter, as they were covered in Chapters 1 and 13.

Under common law the auditor has a contractual relationship with his client – negligent auditing may lead to an auditor being sued for breach of contract.

The auditor also has a common law duty of care towards third parties under the law of tort. This aspect of the auditor's liability is the subject of recent case law and has given rise to much debate (both within and outside the accountancy profession).

1.2 Reasonable skill and care

There is a contractual relationship between an external auditor and his client, and an implied term of the contract is that the auditor will carry out his work with 'reasonable skill and care'. The IFAC Code of Ethics tells auditors that they must act with professional competence and due care.

This term cannot be precisely defined, and ultimately its meaning will be decided by the courts in view of the facts of each particular case. However, the following points are relevant in determining what is a reasonable standard of care:

- applying the most up-to-date accounting and auditing standards
- adhering to all standards of ethical behaviour laid down by the relevant professional bodies
- being aware of the terms and conditions of the appointment as set out in the engagement letter and as implied by law
- employing competent staff who are adequately trained and supervised in carrying out instructions.

Failure to exercise 'reasonable skill and care' constitutes a breach of contract and also may lead to a claim of negligence by the client if the company has suffered financial loss. This type of claim usually arises when an auditor has failed to discover a fraud during the audit. The remedy is usually damages.

There are three main ways that an auditor can reduce the risk of exposure to claims for damages as follows:

- **Limited liability agreements between the auditor and client including liability caps**: The auditor will include a liability cap in the engagement letter that sets a maximum amount they can be sued for by the client.
- **Limited Liability Partnerships**: Most audit firms are now Limited Liability Partnerships (LLP). As a LLP, the partners are not individually liable for any claims.
- **Professional Indemnity Insurance (PII)**: Audit firms must take out PII provides cover for the financial consequences of professional negligence, following a breach of professional duty by way of neglect or error.

1.3 Liability to third parties

It has also been argued that as well as being potentially liable to his client, the auditor might also incur liability to third parties. External auditors can limit their liability to third parties if they include a disclaimer in their audit report. This is referred to as Bannerman paragraph and would include a statement that the 'report is intended solely for the company's members.'

1.4 General duty of care

The case **Hedley Byrne v Heller and Partners** established that a professional person may owe a general duty of care to third parties, where:

- the professional person acted negligently
- the professional person knew or ought to have known that his statement would be relied upon by third parties, and
- the third party suffered financial loss as a result of relying on the professional's statement.

2 Quality control

2.1 Introduction

The following methods of quality control are used in the auditing profession:

- professional regulations issued by RSBs (Recognised Supervisory Bodies)
- the guidance given in the International Standard on Quality Control (ISQC 1) and ISA 220 *Quality Control of an audit of financial statements*
- review procedures
- audit committees (committees of non-executive directors who liaise with the auditors).

In addition, the law goes some way towards ensuring that auditors are competent and independent.

2.2 Professional regulations

The professional bodies expect their members to keep up to date by engaging in Continuing Professional Development (CPD). The bodies discipline individual members under the Joint Disciplinary Scheme.

Under the Companies Act 2006 there is a statutory requirement for the professional bodies to implement and enforce such regulations in order to retain recognition as an RSB.

2.3 Auditing Standards

Quality control policies and procedures should be implemented both at the level of the audit firm and on individual audits.

2.4 Audit firm

Audit firms should establish and monitor quality control policies and procedures designed to ensure that all audits are conducted in accordance with Auditing Standards and should communicate those policies and procedures to their personnel in a manner designed to provide reasonable assurance that the policies and procedures are understood and implemented.

The quality control policies to be adopted by auditors usually incorporate the following:

- **Professional requirements** – personnel adhere to the principles of independence, integrity, objectivity, confidentiality and professional behaviour.
- **Skills and competence** – personnel have attained and maintain the technical standards and professional competence required to enable them to fulfil their responsibilities with due care.
- **Acceptance and retention of clients** – prospective clients are evaluated and existing clients are reviewed on an ongoing basis. In making a decision to accept or retain a client, the auditors' independence and ability to serve the client properly and the integrity of the client's management are considered.
- **Assignment** – audit work is assigned to personnel who have the degree of technical training and proficiency required in the circumstances.
- **Delegation (direction, supervision and review)** – sufficient direction, supervision and review of work at all levels is carried out in order to provide confidence that the work performed meets appropriate standards of quality.
- **Consultation** – consultation, whenever necessary, within or outside the audit firm occurs with those who have appropriate expertise.
- **Monitoring** – the continued adequacy and operational effectiveness of quality control policies and procedures are monitored.

2.5 Individual audits

Any work delegated to assistants should be directed, supervised and reviewed in a manner which provides reasonable assurance that such work is performed competently.

The audit engagement partner and personnel with supervisory responsibilities consider the professional competence of assistants performing work delegated to them when deciding the extent of direction, supervision and review appropriate for each assistant.

2.6 Direction

Appropriate direction of assistants to whom work is delegated involves informing them of their responsibilities and the objectives of the procedures they are to perform. It also involves informing them of matters such as the nature of the entity's business and possible accounting or auditing problems which may affect the nature, timing and extent of audit procedures with which they are involved. Means of communicating audit directions, in addition to briefing meetings and informal oral communications, include audit manuals and checklists as well as the audit programme and the overall audit plan.

2.7 Supervision

Supervision is closely related to both direction and review and may involve elements of both. Personnel with supervisory responsibilities perform the following functions during the audit:

- monitor the progress of the audit to consider whether:
  - assistants have the necessary skills and competence to carry out their assigned tasks
  - assistants understand the audit directions
  - the work is being carried out in accordance with the overall audit plan and the audit programme.
- become informed of and address significant accounting and auditing questions raised during the audit, by assessing their significance and modifying the overall audit plan and the audit programme as appropriate
- resolve any differences of professional judgment between personnel and consider the level of consultation that is appropriate.

2.8 Review

Work performed by each assistant is reviewed by personnel of appropriate experience to consider whether:

- the work has been performed in accordance with the audit programme
- the work performed and the results obtained have been adequately documented
- any significant audit matters have been resolved or are reflected in audit conclusions
- the objectives of the audit procedures have been achieved, and
- the conclusions expressed are consistent with the results of the work performed and support the audit opinion.

3 Review procedures

3.1 Introduction

The standards on quality control do not give details of how monitoring reviews should be carried out. The most common methods are described below.

3.2 Review within the firm

Most common are methods of review within the audit firm.

3.3 Audit review panel

This will comprise a small number of partners and/or technical senior managers. Prior to issuing the audit report they will consider:

- conflicts of interest
- proposed qualifications
- interpretation of law and accounting standards
- contentious matters (e.g. an apparent change of view from one year's audit to the next).

3.4 Second partner review

The second partner should be as independent as possible but should have knowledge of the client. He will:

- comprehensively review all audit files
- form his own opinion based on the work and evidence and compare it to the first partner's opinion. Any conflict must be resolved before the audit report is issued.

This is a more in-depth review, and is therefore more time-consuming and expensive. For this reason, it is sometimes limited to high risk and public interest audits.

3.5 'Hot' review

Performed by a review department before the audit report is issued. Reviewers will:

- check that work done conforms to the firm's standards
- ensure that all review points have been satisfactorily cleared

- confirm that legal requirements and accounting standards have been complied with
- review the report to management in the light of the audit files
- check that the letter of engagement has been complied with
- ensure that the letter of management representation covers all relevant points.

The depth of review undertaken is between that of a second partner review and an audit panel review. Hot reviews are applied to all audits, so all audit work is subject to the same standard of review. The potential disadvantage of this is that the issue of audit reports may be delayed if bottlenecks form.

3.6 Post-audit review ('cold' review)

Checks the extent of compliance with the firm's standards and policies in areas such as:

- auditing procedures
- accounting and reporting principles
- working paper preparation and presentation.

The cold review:

- determines whether the audit evidence obtained is sufficient, relevant and reliable enough to support the audit opinion
- reviews the performance of audit staff and assists them in improving
- identifies areas of weakness in the firm's procedures or in their application, and makes recommendations for improvement
- ensures that unnecessary work is eliminated and efficiency improved.

'Cold' reviews are performed by senior staff or partners from other offices, after the audit report has been issued. It is therefore independent of the staff involved in the audit work. Because of the time involved, 'cold' reviews are undertaken on a rotational basis for selected audits, covering all audit partners and managers.

The review will concentrate on 'problem' audits, for example high risk clients and loss-making assignments.

3.7 External review – peer review

This involves the review of a firm by another firm of auditors or a committee of external experts. This practice is much used in the USA. The review will consider the adequacy of the firm's policies and procedures and the extent to which they are complied with.

3.8 Audit committees

An audit committee is a group of (usually) non-executive directors within the audit client who are able to view a company's affairs in a detached and objective manner and to liaise between the main Board of Directors and the external auditor.

It is argued that they assist in:

- increasing public confidence in the credibility and objectivity of financial statements
- enabling directors to meet their responsibilities in respect of financial reporting
- strengthening the independence of the company's external auditor – the committee can advise on the appointment of the external auditor and provide a channel of communication to the main board
- increasing the non-executive directors' understanding of the financial statements, and all directors' understanding of the nature and scope of the statutory audit.

As yet there is no legal requirement for a UK company to have an audit committee. Supporters of proposals for legislation suggest that audit committees should be required for all companies in which there is a public interest. However, most public companies have set up audit committees in response to pressure from the Stock Exchange following the Cadbury and Greenbury reports into corporate governance.

4 Fraud and the role of the auditor

4.1 Introduction

An auditor has no statutory duty to detect fraud as an end in itself. However, a material fraud may affect the truth and fairness of the financial statements and the auditor should therefore design his work to have a reasonable expectation of detecting material fraud.

This has been a controversial area of audit regulation. The public wish to be reassured that fraud, particularly fraud committed by senior management, is being prevented and detected by the audit. Auditors are reluctant to accept such a responsibility because fraud can be so carefully concealed that it becomes almost impossible to detect. ISA 240 *The auditor's responsibilities relating to fraud in an audit of financial statements* deals with this issue.

4.2 Fraud and error

It is for the court to determine in a particular instance whether fraud has occurred. Auditors need to be alert to conduct which may be dishonest before considering whether it may be fraudulent. Fraud comprises both the use of deception to obtain an unjust or illegal financial advantage and intentional misrepresentations affecting the financial statements by one or more individuals among management, employees, or third parties.

Fraud may involve:

- falsification or alteration of accounting records or other documents · misappropriation of assets, or theft
- suppression or omission of the effects of transactions from records or documents
- recording of transactions without substance
- intentional misapplication of accounting policies
- wilful misrepresentations of transactions or of the entity's state of affairs
- money laundering.

'Error' refers simply to unintentional misstatements.

4.3 Responsibilities

Management is responsible for both the prevention and detection of fraud. Such responsibilities may be discharged by the installation of an effective accounting system and an appropriate system of internal controls, amongst others.

4.4 Audit approach

When planning the audit the auditors should assess the risk that fraud or error may cause the financial statements to contain material misstatements.

Based on their risk assessment, the auditors should design audit procedures so as to have a reasonable expectation of detecting misstatements arising from fraud or error which are material to the financial statements.

4.5 Procedures where there is an indication that fraud or error may exist

When auditors become aware of information which indicates that fraud or error may exist, they should obtain an understanding of the nature of the event and the circumstances in which it has occurred, and sufficient other information to evaluate the possible effect on the financial statements. If the auditors believe that the indicated fraud or error could have a material effect on the financial statements, they should perform appropriate modified or additional procedures.

The auditors should as soon as practicable document their findings and communicate them to the appropriate level of management, the Board of Directors or the audit committee if:

- they suspect or discover fraud, even if the potential effect on the financial statements is immaterial, or
- material error is actually found to exist.

4.6 Reporting to addressees of the auditors' report

Where the auditors conclude that the view given by the financial statements could be affected by a level of uncertainty concerning the consequences of a suspected or actual error or fraud which, in their opinion, is significant, they should include an explanatory paragraph referring to the matter in their report.

Where the auditors conclude that a suspected or actual instance of fraud or error has a material effect on the financial statements and they disagree with the accounting treatment or with the extent, or the lack of disclosure in the financial statements of the instance or of its consequences they should issue an adverse or qualified opinion. If the auditors are unable to determine whether fraud or error has occurred because of limitation in the scope of their work, they should issue a disclaimer or a qualified opinion.

Modifying the audit report or providing an explanatory paragraph provides the auditor with a solution to the dilemma created by knowing that fraud may have been committed. It is unsatisfactory to permit the matter to go unreported because the victims of the fraud will feel that the auditor has let them down. Reporting the fraud to a third party, such as the police, will breach the auditor's duty of confidentiality.

Another advantage of bringing matters to light through the audit report is that the auditor is protected against claims of defamation. If anyone claims to have been libelled in the audit report then the auditor merely has to prove that he has acted in good faith. If the auditor makes a report to a third party and that party subsequently sues the auditor for damages then the auditor would have to prove that the fraud allegations were true, which could be difficult or even impossible given the standards of proof required in criminal cases.

4.7 Reporting to third parties

Where the auditors become aware of a suspected or actual instance of fraud they will normally be prevented from reporting this to a third party because of duties of professional confidentiality. The auditor could, however, have a duty to set this duty aside in order to best serve the public interest. This is a complex issue and the auditor should seek legal advice before doing anything.

The auditor might decide that it is necessary to resign in the light of the facts that have been uncovered. UK company law requires that the auditor file a report of any matters associated with the resignation that should be brought to the attention of the shareholders or payables. That might provide a further means by which the auditor's concerns can be brought to the attention of the company's members.

5 Summary

This chapter has covered:

- the circumstances in which an auditor may be found to be negligent
- the circumstances in which an auditor may be liable to clients and to third parties
- the persons to whom an auditor may be liable
- possible methods of excluding or limiting an auditor's liability (particularly quality control procedures)
- audit considerations regarding the detection and reporting of fraud.

WORKBOOK ACTIVITIES ANSWERS

Workbook Activity Answers

1 Principles of auditing

Workbook Activity 2

1 Statement of financial position.

Statement of profit or loss.

Cash flow statement.

Statement of changes in equity.

Notes to the financial statements.

2 The directors.

3 A failure to disclose some item that is required to be disclosed.

2 Business systems

Workbook Activity 3

1 Paying for goods not received.

2 Theft of inventory.

Workbook Activity 4

3 Sales, purchases and payroll.

3 Planning, controlling and recording

Workbook Activity 2

1 False.

2 True.

3 True.

Workbook Activity 3

1 Reduce.

2 Increase.

3 Increase.

Workbook Activity 4

1	Wayne selling his stake	–	incentive to misstate (Inherent risk)
2	Cash sales	–	lack of an audit trail (Inherent risk).
		–	easier to misappropriate assets (Inherent risk).
3	Perishable inventory	–	may be overvalued on the statement of financial position (Inherent risk).
4	Casual staff	–	may make mistakes due to lack of experience (Inherent risk).
5	Paid cash in hand	–	Proper deductions (e.g. income tax) may not be paid over to HMRC.

6	Leases	–	The type of lease held will affect the way in which it should be accounted for.
7	Seasonal trade	–	may make analytical review difficult if we don't understand the business properly.
		–	if the business cannot pay its bills in the winter months the accounts may be inappropriately prepared on the going concern basis.

4 Accounting systems and internal controls

Workbook Activity 3

1 Checklist.

2 Flowchart.

Workbook Activity 4

1 False.

2 False.

5 Audit evidence, techniques and procedures

Workbook Activity 4

1 Non-current asset register.

2 Goods received records.

Workbook Activity 5

1 Substantive procedure.

2 Test of control.

3 Substantive procedure

7 Audit verification work 2 – Inventory

Workbook Activity 3

Vouch a sample of entries for material to invoices.

Vouch a sample of entries for wages to payroll records.

Trace a sample of invoices to costing records.

Trace a sample of timesheet details to the costing records.

Reperform the overhead percentage calculation.

For a sample of contracts in progress at the year-end compare actual costs to:

- Contract price to identify losses.
- Budget to identify cost overruns and potential losses.

Workbook Activity 4

1 False.

2 True.

3 False.

8 Audit verification work 3 – Non-current assets

Workbook Activity 1

(i) **Consequences**

Equipment recorded in the register may not exist

Equipment may be fully written down but still in use

Depreciation charges may be inappropriate

Equipment in existence may not be recorded.

(ii) **Recommendations**

Periodic reconciliation of:

- Physical equipment to register to ensure completeness.
- Entries in the register to physical equipment to ensure existence.

Differences to be investigated.

Monitoring of procedures to ensure checks are undertaken.

Workbook Activity 2

1 Physical asset

2 Purchase invoice

9 Audit verification work 4 – Receivables, cash and bank

Workbook Activity 1

No further action as it is immaterial and is clearly due to human error.

Workbook Activity 2

(a) Deducted from.

(b) Deducted from.

10 Audit verification work 5 – Liabilities, shareholders' funds and statutory books

Workbook Activity 3

(i) **Risks**

Incorrect classification of the lorries within non-current assets.

Incorrect classification of the finance agreement within liabilities.

Incorrect calculation of the finance.

Inappropriate depreciation policy.

Incorrect calculation of depreciation.

Inaccurate cost figures used.

Incorrect calculation of the interest on the loan.

Incorrect disclosure of the loan terms and interest.

Recording purchase in the wrong period.

Failure to record new assets at all.

Failure to record loan payments.

(ii) **Procedures**

Check date of purchase to invoice.

Check amount capitalised to invoice.

Check recorded under motor vehicles in non-current assets note.

Agree accuracy of entry in non-current asset register.

Obtain depreciation policy and review for reasonableness.

Recalculate depreciation for the year on lorries.

Recalculate interest paid on loan.

Agree interest calculated to statement of profit or loss.

Calculate split of loan between less than one year by reference to the loan agreement.

Agree loan split to liabilities note.

Agree interest payment to bank statement and cash book.

Agree loan repayment to cash book and bank statement.

11 Completion stages of an audit

Workbook Activity 1

Any 3 of the following:

- Liabilities exceed assets.
- Loss of key customer/supplier/staff.
- Breach of loan covenants.
- Fundamental changes.
- Major litigation.

12 The reporting function

Workbook Activity 2

Refer to supervisor. The managing director is fraudulently using the company's money to pay for his children's school fees.

Workbook Activity 3

(i) **Consequences**

Equipment recorded in the register may not exist or may have been stolen.

Equipment in existence, acquisitions or disposals may not be recorded.

Equipment may be fully written down but still in use.

Equipment may be impaired and consequently overvalued.

Depreciation charges on the equipment may be inappropriate.

(ii) **Recommendations**

Periodic reconciliation of physical equipment to register to ensure completeness of recording.

Periodic reconciliation of entries in the register to physical equipment to ensure existence and in good condition.

Reconciliation to be performed independent of custodian.

Differences to be reported and investigated.

Monitoring of procedures to ensure checks are undertaken.

Workbook Activity 4

1 The accounting treatment adopted by the company does not agree with the relevant accounting standard. This should be discussed with management who should be requested to comply with the accounting standard. If they refuse to do so this should be referred to in the report to management.

The adjustment represents 0.67% of profit and 0.94% of total assets. Based on this, it does not appear to be material to the accounts. As the adjustment is not material, the accounts show a true and fair review and therefore there will be no adjustment to the audit opinion or audit report.

2 The issue here is one of a limitation of scope. Due to the loss of the physical inventory count records the auditor will not be able to perform normal audit procedures in this area.

The inventory balance is clearly material to the accounts as it represents 70% of profit and 12% of total assets. However in this instance the issue is the extent to which the inventory balance quoted is incorrect. As the limitation of scope leads to uncertainty, it is not possible to quantify exactly the size of any adjustment.

Assuming the limitation of scope is material but not so material or pervasive the audit report would be modified as we would give a qualified opinion based on the limitation of scope.

3 There is a significant uncertainty at the year-end in respect of whether or not the company is a going concern. This is dependent on the renewal of the contract which is significant to the viability of the company. The auditor needs to establish the likelihood of renewal. If the company is not a going concern then the accounts should be prepared on the break-up basis.

No information has been provided to quantify the adjustments but these are likely to be material.

There are a few possible impacts on the audit report as follows:

(i) Assuming the accounts are prepared on a going concern basis and if the auditor agrees and is satisfied that the disclosure is appropriate, an unmodified audit opinion would be given but the audit report would be modified by inserting an emphasis of matter paragraph in to explain the significant uncertainty.

(ii) Assuming the accounts are prepared on a going concern basis but the auditor disagrees then an adverse opinion would be given as this is likely to be deemed so material or pervasive.

(iii) If the accounts are prepared on the break up basis and the auditor agrees with this and the disclosures then an unmodified audit opinion would be given but the audit report would be modified by inserting an emphasis of matter paragraph in to explain the significant uncertainty.

4 A qualified opinion will be given based on disagreement. As the reporting partner disagrees with the size of the provision necessary.

13 The legal and professional framework

Workbook Activity 1

Answer (b)

If at the conclusion of the AGM no auditor has been appointed then the Secretary of State will step in. This is very rare.

MOCK ASSESSMENT

1 Mock Assessment Questions

Task 1.1

Auditors use tests of controls and substantive procedures.

For each of the following, select whether it is a test of control or substantive procedure.

		Test of control	*Substantive procedure*
1	Performing analytical procedures on the revenue balance.		
2	Observing the payroll clerk add a new staff member to the database.		
3	Reconciling the cash book balance to the bank statement closing balance.		

Task 1.2

Accounting systems have control objectives and control procedures to mitigate the risks that the control objective is not met.

For each of the following select whether they are a control objective, risk or control procedure.

		Control objective	*Control risk*	*Control procedure*
1	Customers fail to pay for goods received			
2	Al goods leaving the warehouse are invoiced			
3	Sequence check on dispatch/delivery note numbers			

Task 1.3

Complete the following definition on internal controls by filling in the gaps from the picklist below.

Picklist
Absolute
Accounting and reporting standards
Accounting records
Financial reporting
Laws and regulations
Reasonable

The process designed, implemented and maintained by those charged with governance, management and other personnel, to provide:

1 ________________ assurance about the achievement of an entity's objectives with regard to the reliability of

2 ________________ effectiveness and efficiency of operations and compliance with applicable

3 ________________.

Task 1.4

State whether the following statements are true or false in respect of assurance.

		True	*False*
1	A reasonable level of assurance means that the auditor has tested 100% of the balances.		
2	A reasonable level of assurance is used when reviewing forecasts and business plan.		

Task 1.5

The external auditor of Cross Ltd uses an internal control questionnaire to assist him in his evaluation of internal controls over the revenue cycle.

Identify, for each of the following questions and answers, whether the answer indicates a control, or a lack of control by selecting the appropriate option.

		Control	*Lack of control*
1	Are customers required to sign on delivery of orders? **YES**		
2	Does the sales ledger clerk perform a monthly reconciliation between the sales ledger balances and the balance on the sales ledger control account? **NO**		

Task 1.6

Select whether the following contribute to a strong control environment, a weak control environment or have no effect.

		Strong	*Weak*	*No effect*
1	Management established an internal audit function last year on the recommendation of the auditors.			
2	The finance director left last year and has still not been replaced. At present, the sales director is overseeing the finance team			

Task 1.7

The external auditor may seek to place reliance on internal controls in order to restrict substantive testing.

In each of the following circumstances select whether the auditor is likely to place reliance or no reliance on internal controls.

		Reliance	*No reliance*
1	A company where the processing of accounting transactions is undertaken by one person.		
2	A company which has an internal audit function which monitors operational and financial controls.		
3	A company which has internal controls with a history of management override.		

Task 1.8

The following are descriptions of procedures within the payroll system of Delaware Ltd.

For each procedure select whether it is a strength or a weakness.

		Strength	*Weakness*
1	The computerised payroll is processed weekly by Amelia who is also responsible for amending the standing data such as the addition of new employees and changes to wage rates		
2	The managing director, David Delaware, reviews the BACS listing of net pay details per employee and signs the listing before authorising the assistant accountant, Marie, to transmit the details to the company's bank		

Task 1.9

The external auditor is required to undertake analytical procedures as part of the planning process in order to identify the risk of misstatement of figures in the financial statements. The results of the analytical procedures conducted on trade receivables and trade payables in the financial statements of an audit client are listed below.

Select whether the results indicate that trade receivables and trade payables might have been under or overstated.

The results show that, compared to the previous year:		*Understated*	*Overstated*
1	Trade receivables have increased by 20% and revenue has increased by 5%.		
2	Trade payables have decreased by 10% and purchases have decreased by 7%.		

Task 1.10

When selecting items in order to perform tests of detail, the auditor has to consider a number of factors.

For each of the following factors, select whether they will result in an increase or decrease in sample size.

		Increase	*Decrease*
1	An increase in the auditor's assessment of risk of misstatement.		
2	An increase in the use of other substantive procedures directed at the same assertion.		
3	Stratification of the population being tested.		

Task 1.11

Auditors use tests of control and substantive procedures to gather audit evidence.

For each of the procedures listed below, select whether it is a test of control or a substantive procedure.

		Test of control	*Substantive procedure*
1	Comparison of the current year's revenue figure with the previous year's figure.		
2	Observation of the despatch procedures in respect of goods leaving an entity's warehouse.		
3	Vouching of an addition to non-current assets to the supplier's invoice.		

Task 1.12

An audit junior performed direct confirmations on a sample of trade receivables balances of Elm Ltd at 31 March 20X9 and has reconciled the balance on one customer's reply to Oak Ltd's receivables ledger balance as follows:

Balance outstanding per customer's reply		25,200
(i)	Credit note issued 29 March 20X9 received by customer on 1 April	(5,400)
(ii)	Sales invoice 27 March 20X9 not yet processed by the customer	10,000
Balance outstanding per Oak Ltd's receivables ledger		29,800

The audit junior has asked for guidance on the further work to be performed in respect of this reconciliation.

Using the table below, indicate which of Oak Ltd's accounting records each of the reconciling items should be checked to.

		Pre month end credit note file	*Post month end credit note file*	*Pre month end invoice file*	*Post month end invoice file*
1	Credit note issued 29 March.				
2	Sales invoice not yet processed.				

Task 1.13

During the year ended 31 December 20X9, Becks Ltd took out a bank loan of £1 million to fund a capital project. The terms of the loan require:

- Capital repayments, over 5 years, in monthly instalments commencing 1 July 20X9
- Interest at 9% per annum payable monthly
- Profit before interest and tax in the monthly management accounts to cover interest at least four times

Set out in a manner suitable for inclusion in the audit plan the audit risks relating to the loan.

Task 1.14

As part of verification techniques in respect of purchases, an auditor will inspect purchase invoices. The auditor will gain assurance about different assertions depending on the information on the invoice.

In respect of the information below, select the assertion for which the information will provide assurance.

		Assertion
1	Date of the invoice.	
2	Description of the item purchased.	
3	Monetary amount.	

Task 1.15

Two types of computer-assisted audit techniques (CAATs) are test data and audit software.

For each of the procedures listed below, select the type of CAAT which would be used to perform that procedure.

		Test data	*Audit software*
1	Comparison of the cost and net realisable value of inventory items to determine the lower value.		
2	Input of data with false inventory code numbers to check that the system rejects such data.		
3	Extraction of inventory balances over £5,000 in order to carry out further testing.		

Task 1.16

Identify whether each of the following factors would be likely to cause the auditor to exercise a greater or lesser degree of professional scepticism by selecting the appropriate option.

		Greater	*Lesser*
1	The audited entity's management provides thorough comments on the management letter provided by the auditors that identifies deficiencies noted throughout the course of the audit and the proposed recommendations.		
2	The finance team is made up of unqualified accountants and the Finance Director has been on sick leave for 3 months.		

Task 1.17

External auditors use a number of methods to document their understanding of control systems, including flowcharts, internal control questionnaires and internal control checklists.

For each of the following descriptions, select whether it represents a flowchart, internal control questionnaire or internal control checklist.

		Flowchart	*Internal control questionnaire*	*Internal control checklist*
1	A list of questions for the auditor to ask the client in order to understand how the control works			
2	A pictorial presentation of the complete control process			

Task 1.18

State whether the following statements in respect of working papers are true or false.

		True	*False*
1	Working papers are the property of the client once the audit is completed.		
2	Working papers must contain the name of the client, the name of the person who performed the work and the date the work was performed on.		

Task 1.19

SJB Ltd is a package tour operator offering holidays to South Africa. During the year, a customer started legal proceedings against them as a result of poor service and problems on their holiday. Legal opinion is divided as to what the outcome will be. The client has disclosed this matter within the notes to the financial statements.

Select the most appropriate response.

(a) Issue a qualified opinion

(b) Issue an adverse opinion

(c) Include an 'other matter' paragraph, or

(d) Include an 'emphasis of matter' paragraph.

Task 1.20

Jasmele Ltd is a company which hires out various items of equipment to a range of customers ranging from small customers to very large building companies. The hire periods range from one day to six months and there is great variety in the number of items hired at any one time per customer. For individual items and hire periods of less than one month, Jasmele issues an invoice on completion of the hire period. For hire periods greater than one month a progress invoice is issued at each month end. The credit period is 30 days.

Set out in a manner suitable for inclusion in the audit plan, the audit procedures to be undertaken in order to ensure that receivables is fairly stated in the financial statements.

Task 1.21

During the external audit of DJB Ltd, the auditor identified three instances where the finance director had failed to sign cheques over £5,000 in accordance with company policy. On further investigation, the auditor discovered that the finance director had been unwell.

In respect of this matter, select whether the auditor should take no further action or refer to their supervisor.

Task 1.22

The error listed below has been detected during the audit of Peppa Ltd and the directors are refusing to amend this error. Materiality has been set by the auditors as 5% of profit before tax and profit before tax for the year is £500,000.

Select whether or not the following error requires to be adjusted or not in order to issue an unmodified opinion.

	Requires to be adjusted	*No adjustment*
An overstatement of receivables amounting to £50,000 due to a cut-off error.		

Task 1.23

During the audit of Dijkman Ltd, a large firm of PR consultants, the following issues were discovered:

- You have found a total of £18,000 of unauthorised expenditure on IT equipment. Any IT expenditure in excess of £150 has to be authorised by a director.
- Large sums for travelling expenses are not being authorised when in excess of nightly limits set. Four executives spent a total of £25,000 in excess of their limits.
- When overtime forms are submitted, any amounts of more than three hours per month need to be authorised. This is rarely done and the company paid out £180,000 in unauthorised overtime.

Prepare extracts, suitable for inclusion in a report to management of Dijkman Ltd, which set out

(i) the possible consequences; and

(ii) the recommendations that you would make in respect of this matter.

Task 1.24

ISA 265 Communicating deficiencies in internal control defines a significant deficiency in internal control as a deficiency or combination of deficiencies in internal control that, in the auditor's professional judgement, is of sufficient importance to merit the attention of those charged with governance.

Identify whether or not the following deficiency is a significant deficiency by selecting the appropriate opinion:

		Significant deficiency	*Not significant*
1	No credit checks are run as the sales manager knows most of his customers personally.		

Task 1.25

The errors listed below have been detected during the audit of Taurus Ltd. The directors of Taurus refuse to make an adjustment to correct the errors. The audit firm Able Khan LLP uses 5% of profit before tax as the yardstick to determine whether errors are material. Taurus Ltd's profit before tax is £100,000.

Select whether the following errors require adjustment in order to issue an unmodified audit opinion on the financial statements.

		Requires adjustment	*No adjustment*
1	An overstatement of inventory amounting to £4,200 and an overstatement of receivables amounting to £3,800.		

Task 1.26

Select whether the following statements are true or false with respect of confidential information.

		True	*False*
1	When a member changes his firm of employment, he is entitled to use confidential information acquired there.		
2	A member acquiring confidential information in the course of his or her work may not use this for their personal advantage.		

Task 1.27

Complete the following statement on the overall objectives of the external auditor in conducting an audit of financial statements, by filling in the gaps from the picklist below.

Picklist
Absolute
All
An applicable financial framework
Express an opinion
International Standards on Auditing
Material
Provide a guarantee
Reasonable

The overall objectives of the external auditor are to obtain

1 ___________________ assurance about whether the financial statements are free from

2 _________________ misstatement, whether due to fraud or error, thereby enabling the auditor to

3 _________________ on whether the financial statements are prepared in all material respects in accordance with

4 ___________________.

Task 1.28

State whether the following statements are true or false in respect of external auditors' liability.

		True	*False*
1	External auditors are liable to anybody who relies solely on the audit report in financial statements when making investment decisions.		
2	External auditors may limit their liability to third parties if they include a disclaimer of liability in their audit report.		

Task 1.29

Which *one* of the following best describes the role of the International Auditing and Assurance Board (IAASB)?

1	Setting auditing standards which are compulsory throughout the world.	
2	Monitoring auditors to ensure that they comply with auditing standards.	
3	Investigating and disciplining auditors who fail to comply with auditing standards.	
4	Setting auditing standards which facilitate the convergence of national and international auditing standards.	

Task 1.30

Select whether the following factors are likely to lead to the auditor assessing that there is an increase or decrease to control risk.

		Increase	*Decrease*
1	The finance department is made up of temporary staff who are inexperienced in their understanding of accounting principles.		
2	An internal audit function was established 5 years ago and they produce monthly reports.		
3	Management has a positive attitude towards enforcing controls and disciplinary action is taken against any member of staff who contravenes these controls.		

Task 1.31

Select whether the following statements in respect of performance materiality are true or false.

		True	*False*
1	Performance materiality should be set at a level below the level of materiality for the financial statements as a whole.		
2	Once established, performance materiality must not be changes as the audit progresses.		

Task 1.32

Complete the following statement in respect of the reliability of information provided by the client by selecting the appropriate option.

The statement by the financial controller that accounting estimates are reasonable and prudent.

(a) Reliable

(b) Not likely to be reliable

2 Mock Assessment Answers

Task 1.1

		Test of control	*Substantive procedure*
1	Performing analytical procedures on the revenue balance.		✓
2	Observing the payroll clerk add a new staff member to the database.	✓	
3	Reconciling the cash book balance to the bank statement closing balance.		✓

Task 1.2

		Control objective	*Control risk*	*Control procedure*
1	Customers fail to pay for goods received		✓	
2	Al goods leaving the warehouse are invoiced	✓		
3	Sequence check on dispatch/delivery note numbers			✓

Task 1.3

1 Reasonable

2 Financial reporting

3 Laws and regulations

Task 1.4

		True	False
1	A reasonable level of assurance means that the auditor has tested 100% of the balances.		✓
2	A reasonable level of assurance is used when reviewing forecasts and business plan.		✓

Task 1.5

		Control	Lack of control
1	Are customers required to sign on delivery of orders? **YES**	✓	
2	Does the sales ledger clerk perform a monthly reconciliation between the sales ledger balances and the balance on the sales ledger control account? **NO**		✓

Task 1.6

		Strong	Weak	No effect
1	Management established an internal audit function last year on the recommendation of the auditors.	✓		
2	The finance director left last year and has still not been replaced. At present, the sales director is overseeing the finance team		✓	

Task 1.7

		Reliance	No reliance
1	A company where the processing of accounting transactions is undertaken by one person.		✓
2	A company which has an internal audit function which monitors operational and financial controls.	✓	
3	A company which has internal controls with a history of management override.		✓

Task 1.8

		Strength	Weakness
1	The computerised payroll is processed weekly by Amelia who is also responsible for amending the standing data such as the addition of new employees and changes to wage rates		✓
2	The managing director, David Delaware, reviews the BACS listing of net pay details per employee and signs the listing before authorising the assistant accountant, Marie, to transmit the details to the company's bank	✓	

Task 1.9

The results show that, compared to the previous year:		Understated	Overstated
1	Trade receivables have increased by 20% and revenue has increased by 5%.		✓
2	Trade payables have decreased by 10% and purchases have decreased by 7%.	✓	

Task 1.10

		Increase	*Decrease*
1	An increase in the auditor's assessment of risk of misstatement.	✓	
2	An increase in the use of other substantive procedures directed at the same assertion.		✓
3	Stratification of the population being tested.		✓

Task 1.11

		Test of control	*Substantive procedure*
1	Comparison of the current year's revenue figure with the previous year's figure.		✓
2	Observation of the despatch procedures in respect of goods leaving an entity's warehouse.	✓	
3	Vouching of an addition to non-current assets to the supplier's invoice.		✓

Task 1.12

		Pre month end credit note file	*Post month end credit note file*	*Pre month end invoice file*	*Post month end invoice file*
1	Credit note issued 29 March.	✓			
2	Sales invoice not yet processed.			✓	

Task 1.13

- Inappropriate split between current and non-current liabilities.
- Incomplete disclosure in the notes to the financial statements.
- Going concern risk if company fails to comply with the terms of the loan.
- Inflation of profits to ensure compliance with the interest cover requirement.

Task 1.14

		Assertion
1	Date of the invoice.	Cut-off
2	Description of the item purchased.	Classification
3	Monetary amount.	Accuracy

Task 1.15

		Test data	*Audit software*
1	Comparison of the cost and net realisable value of inventory items to determine the lower value.		✓
2	Input of data with false inventory code numbers to check that the system rejects such data.	✓	
3	Extraction of inventory balances over £5,000 in order to carry out further testing.		✓

Task 1.16

		Greater	*Lesser*
1	The audited entity's management provides thorough comments on the management letter provided by the auditors that identifies deficiencies noted throughout the course of the audit and the proposed recommendations.		✓
2	The finance team is made up of unqualified accountants and the Finance Director has been on sick leave for 3 months.	✓	

Task 1.17

		Flowchart	*Internal control questionnaire*	*Internal control checklist*
1	A list of questions for the auditor to ask the client in order to understand how the control works		✓	
2	A pictorial presentation of the complete control process	✓		

Task 1.18

		True	*False*
1	Working papers are the property of the client once the audit is completed.		✓
2	Working papers must contain the name of the client, the name of the person who performed the work and the date the work was performed on.	✓	

Task 1.19

Answer (d).

Include an 'emphasis of matter' paragraph.

Task 1.20

- Stratify the population in order to conduct sample testing.
- Perform a direct confirmation of a sample of receivables.
- Obtain aged receivables analysis and cast for accuracy.
- Review reconciliation from receivables ledger control account to receivables ledger.
- Perform after dare cash test on a sample of receivables.
- Calculate receivables days and compare to prior year.
- Compare ageing of receivables with prior year.
- Review aged debt receivables list for any overdue debts
- Review above debts for inclusion in specific bad debt provision.
- Enquire as to methodology behind any general bad debt provision.
- Recalculate general bad debt provision based on clients methodology.
- Agree receivables figure to draft FS.
- Agree ageing of sample of specific receivables to invoices.
- Review receivables ledger for any credit balances.

Task 1.21

Take no further action.

Task 1.22

		Requires to be adjusted	*No adjustment*
1	An overstatement of receivables amounting to £50,000 due to a cut-off error.	✓	

Task 1.23

Consequences:

The IT expenditure is uncontrolled and investment is not always clearly for the benefit of the company.

Loss of profits due to excessive travel expenditure.

Excessive overtime costs are adversely affecting profits.

Recommendations:

Purchasing department to be warned that no IT expenditure should be incurred without authorisation; otherwise disciplinary action could result.

Travelling expenses should not be reimbursed when limits are exceeded, unless prior consent has been received.

Overtime over one hour per week should be authorised prior to the work being undertaken, and should then be authorised once the timesheet is submitted.

Task 1.24

		Significant deficiency	*Not significant*
1	No credit checks are run as the sales manager knows most of his customers personally.	✓	

Task 1.25

		Requires adjustment	*No adjustment*
1	An overstatement of inventory amounting to £4,200 and an overstatement of receivables amounting to £3,800.	✓	

Task 1.26

		True	*False*
1	When a member changes his firm of employment, he is entitled to use confidential information acquired there.		✓
2	A member acquiring confidential information in the course of his or her work may not use this for their personal advantage.	✓	

Task 1.27

1 Reasonable

2 Material

3 Express an opinion

4 An applicable financial reporting framework.

Task 1.28

		True	*False*
1	External auditors are liable to anybody who relies solely on the audit report in financial statements when making investment decisions.		✓
2	External auditors may limit their liability to third parties if they include a disclaimer of liability in their audit report.	✓	

Task 1.29

1	Setting auditing standards which are compulsory throughout the world.	
2	Monitoring auditors to ensure that they comply with auditing standards.	
3	Investigating and disciplining auditors who fail to comply with auditing standards.	
4	Setting auditing standards which facilitate the convergence of national and international auditing standards.	✓

Task 1.30

		Increase	*Decrease*
1	The finance department is made up of temporary staff who are inexperienced in their understanding of accounting principles.	✓	
2	An internal audit function was established 5 years ago and they produce monthly reports.		✓
3	Management has a positive attitude towards enforcing controls and disciplinary action is taken against any member of staff who contravenes these controls.		✓

Task 1.31

		True	*False*
1	Performance materiality should be set at a level below the level of materiality for the financial statements as a whole.	✓	
2	Once established, performance materiality must not be changes as the audit progresses.		✓

Task 1.32

(a) Reliable

INDEX

A

Accounting
  estimates, 141, 147, 234
  systems, 81, 82, 110

Accruals, 226, 229

Accuracy, 116

Adverse opinion, 265, 278, 279

Allocation, 144

Analytical procedures, 49, 70, 71, 113, 120, 131, 132, 134, 136, 138, 143, 196, 197

Application controls, 96

Appointment of auditors, 287, 291

Assurance, 2, 3, 9

Audit
  approach, 49, 54, 58, 63, 71, 73, 77
  committees, 306, 311
  evidence, 113, 114, 116, 118, 138
  objectives, 117, 122
  planning memorandum, 49, 57
  programme, 151, 165, 166
  risk, 49, 57, 60, 63, 64, 65, 67, 70, 71, 72
  sampling, 113, 120, 121, 122, 123, 124, 138

Audit software, 99, 111

Auditor's report, 2, 3, 4, 7, 12, 250, 253, 259, 264

Auditor's removal, 293

B

Balance sheet, 276, 277

Bank
  confirmation letter, 213
  reconciliation, 213, 217, 223

Basis of audit opinion, 274

Block sampling, 128

C

CAATS, 99

Cash
  and bank, 194, 220
  system, 15, 38

Classification, 144, 145, 181, 226

Classification and understandability, 116

Cold review, 310

Companies Act 2006, 3, 6, 53, 59, 68, 82, 189, 232, 241, 242, 253, 254, 255, 259, 260, 273, 274, 275, 276, 279, 287, 288, 289, 294, 295, 296, 304, 306

Completeness, 115, 144, 145, 181, 182, 191

Completion, 249, 250, 252, 253, 266

Computation, 119, 142

Computer assisted audit techniques, 99

Computer environment, 96

Confidentiality, 58, 300, 301

Continuous stocktaking, 154, 172

Control
account, 195
environment, 82, 94, 95
objectives, 19, 25, 34, 40, 43
procedures, 95
risk, 63, 64, 65, 66, 72, 73, 124

Credit transactions, 256

Current assets, 175, 176, 177, 178, 180, 181, 184, 185, 186, 189, 191

Current audit file, 76

Cut-off, 116, 144, 158, 159, 160, 166, 168

D

Debenture loans, 226, 230

Depreciation, 179

Detection risk, 64, 124

Direct circularisation, 193, 197

Directors'
loans, 254, 255
remuneration, 255

Disclaimer, 266, 271, 280
of opinion, 278, 279

E

Emphasis of matter, 265, 280, 281

Engagement letter, 11, 49, 52, 53

Enquiry, 119, 142

Evaluation of misstatements, 273

Existence, 116, 144, 145, 181, 182, 185, 187, 191

Expectation gap, 8

Expected error, 123, 124, 126

F

Financial statement assertions, 115, 117, 132, 134, 135, 143, 144, 149

Financial statements, 2, 4, 249, 250, 253, 254, 255, 256, 258, 259, 260, 261, 262, 264, 265, 266

Flowcharts, 83, 84, 92

Fraud, 303, 311, 312

G

Going concern, 249, 262, 263, 264, 265, 266

Goodwill, 188

H

Haphazard selection, 128

Hot review, 309

I

IAASB, 9

ICQ, 102, 106

IFAC, 297, 300

IFAC, 304

Income statement, 178, 180, 182, 183, 187, 191, 243, 254

Independence, 287, 297

Independent auditor's report, 274

Inherent risk, 64, 65, 121, 124

Inspection, 119, 142

Intangible non-current assets, 175, 176, 177, 187

Internal audit, 81

Internal control(s), 81, 94
evaluations, 106
questionnaires, 83, 101
system, 94, 100, 108

International Accounting Standards(IASs), 253

International Standards on Auditing (ISAs), 3, 4, 5, 8, 9

Inventory, 7, 16, 18, 19, 23, 24, 25, 26, 28, 29, 41, 42, 43, 44, 45, 46, 56, 57, 58, 59, 64, 66, 69, 76, 95, 99, 103, 104, 114, 116, 119, 134, 136, 137, 142, 144, 147, 151, 152, 153, 154, 155, 156, 157, 158, 160, 161, 162, 163, 164, 165, 166, 167, 168, 169, 170, 171, 172, 183, 191, 206, 220, 228, 235, 237, 261

Inventory system, 41

ISA 450 Evaluation of Misstatements Identified During the Audit, 273

L

Letter of representation, 234

Limited Liability Partnerships, 305

M

Management
- letter, 251, 253
- representation letter, 252, 259
- representations, 249, 257

Manual controls, 96

Material deficiency, 270

Material misstatement, 114, 135

Materiality, 6, 49, 57, 60, 67, 68, 69, 77, 115, 121, 126, 273

Modified, 269, 276, 277, 278, 280, 283
- opinion(s), 63, 269, 277

N

Narrative notes, 83

Net realisable value, 153, 164

Non current assets, 136, 137, 144, 175, 176, 177, 186, 189, 206, 241, 243, 244, 278

Non-current asset investments, 176, 177, 189

Non-satistical sampling, 131

O

Objectivity, 298, 299

Observation, 119, 142

Occurrence, 115, 144, 145

Other matter paragraph, 281

Overheads, 163

Ownership, 181, 182, 185, 190, 191

P

Patents, 188

Payables, 24, 27, 122, 199, 225, 227, 228, 229, 235, 236, 237, 238, 245, 293, 294, 314

Payroll cycle, 15, 30

Peer review, 311

Performance materiality, 67

Periodic stocktaking, 155, 172

Permanent audit file, 75

Planning, 49, 50, 54

Population, 122, 124

Positive circularisations, 199

Professional scepticism, 109, 110

Provisions, 225, 231, 232

Purchases cycle, 15, 22

Q

Qualified opinion, 278

Quality control, 303, 306

Quasi-loans, 255, 256

R

Random selection, 127

Reasonable assurance, 5, 7, 8

Receivables circularisations, 193

Receivables, 18, 21, 46, 76, 97, 102, 103, 116, 119, 122, 123, 128, 129, 131, 134, 135, 136, 143, 144, 147, 193, 194, 195, 196, 197, 198, 199, 202, 203, 205, 206, 207, 208, 209, 210, 211, 212, 223, 228, 240

Recognised Supervisory Body (RSB), 290, 306

Representation letter, 251, 253, 257, 259, 260

Research and development, 187

Rights and obligations, 116, 144

S

Sales cycle, 15, 16, 17

Sample
  size, 123, 125

Sampling risk, 123, 124, 125, 126, 130, 131
  units, 123

Share capital, 225, 240, 241, 242, 244

Statement of financial position, 4, 56, 64, 76, 145, 152, 172, 176, 178, 180, 182, 183, 186, 188, 191, 198, 211, 232, 240, 243, 254, 274, 294, 296

Statement of profit or loss, 294, 296

Statistical sampling, 130

Stock system, 15

Stocktake, 151, 152, 154, 158, 166, 168, 172

Stratification, 124

Subsequent events, 148, 234, 235

Substantive procedures, 73, 114, 115, 117, 122, 124, 125, 126, 127, 130, 132, 134, 135, 137, 157, 227

Substantive tests, 72

Systematic selection, 127

T

Tangible non-current assets, 175, 176, 177, 178, 181, 183, 190

Test data, 99, 111

Tests of control, 72, 82, 108, 114, 115, 117, 122, 123, 124, 125, 126, 127

Tolerable error, 123, 124, 126

Tort, 303, 304

Trade marks, 188

Trade payables, 227, 235, 236, 237, 238, 239

True and fair view, 2, 3, 5, 6, 13, 274, 275, 276, 279

U

Uncertainties, 281, 282

Unmodified, 269, 278, 279, 281, 282
  opinion, 63, 274

V

Valuation, 115, 144, 145, 152, 177, 178, 179, 181, 182, 186, 189, 190, 191

W

Working papers, 74, 77, 249, 250, 251, 252

Work-in-progress, 152, 162

Written representation, 259